THE ULTIMATE GUIDE
TO DEER HUNTING

OTHER BOOKS BY THE AUTHOR

A Child's Introduction to the Outdoors
Complete Guide to Lake Fishing
Dardevle Guide to Fishing
English Language Fishing, Hunting & Natural History Books:
  A Bibliography & Price Guide (A-K)
Hunting Fringeland Deer
Getting Hooked on Fishing (with Jerome Knapp)
Great Lakes Steelhead Flies
How & Where to Fish the Great Lakes
How to Catch Trophy Freshwater Gamefish
Hunting Michigan Whitetails
Sea Run (contributing author)
Shakespeare's Guide to Great Lakes Fishing
Steelheading for Everybody
Steelheading in North America
The Brown Trout Fisherman's Guide
The Fly Hatches
The Small-Boat Handbook
Trout Fisherman's Digest
Trout of Michigan

THE ULTIMATE GUIDE TO DEER HUNTING

DAVID RICHEY

The Lyons Press
Guilford, CT
An Imprint of Globe Pequot Press

The Lyons Press is an imprint of The Globe Pequot Press.

Originally published as *Hunting Fringeland Deer* by Outdoor Life Books

Printed in the United States

Cover design by Yann Keesing

Photographs by David Richey, unless otherwise noted

10 9 8 7 6 5 4 3 2

The Library of Congress Cataloging-in-Publication Data is available on file.

DEDICATION

For
The late Max Donovan

Max was my mentor. He taught me about fishing and hunting at a very early age. He was never long on praise, always abrupt when I did something wrong, and through it all I came away with a greater knowledge of the outdoors and why game animals, birds and fish do what they do. Max was North America's oldest living hemophiliac upon his untimely death, and his sharing of wisdom with a

Max Donovan of Clio, Michigan was my friend and mentor.

tow-headed skinny kid meant more to me than I ever thought possible. I think of Max often, recall our fishing and hunting trips with fondness, and when my days end I hope he'll be waiting to greet me with open arms and an eternity of lengthy conversations about the sports we both loved. I wouldn't be writing this book had it not been for his unwavering confidence in me. Thanks Max!

CONTENTS

ACKNOWLEDGMENTS

Who a writer hunts with and where, and how the hunt goes, represent the flesh and bones upon which the body of a book is built. The imput of many people, and in some cases their companies, provide the framework of its contents.

This book is no different. From my first bumbling beginnings as a deer hunter 45 years ago until now, hundreds if not thousands of different voices have been heard. Some imput was hand-me-down garbage that has been passed from one generation to the next, and much has been discarded as useless.

None of the people who provided that childish pablum are mentioned here.

However, it's been my extremely good fortune to have hunted with some mighty fine sportsmen. I learned long ago to pick the brains of savvy people, learn what they know, and apply that solid information during my hunts and between these pages.

One thing I've learned over time from the farmlands and deep woods of my native Michigan to the rolling hills of Iowa, from the cottonwood canyons of Montana to the palmetto swamps of Alabama, is that each person has an in-depth knowledge or technique that works. I'm indebted to many for sharing their knowledge.

Among these savvy whitetail hunters are people like Claude Pollington of Marion, Michigan. Pollington is the man *Outdoor Life* magazine once called "The Whitetail Wizard." He owns 1,500 acres of prime whitetail habitat that has been my study ground for over 20 years. He is kind, gentle and soft spoken, but his knowledge of whitetails, what they do and why they do it is encyclopedic and always correct.

Roger Kerby of Honor, Michigan, is another accomplished deer hunter. His specialty is organizing and executing deer drives.

This particular hunting method is far more complicated than many sportsmen realize, and a hunter only has to be told to take a stand in a specific location, remain quiet and not move, and then watch as Kerby nudges a buck within firearm range to know that he has an uncanny hunting skill. I've often felt that Kerby knows more about what a buck will do in a deer drive than the animal. He's the best drivemaster I've seen.

Lee Blahnik of Elberta, Michigan, may have forgotten more about whitetail deer and their habits than many hunters ever learn. He is generous to a fault, and many times I've seen him give a key location to a first-time hunter and then stand by with a smile on his face as the sportsman shoots his first buck. He has taken more deer than he can remember, and receives more enjoyment from the success of others than his own.

Herb Boldt of East Tawas, Michigan, is a deadly one-shot deer hunter. He is the epitome of a hard-boiled newspaper man, and over 20 years ago hired me as *The Detroit News'* staff outdoor writer. He loves swamp hunting more than anything else, and he has an uncanny knack for picking the right spot to sit.

Once, many years ago, I had been hunting a big 11-point for five weeks with a bow before ultimately missing my only chance. Boldt showed up for opening day of the firearm season, and picked himself a good spot while I went in search of the big buck. He shot what I considered "my" 11-pointer that day and has never let me forget it. He's a good friend and one I enjoy deer hunting with whenever we get together.

Tom Edwards of Superior Wildlife Feed Company in Livonia, Michigan, worked with me and my neighbor so we could plant three Imperial Brand Whitetail Clover food plots and two farm lanes to the protein-rich clover. They sprouted like fresh flowers, and the deer homed in on it quickly. Our combined four acres now produces heavy crops of clover each spring, and Tom's knowledge made it work.

Tony Knight of Centerville, Iowa, is a man I respect highly as a deer hunter. We've prowled Iowa's hills and several other states in search of whitetails, and he is mostly responsible for turning me into a muzzleloader hunter. His original in-line MK-85 Modern Muzzleloading rifle made superb blackpowder accuracy possible, and he and I have shared countless hunts together. He has become a legend in his own time among frontloader sportsmen, and has taught me much about hunting Iowa bucks.

Dave Lyons and Jim Mason of Hayneville, Alabama, own Southern Sportsman's Lodge in the middle of Alabama's famous "Black Belt" deer range. Between them, they have worked with and showed me how to hunt the palmetto thickets in their area. It's not their fault that the huge (175-class) 12-pointer they set me up on chose to run past me with his body screened by palmettos. I didn't get that buck, and to my knowledge, no one else has but they provided the opportunity. I enjoy their company, their fine hospitality, and hunting their land is great fun during the January rut.

Billy McCoy of Lineville, Alabama, is another southern hunter who has shared his deer hunting skills with me. He is a hunting guide, knows how and why deer move as they do, and he has an uncanny sense for knowing when deer will move to hunters.

The late Art LaHa of Winchester, Wisconsin, was as fine a wounded deer trailer as anyone in North America. On one occasions he proved his worth in tracking down an animal wounded by another hunter. I watched him follow a buck that wasn't leaking blood. LaHa, and his friend, Marge Engle, conducted the tracking job like professionals. They took it one step at a time, finding first a partially overturned leaf and then a single berry of blood on the underside of a grass stem. They methodically examined the forest floor and could read sign of the buck's passage that no one else could see. That trailing job may have taken hours but the hunter was able to tag the animal.

George Gardner of Southgate, Michigan, was an archery tackle sales representative for many years, and I've shared several hunts with him. He is knowledgeable about bows, arrows and the accessories used by bowhunters, and he's helped me sort out the complexities of matching the proper arrow to a bow.

Pat Marino of Williamsburg, Michigan, is a hunting buddy. I use a compound bow and he favors a recurve. He keeps me clued in to the art of shooting a recurve or long bow, has a great sense of humor, and takes wonderful photographs. We've hunted together for several years and enjoyed our outings immensely.

Gary Baynton of Buckley, Michigan, is another friend who accompanies me on bow and firearm hunts for deer and caribou. He has some of the keenest vision I've seen in a human, and he never misses spotting deer. His theory of seeing deer is like mine: look as far into brush as possible, and anything moving in between, will be seen.

Jean-Paul Bisson of Le Chateau Montebello in Montebello, Quebec. This man was a wonder at finding deer in areas with very few animals. He performed a one-man drive for me years ago that produced a 140-point (Boone & Crockett) buck that was mincing along 100 yards in front of him. He knew the deer was close, and bellowed twice like a beagle on a hot track to alert me, and I was ready when the buck stepped out.

My twin brother George Richey of Honor, Michigan. He hasn't been bitten by the deer hunting bug like me but we get together several times each year to hunt whitetails with a bow, muzzleloader or centerfire rifle. Sharing a hunt with him ranks high on my list of things to do, and we enjoy each other's company even if we don't score.

Arnold DeMerchant of Perth, New Brunswick. I've never hunted with him but he guided me for Atlantic salmon several times. He regaled me with stories of deer hunting when his job was the primary meat producer for a lumber camp. His job was to shoot at least two deer daily to feed the workers, and he's the only man I know who has taken two bucks with one shot several times, three deer with one shot twice, and probably shot more deer than any man alive. His tales of hunting and woodsmanship were true because I saw photos of some of his exploits from years ago.

John McKenzie of Millington, Michigan. He and I teamed up 30 years ago to hunt whitetails near Flint, Michigan's second largest city. We learned that many farmland bucks are like circuit riding preachers in the Old West, and would be found in one section today and two or three miles away the next day. We choreographed their daily movements, and ambushed them on opening day.

The late Max Donovan of Clio, Michigan. Max was my mentor 45 years ago and taught me a great deal about fishing and hunting. Those lessons learned over four decades ago remain as fresh in my mind now as if they had happened yesterday. At that time, Max was North America's oldest living hemophiliac and walked on one good leg and one wooden leg. His powers of observation were deeply instilled in me at an early age, and his advice on deer hunting was simple: "Hunt deer where they eat, sleep and travel." That pretty much sums up deer hunting then and now and I miss him greatly.

Matt Pollington and Ross Richards of Marion, Michigan. Matt is Claude Pollington's son and Ross is Claude's grandson. I've watched both men grow from teenagers into adults, and both are superb bowhunters and rifle shots. I've watched their hunting skills progress with great admiration. I can remember countless times when my wife and I took each of them out hunting years ago, and watched them blossom into ardent and successful deer hunters.

My wife Kay Richey. I turned this poor Idaho-raised girl from an apartment dweller into a hunter, and for the past 24 years we have shared many deer hunting trips in Alabama, Georgia, Iowa, Kentucky, Michigan, Missouri, Tennessee, Wisconsin and other states. She is one of the most accurate rifle shots with her scoped Thompson-Center

.243 I've seen, and since she uses a single-shot rifle, she concentrates on making each shot count. We've lost count but I know she has made more than 75 one-shot rifle kills in the past 24 years, and probably an equal number of one-shot bow kills. She's my constant hunting buddy, and we enjoy hunting together.

Jim Riley of Northville, Michigan. Jim is an avid deer hunter who has hunted with my wife and me on several occasions, and an expert on handloading, ballistics and shooting centerfire rifles. His knowledge of firearms and ballistics is encyclopedic, and he is a good friend.

Carl Salling of In-Seasons Adventures in Mesick, Michigan. He has turned me on to South Texas deer hunting where the limit is five deer. I took my largest desert whitetail with him several years ago, and the 10-pointer is a beauty.

Gary Todd of Pro-Release. His release aids for bowhunters have enabled me to smoothly shoot many nice bucks. I've hunted in Texas and Michigan with him, and found him knowledgeable about deer hunting and fun to spend time with in camp.

Bob and Cathy Beutler are two good friends with whom I've shared countless Michigan deer hunts. Both are avid bowhunters, good shots and have spent countless days with my wife and me in the deer woods. We both enjoy hunting with them.

Doreen Easterbrook is a special lady in our lives. She loves to hunt, and we enjoy having her in our deer camp. We shared in her teary delight when she took her first buck with a bow, and it was a moving moment to remember.

Keene Maddy of Iowa is one of the finest deer drivers I've seen. It's been my pleasure to watch him move deer and he has an uncanny sense for putting people in the right spot to shoot one of those big corn-fed bucks.

There have been countless other people who have shared their knowledge and made me a better hunter. In fact, if all were mentioned here, this book would be filled with names and comments about people. My thanks to one and all.

Many companies have helped in other ways. Product testing is an important part of company business, and thoughts from writers like myself have made it possible for many to improve their products.

People like Bill Jordan of Advantage Camo (camo clothing); Tommy Akin of Akin Promotions (deer scents); Paul Meeks of API Outdoors (treestands); Kurt von Besser of Atsko-Sno Seal (Sport-Wash and U-V Killer); Brian Johanson and Phyllis Garbow of Buck Stop Lure Company (deer scents); Bruce Watley of Bug-Out Outdoorwear (bug-proof clothing); Barbara Mellman and Bill McRae of Bushnell Sports Optics (binoculars and scopes); Jim Reid of The Coleman Company (catalytic heaters and sleeping bags); Andy Sturdevant of DeLorme Mapping Company (state maps); Mike Larsen of Federal Cartridge Company (Federal Premium rifle cartridges); Bob Eastman and Lennie Rezner of Game Tracker (Game Tracker string tracking devices, broadheads, knives, arrows and treestands); Joe Pundzak of Hunter's Specialities (deer scents); Tony Knight, Michele Bartimus and Mike Murphy of Knight Rifles (in-line muzzleloading rifles and supplies); Kevin Kreh of Hawgs Lures (man-made deer scents and cover-up sprays); Jim D'Elia of Nikon Sport Optics (binoculars and scopes); Jimmy Johnson of Ol' Man Treestands (treestands); Claude Pollington of Oneida Labs (Oneida bows) and Pollington Pro-Products (red-dot sights and bow releases); Larry Rickard of Pete Rickard, Inc. (deer scents); Bruce Stanton of PRADCO (Knight & Hale Game Calls and Code Blue deer scents); Dave Kirby of Quaker-Boy Game Calls (deer calls); Bill Robinson of Robinson Laboratories (Scent Shield spray and Scent Blocker clothing); Dave Lyons and Jim Mason of Southern Sportsman Lodge (deer hunting); Robert Pitman of White Oaks Plantation (deer hunting); Johnny Lanier of Bent Creek Lodge in Alabama (deer hunting); David Morris, formerly of Georgia's Burnt

Pine Plantation (deer hunting); Steve Scott of Alabama's Whitetail Institute of North America (Alfa-Rack, Imperial Brand Whitetail Clover and No-Plow seeds plus Cutting Edge and 30-06 mineral supplements); and Rick and Russ Markesbery (Rusty Duck products).

INTRODUCTION

Make no mistake about it—North American whitetail deer are here to stay. They not only are available across most of the United States and many Canadian provinces, but their numbers have increased dramatically over the past 20 years.

There are many reasons for the whitetails' population explosion. More and more farmland has gone to seed and grown into second-growth edge cover that deer prefer. This edge cover, as wildlife biologists and deer specialists call it, is nothing more than the "edges" of thin and heavy cover. It is found in urban and suburban areas, and in the country and in dense northern thickets . . . wherever whitetails are found.

There are hundreds of times more whitetails now than when North America was first settled. Native Americans and the first immigrants found whitetails in many locations but not in the numbers seen today.

Man created fine deer habitat when he began clearing land for farms and building homes. Once the timber era ended, and farming began, deer prospered.

Whitetail numbers reached a low point in the mid-1800s when huge timber stands, often covering countless miles in each state, province or territory, stood proud and tall and afforded little whitetail cover or food. Timber companies began cutting trees like farmers level standing cornfields, and when they ran out of timber and moved on, little remained of the former forest.

What did remain were young and tender shoots which rapidly grew into second-growth timber and undergrowth, and this provided food for the few surviving whitetails. As more land was cleared and timber was harvested, more edge cover developed, and whitetails thrived and their numbers doubled, tripled and quadrupled until now they are far too plentiful for their available habitat and food supply.

Michigan, where I live, is a good example. The state wildlife biologists vowed in the mid-1970s that by 1980 the state would have 1 million deer. They erred slightly; by 1980 nearly 1.5 million whitetails were roaming the fields, swamps and woods. By 1988, the state boasted 2 million deer. Car-deer accidents increased in rapid fashion, farmers and orchardists grumbled about "too many deer" and the annual hunter kill jumped from 140,000 in the mid-1980s to 505,000 in 2000.

Bow seasons have been expanded, more liberal antlerless deer harvests have been allowed, and as more land clearing and development occurs, more deer are being squeezed into an ever-decreasing amount of available habitat.

The result is more crop damage, more car-deer crashes, and the possibility of disease. Biologists now are trying to reduce Michigan's deer numbers by 30 percent.

New-age values, a hunter population that is growing older by the year with too little recruitment of younger hunters, has made it increasingly difficult for many states—Michigan included—to properly manage an ever growing deer population. Deer have learned how to live in close proximity to man, and there are thousands of reports across the country of urban deer populations nibbling on backyard shrubs and flowers.

Deer no longer are creatures of the deep woods. They live in small and large cities, and on numerous occasions I've seen whitetails in fields within the city limits of Detroit, Michigan's largest city. Some cities have had to adopt urban hunting rules, usually with a bow, to help control in-city deer problems.

Sure, Michigan and many other states or Canadian provinces own some deep woods or heavily forested areas where whitetail numbers are low. These areas represent only a minute portion of the state's land resources, and the rest is a generous mix of farmland and wooded areas that provide edge cover. This mix of urban, suburban, farmland and wooded terrain represents 50 to 95 percent of most states' land resources, and it's in such areas where most whitetails live.

Just what is this edge cover? By my definition, it is what many sportsmen would term farmland with open woodlots, acres of fields under cultivation, sparse clumps of heavy cover surrounded by fallow fields, and bits and pieces of heavy and sparse cover near a smorgasbord food source.

However, it is much more. It's abandoned apple orchards, drainage ditches traversing thick or thin cover, and winding two-tracks through second-growth land.

It also is a mix of open land and cattail marshes, wooded pocket covers, damp swales, tag alder thickets, abandoned railroad rights-of-way and tangled creek or river bottoms. It also is rolling hills and fertile farmland—everything but deep impenetrable forests with tall trees and little undergrowth.

The key to learning from this book, and to successfully hunting whitetails in this semi-open cover, is to remember that deer need a stable and healthy food source—whether agricultural or wild—near heavy cover where they can hide or rest, raise fawns and exist without constant human contact.

Again, quoting several Michigan wildlife biologists although the same can be said for hunters in any populous state, more whitetails are found on private lands than on public lands. Michigan wildlife biologists feel 75 to 80 percent of our 2000 deer herd live on private rather than public, state or federal lands.

This ideal whitetail habitat is far more common than many hunters believe. Look around, and you'll find the heaviest deer numbers near areas where human population is the highest. The reason is simple: Deer live where edge cover is plentiful, and where they can wax fat on plentiful foodstuffs while remaining out of touch with humans. It's important to realize that deer need little cover to survive.

Before writing this book, I polled every state and province, and turned up some startling statistics. For instance: Sportsmen who hunt the following states may not realize just how abundant edge cover may be in their area.

"Consider that most of this state is made up of edge cover along the fringes of heavy and agricultural land," said a Vermont game biologist. Kansas reports "95 percent of the state is agricultural with some wooded cover, and the balance is deep forest and federally owned land."

Tennessee boasts only 40 percent of their land falling into this category while Delaware feels 70 percent of its huntable land is this type of terrain. South Dakota figures 80 to 90 percent of its land east of the Missouri River falls within my definition, and most of it is open farmland.

It's an undeniable fact that hunting opportunities in this mixed cover are at their peak in North America, and a knowledge of the habits of whitetail deer and how they react to hunting pressure is important to continued hunting success.

There are many ways to learn more about deer hunting in areas with a generous mixture of edge cover near farmland and woods. One is to develop a rapport with the local game warden or a wildlife biologist. Learn where the heaviest deer numbers are found, and use some of the specialized hunting tactics listed in this book.

Good luck!

David Richey
Grawn, Michigan

KNOW YOUR FOODS

The buck moved like a night-prowling tomcat looking for field mice. He would stop and start, and pause to look around or to wind-check the air with quivering nostrils for a hint of human scent.

This deer was cautious; I'd been watching him from my ground blind as he fed along a cornfield edge. Twilight had switched from a promise to reality, and as darkness crept across the field with long purple shadows, the buck stopped feeding on corn and moved to the next food site.

I wanted him in front of my blind, within rifle range. He stopped once at 50 yards but was screened by low sumac bushes. Then he moved closer as my heart leapfrogged into my throat.

"Just a few more feet," I muttered to myself while urging him on. "Just take two more steps."

The buck headed for an abandoned apple orchard behind me. He'd fed on corn and now was going to top off the evening meal with a whitetail's version of apple pie.

I snuggled the rifle's buttstock to my shoulder, settled the Weaver crosshairs low behind his near shoulder, and when everything looked right I squeezed the trigger of my Model 70 Winchester. The .264 Magnum with its 140-grain softpoint roared. When the dust settled the buck was down.

He wasn't a trophy with antlers spread like wheelbarrow handles, but he was the handsome 8-pointer I'd been watching for two weeks during the preceding bow season.

Big deal! The guy watches a buck for 14 days and shoots him on opening day of the firearms season. Some hunt!

Whoa! Let's hold up here for a minute. Sure, the buck had been scouted, and watched intensively. But more importantly, I had learned his feeding habits, which explains why I was hunting near the apple orchard.

The important lesson in deer hunting is to know what deer in your locale feed on. If a hunter knows deer foods, knows where seasonal foods are located, and knows when and where whitetails feed, that person will be well on his way to scoring on antlered venison. A knowledge of food sources is the first step to becoming an accomplished hunter.

Many bow or firearm deer hunters are dealing with farm-fed whitetails. Any sportsman worthy of the name knows that deer eat corn, oats, rye, winter wheat and other farmland crops but very few know *when* deer have an appetite for the foodstuffs.

Fewer still are the hunters who know what wild foods whitetail deer eat in their state or province, and during which season these foods are consumed. Any hunter worth his deer tag will study deer, their habits, and learn when, where and how local deer eat

Farmland whitetails like this buck and doe are common sights in open fields before the hunting season begins. They often feed during the day in fields to augment their diet of natural browse.

and what they munch. Believe it or not, this key factor is ignored by about 95 percent of North America's hunters.

And some sportsmen wonder why they never score on white-tails. Savvy hunters know and study these things; unsuccessful sportsmen could care less and always blame their bad luck on the weather.

This hunter in Alabama knew that bucks like this often feed on acorns. He found the area where they were feeding, set up a stand and shot this fine buck.

Dr. Reuben Trippensee, in Volume I of his two-volume series, *Wildlife Management* (McGraw-Hill Book Co., New York) states: "Whitetail deer have been described rather aptly as 'random tip browsers plucking at a twig here and a leaf there in an apparently thoughtless and unsystematic manner.'"

How true, but there is much more to learn than just what leaves or twigs a whitetail will consume. Farm-grown crops are systematically eaten by deer in many areas. In some cases sportsmen have learned that farmland and other edge-cover deer will consume more of a farmer's crop than can be harvested, and this leads to crop-damage complaints and herd thinning by the landowner or state conservation agency.

Deer are reasonably catholic in their approach to crops or wild foods, and will eat almost anything. Consider the following wild foods consumed during winter months based on a sampling from widely scattered states: acorns, apples, blackberries, chestnuts, dogwood, dwarf sumac, greenbrier, hazelnut, mountain laurel and orchard grass from Ohio. New York counters with apples, basswood, round-leafed dogwood, staghorn sumac and witch hobble. Massachusetts deer favor apples, black cherries, dwarf raspberry, ground hemlock, hazel, hemlock, red maple, red oak and wintergreen at certain times.

South Dakota's deer flourish on foods not common east of the Mississippi River. In winter they eat bearberry, bur oak, buckbrush, Oregon grape, serviceberry and wild rose. Michigan deer prefer wild foods like ground hemlock, red osier dogwood, red maple, and white cedar. Second-class deer foods include aspen, hard maple, jackpine and white birch, but the tips are most commonly eaten in the winter.

It requires about seven pounds of food to sustain a deer each day during the winter months. They will eat buds, catkins or twigs, but a mountain of poor forage like balsam, spruce or tamarack are considered stuffing foods, food with no nutritional value. In bad weather a deer can starve to death on a full-belly ration of such foods.

Deer in North Carolina's Pisgah National Forest munch on basswood, black locust, chestnut, fetterbush, flowering dogwood, greenbrier, mountain pepper bush, red maple, red oak, saw brier, witch hazel and wild grape when truck crops aren't available.

The reason deer numbers have increased and whitetail numbers in heavily forested areas have decreased in most areas is because of the available natural food supply. Unlike humans who can grow their own food, deer cannot. The food has to grow naturally in the wild and be abundant enough to provide adequate forage for the animals in the area or they must subsist on someone's garden or crop lands . . . or die.

It isn't common knowledge but a 100-pound winter deer needs about seven pounds of daily food to keep its winter fat reserves intact. Once the fat goes, and the fat in bone marrow is diminished, the deer will die. Once a deer loses over 30 percent of its body weight, the critter is ready for the boneyard. In Michigan and other northern tier states deer often yard up (herd together) during the winter. Many deer yards have been picked clean of wild food by countless preceding generations.

Wild foods can and will sustain wild deer, but farm crops often do a better job during winter's slim pickings. The list of home-grown crops is nearly endless once all states and Canadian provinces are considered, but common truck crops like alfalfa, apples, barley, beans, celery, cherries, clover, corn, grapes, oats, peas, rye, rye grass, sassafras, soybeans, strawberries, winter wheat and others constitute a large portion of a whitetail's diet in many areas. If someone grows it, a whitetail probably eats it and flourishes in the process.

Commercially prepared clover mixes are available for sportsmen to plant in fields and wooded openings. Steve Scott of the

Winter deer in northern areas often gather in a winter deer yard to feed on white cedar once the snow gets too deep to move to agricultural fields. If a deer yard is browsed too heavily, the browse line grows out of reach of many young deer and leads to starvation.

Whitetail Institute of North America has this to say about the clovers and clover blends they sell.

"We worked with and studied various clovers for many years," Scott said. "We've learned how to grow clovers that are made for various parts of the country. Some grow well in the northern tier of states and parts of southern Canada where the winters are bad. These clovers are cold and snow resistant for the north and drought resistant for southern states and their warmer temperatures."

Scott said a deer needs 17 percent protein in its daily diet. A deer's diet requires about 0.45 percent calcium and 0.35 percent

Kay Richey (left) and Steve Scott walk up to a 12-point buck she shot while hunting a lush clover plot in central Alabama. Imperial Brand Whitetail Clover is produced for regional climates so southern seeds are drought-resistant while northern seeds are cold-resistant.

phosphorous for a well regulated antler and body growth. Their Alpha-Rack, Imperial Whitetail Clover, and No-Plow clovers, when planted on properly limed and fertilized soils, produce 30 to 35 percent protein. Their mineral supplements—30-06 and Cutting Edge—add even more of the minerals needed to produce superb antler growth. Phone (800) 688–3030 for more information.

"Much of the wild forage is good but nothing adds healthy nutritional benefits and sorely needed trace minerals like our clovers and mineral supplements," he said. "Whitetail testing has proven that protein is vitally important in the spring. The initial burst of protein goes into body development, and anything left over will go into antler growth. If a deer needs 17 percent protein to live and grow body weight, anything that provides 30 percent protein will put approximately 13 percent more protein into antler and body development."

I planted Imperial Whitetail Clover in four locations on my land and my neighbor's land two years ago. The ground was first tested, and soil tests returned with a recommendation to add lime and fertilizer before planting began.

Soil in a food plot must be fertilized and limed to bring its pH to near seven (7). Here our food plot is being fertilized and limed with a tractor and properly set spreader.

My neighbor and I spent a month cutting up sod and native grasses, and removing about 20 tons of big rocks. The land was then disced, limed and we added the fertilizer, and then waited for the optimum planting time.

The plantings were made in mid-May after spring rains had percolated the lime and fertilizer into the soil. The clover seed should only contact the ground, and must never be buried in dirt. A compacter pressed the seeds into the ground. Two days later a soft rain fell and within seven days we saw the first green clover shoots growing.

We tended the clover like a new mother doting on her first-born, and the clover grew and spread and within a month was several inches high. It didn't take long for the deer to find the succulent new growth, and by our first hunting season we were seeing more deer and bucks with bigger racks.

The second growing season was unbelievable. The deer ate paths through the clover, and continued to feed on the clover from green-up until the first snow dusted the ground. We could see craters made by pawing and feeding deer even when 10 inches of snow covered the ground.

We added several mineral deposits across our combined land. We dug shallow (six inches deep) elongated holes and filled them with Cutting Edge and/or 30-06, and the deer ate the mineral supplement like a kid eating a bag of Halloween candy. The combination of dense clover and mineral placement led us to feel that we are putting something back into our deer hunting. We also learned that what is good for deer will benefit game animals and game birds as well as local songbirds.

And best of all, we feel our deer hunting will improve as we protect young bucks and thin out excess antlerless deer. Planting green fields is only part of the overall deer management philosophy; the rest of it is learning how to manage deer on our land. We hope to

Steve Scott of the Whitetail Institute of North America in Pintlala, Alabama shows how dense and lush a field of Imperial Brand Whitetail Clover can be. Deer love the clover, and it is high in proteins.

eventually get our buck-to-doe ratio down to two does per buck, which would provide a greater number of larger antlered deer.

Every deer hunter wants to shoot a buck. Granted, arguments are in favor of thinning the deer herd in certain areas through an antlerless harvest of does and fawns, but many sportsmen still live for those days when an antlered buck walks in front of their bow or firearm sights.

It's sad but true that some bucks may get 17 percent or more protein from natural forage but some will not, and those animals that do not get enough to eat with a good balance of protein and trace minerals often have small antlers and are somewhat smaller in body structure than whitetails feeding on better range.

Two time periods are important for whitetails, and especially for bucks of six months to 1½ years—April through September and December through March. The first period is when bucks are re-building body weight after a long winter or when newborn fawns are first putting on weight. Older bucks of breeding age must feed heavily during the earlier and latter periods to carry them through the rut, and the better quality food they eat, the more likely they will enter the rut with heavy antlers and more body fat.

The second period also is critical to a rutting-age buck. The animal may lose up to 30 percent of its total weight during the rut, and it must be replaced before winter becomes severe. Some bucks never recover.

Old bucks that have spread their seed through the local doe population over a period of two months may not be able to regain lost weight and may perish during a severe winter in northern states. Winter kill of rutting-age bucks can be very high in normal climates when snow falls in November and December, and deer are yarded up in conifer swamps by New Year's Day.

A common fallacy among hunters is that 1½-year-old bucks will have spike antlers, and older bucks will carry four or more points.

Scott feels that nothing could be further from the truth. A spike buck usually is a buck with poor forage and/or genetics. If a spike-horn buck has enough protein-rich food to eat, the following year it will gain weight and will likely produce antlers that will blossom like flowers after a summer rain.

A normal whitetail buck at 1½ years of age, on good range with proper food containing adequate trace minerals, will have from four to eight points. A young deer may have a spindly rack and points with very little spread, but each year the animal lives the spread increases as does the diameter of each point on both antler beams.

However, an overpopulation of whitetails on any range (especially if the buck-doe population is heavily weighted in favor of does) can lead to a year-by-year reduction in antler size. Does will eat most of the available forage, and thereby reduce food possibilities for small bucks in the area. The male deer may suffer a decrease in antler size from one year to the next if natural forage is scarce or the winter is long.

Natural food on prime whitetail lands can support only so many deer, proving the law of supply and demand. An overpopulation of deer on the summer and winter range can lead to weakened animals and unnecessary winter kill in colder, snowier climates. Deer should be managed for quality rather than quantity, but this management policy is lost on many state conservation agencies. If numbers of deer over quality of deer is what people want (as usually is the case), and what state agencies wish, then a state's deer range should be managed to produce more food of better quality.

Unfortunately, many state wildlife agencies manage for quantity. It helps sell licenses, and put sorely needed money into state coffers. What sells deer hunting to many hunters who are afield only two or three days a year is seeing more deer. They often shoot the first antlered buck seen, regardless of body or rack size, because it allows bragging rights. Sadly, many of these people should be taking

Bucks in velvet like this one will eat natural browse and crops from a farmer's field. High protein levels can help a buck grow large antlers. This buck will be a dandy once his antlers harden.

antlerless deer rather than small bucks because that action would help reduce excess deer numbers, offer some protection to over-browsed deer yards and benefit the overall deer herd.

Grouse hunters have long known that what ruffed grouse eat will dictate where the birds will be found, but this knowledge seems lost on many deer hunters. They bop out into the woods, pick a spot that "looks good" and wait patiently for a buck to meander by within easy shooting range.

This tactic may work on occasion in some areas but it seldom produces well. Those people who always shoot bucks know where and when to hunt certain food areas.

A case in point. One year I was bowhunting on state land in northwestern Wisconsin, and acorn mast was plentiful. I had scouted the area thoroughly, and on two occasions had watched a handsome six-point buck sneak across a two-track trail ahead of my car.

I suspected he was gobbling acorns, and backtracked to a beautiful oak stand. A thick spruce stood like a sentinel at the edge of the oak grove, and a faint deer trail followed the edge. I felt the buck might be using that trail to cross the road to water.

Three choices were considered—hunt the food, hunt the trail or hunt near the water. Time was running out on this hunt; I had but one day left before the Wisconsin firearms season opened. I couldn't return for another hunt, and it was now or never.

The choice was an easy one. I'd hunt near the food source. That afternoon I hoisted my Summit treestand into the spruce and anchored it so it would offer a broadside shot if the buck fed past me the next day. I planned to return the next morning long before dawn in hopes of being in front of the feeding buck.

I arrived far too early the next morning, and spent a cold and miserable six hours in the tree. My butt felt like a practice field for the Detroit Lions' place kicker, and I soon wearied of waiting.

Shortly after noon the buck materialized like a ghost. One minute the oak ridge was empty, and the next time I looked up he was head-down and feeding my way at a distance of only 40 yards. The wind was in my face, and unless I moved prematurely or at the wrong time, I would have a chance to dust his hide with an arrow.

This buck sneaked across a two-track trail in front of me and gave me a clue the animals were feeding in the acorns. Knowing what deer eat helps in finding their feeding grounds.

The buck fed slowly for 30 minutes without seeming to move two steps, and I kept thinking he'd soon have his fill of acorns and would head past me and across the trail to water. That's what thinking did for me.

He continued to feed, and then either ran out of acorns or decided another location might offer better foraging. In short, he started moving slowly toward me with unhurried steps.

The buck bent over to nibble more mast, and then swiveled his head around at some unheard sound. I suspected more deer, but used that opportunity to lift my bow into position for a shot should the buck continue on his present course.

He turned, seemed to bore holes through me with a direct look, glanced over his shoulder again at other deer making their way through the oak grove, and then after satisfying himself that all was well, began striding down the trail. I'd guessed right; he was heading for water, and was following the same trail I had seen him on before.

The buck was allowed to walk past my treestand at 15 yards before I came to full draw. The sight pin nestled behind his shoulder, and when his near front leg reached forward for another step I made a smooth release.

The broadhead sliced through the buck and stuck six inches in the ground on the far side. He whirled, seemed to sag for a moment and then raced off in the direction from which he'd come. He covered 75 yards, and folded up in plain view. It had been a clean kill, and later his nut-sweet chops and steaks were superb.

Luck? Maybe, but I prefer to think of it as knowledge combined with an average amount of skill. If I hadn't seen the buck cross the road I may never have found the food source, and without his groceries I never would have shot that buck.

Mast such as acorns, beechnuts, chestnuts, hickory nuts and soft mast like berries and berry leaves figure highly in a whitetail's diet. States with mild winters or very little snow often have bucks, does and fawns feeding all winter on these natural food sources. An Ohio buddy of mine kills a buck each year under the same oak tree, and he does it in late December. Another buddy, this time from

South Carolina, loves to hunt in September and he shoots bucks each year that forage on berry leaves.

Bob, the Ohio hunter, told me: "Winter bucks will scratch through snow to get to acorns, and you can almost see a horizontal browse line crossing the ground where deer have dug up nuts. Deer seem to follow a daily progression, and by the time that on-ground browse line gets near my tree, I know it's time to go hunting. I watch the browse line daily, and never hunt until it reaches my treestand location."

His last buck, a big wide-beamed 10-pointer, was shot during midday from his favorite stand. Such tactics are not a result of luck, but come from knowing a deer's habits and which foods they prefer to eat at specific times of the year.

He knew from past experience that whitetails would be feeding on mast, and he also knew from which direction they would appear. It was only a matter of time before his big buck would graze within easy bow range and offer a shot.

Many hunters depend on luck. Savvy hunters make their own luck.

Many deer hunters do not have or know about distinct areas where bucks amble along like milk cows heading for the barn. Few sportsmen have locations where whitetails literally feed on acorns along a prescribed route, and eventually line themselves up for a close treestand shot. The majority of us just are not privy to such made-to-order situations.

However, we are granted a God-given amount of gray matter between our ears. It's this ability to think, and to solve how, when and where whitetails feed that makes man the supreme predator. This doesn't mean we score each time we go hunting. If such were the case we'd soon tire of hunting, and take up some mundane sport like racquetball or squash or sit home watching sitcoms on television.

Hunting appeals to sportsmen because it places a heavy premium on knowing something about the quarry we seek: where it

This Kentucky deer hunter knows the value of understanding local food sources. He placed his treestand in an area where deer are foraging on acorns from nearby oak trees.

lives, how it reacts, what it feeds on and where it goes in times of danger. Humans, for all our brains, often commit errors in judgment which allow trophy whitetails to live long enough to instill big-deer genes in enough fertile does to perpetuate the species.

Granted, everyone knows what corn or soybeans look like, but if you transplanted this Yankee down South I would be hard put to immediately be able to identify mountain laurel, witch hazel or

This well-formed 8-pointer from Wisconsin, if he makes it through the winter, will sport a much heavier rack the following year if nutritious food is available.

other southern wild foods. I'm confident that within two weeks I could identify those foods and learn how to hunt near them.

Every state conservation or natural resources agency could supply a courteous sportsman with a list of local wild foods. Learning to identify them would be up to you.

A hunter's ability to become a proficient whitetail hunter rests solely on just how informed that person wishes to be. Wild deer foods and truck crops can be learned overnight without pain or strain. Just remember that truck-crop food sources may change from year to year in a specific locale, but a quick check in soft earth near each food source will reveal whether deer are utilizing these foods. Take time to learn where each food type is consumed by deer, where the animals feed on wild foods, and where they bed down and you'll be a leg up on other deer hunters.

Whitetail foods are important, but this knowledge is only one small piece of the deer hunting puzzle. But agricultural and wild foods are two key pieces around which deer hunting success is built, and this information is required knowledge for the other deer hunting puzzle pieces to fall into place.

2

TERRAIN: A KEY TO DEER HUNTING SUCCESS

I t's important for deer hunters to realize that hunting success comes to those people who are intimately familiar with local whitetail terrain. They know where deer feed, where they bed, which travel routes they follow to and from bedding and feeding areas, and which escape routes are favored when danger threatens.

Learning these facts from a book is like knowing that Bill Gates has money. How the computer mogul made his bucks is well known, but learning how terrain differs is meaningless unless a hunter is willing to lay down boot leather to learn the local terrain as well as they would know the dimensions and layout of their home. Only time and experience can teach deer hunters how to recognize excellent whitetail habitat at a glance.

One habit of mine while driving 50,000 to 60,000 miles each year is to study the land as it passes the windshield of my car. I note the presence of natural forage or croplands, and it's instinctive to look for terrain features that cause whitetail deer to travel in certain directions. I've been known to stop, stretch my legs, and walk the shoulder of the road in search of deer tracks. Do this enough times and in enough places, and you instinctively begin sizing up the land for hunting potential even though you may never hunt there.

North America is a maze of differing terrain features. Habitat where whitetails thrive in the Midwest is often much different from that commonly found in northern Minnesota or along the Missouri Breaks. Where whitetails live in eastern Tennessee along the Great Smoky Mountains will differ from what hunters can expect to find in northern Maine.

Compare the prime whitetail habitat of Alberta, Manitoba or Saskatchewan and it will differ greatly from southern states like Alabama, Georgia, Louisiana or Mississippi. The cottonwood canyons along streams in western Idaho or Montana will be far different than a hunter would find in South Carolina's tangled woods.

Hunters should have learned in the previous chapter about how important it is to recognize local natural forage and farm crops, and the same holds true in this chapter. Putting preferred deer foods together with certain terrain features is somewhat like putting together a meal of bacon and eggs. Putting food and terrain together into a cohesive package of information is important to continued hunting success.

One of the most important things I thought I had learned was given to me by an old codger many years ago when deer hunting was but a distant glimmer of hope in my teenage mind. The old-timer had shot a few deer, as I recall, but he didn't rack up a kill each year and was seldom seen in the woods.

"Find yourself the highest hill in the area and sit tight," the old coot said. "Them deer, why, they be crawlin' all over ya as soon as the opening-day guns go bang."

Larry Barrett knows about examining terrain features, and found this buck trail leading through cattails. He hung a treestand nearby, and nailed the buck using an escape route into the vegetation.

"Oh, yeah," I asked. "Why's that?"

"Them deer will be leaving the co'nfields and tryin' to get up high where they can watch the redcoats."

"No kidding? I always thought they headed for thick cover."

"No sirree. They go up topside to keep a sharp lookout for hunters, and that's where ya should be sittin' with your shotgun. Get 'em when they come over the crest of the hill."

Amazing, I thought. Here was my chance to be the first kid on my block to waylay a deer, and the old gent had felt enough pity for my scrawny hide to pass along his cherished words of wisdom.

Well, the opening-day guns went bang and I could see the redcoats. They were sitting in ground blinds near the "co'nfields," and they were shooting deer. Whitetails scooted off in every direction, but if memory serves me correctly the scurrying deer seemed to be following a prescribed course toward safety . . . through heavy cover. I figured that perhaps I had chosen the wrong hill to defend against the deer.

I didn't shoot a buck that year while sitting on the highest hill in the area, and I didn't take one the following year from the same spot. Perhaps in my teen-age years with the scrambled hormones of puberty a recent memory, I wasn't a quick study or at least that is what the old-timer alluded to when I complained about my wonderful lack of deer-hunting success.

The old-timer bad-mouthed me, insinuating that some movement of mine must have spooked any bucks heading my way. The second year I didn't move a muscle, and that hilltop was as dreary as a Russian love story and as empty of deer as the Sahara Desert.

The only whitetails I saw that year looked about the size of a gnat's backside as they scrammed away from the hill. I did see a few bucks, but other deer hunters had them securely fastened to the roofs of their vehicles for the long drive home. When questioned, they said they ambushed the deer as they tried to move into heavy cover.

After my second opening-day fiasco, I spent every waking moment possible reading anything I could find about whitetail deer habitat and how to hunt various types of terrain. That winter was a real eye-opener for me, and had castration or death been positive alternatives, I would have practiced one or both on the old goat.

My reading and studying was more important than my algebra class, and infinitely more fun that trying to learn Latin. I wanted to know when and where deer fed, how they made babies, when antlers grew and fell off, and any other tidbit that could be obtained from what was then the Michigan Conservation Department.

I was like Sherlock Holmes tracking down clues. The wildlife biologists must have taken pity on me, and sent me a raft of material dealing with Michigan's whitetails. I devoured it in throat-choking chunks.

Whitetail information was absorbed like a new kitchen sponge wiping up spilled water. I discarded worthless information such as the well-meaning old-timer offered. I learned that in Western states mule deer and whitetails do go high and squirrel themselves back into secure corners where they can watch their backtrail and escape over the top without being seen. I also learned that deer found near urban, suburban or rural areas where farm crops are a major part of their diet seldom go high.

Such deer become adept at diving into the puckerbrush. They also frequent thickets so dense a bunny would have trouble getting through, and they hide out in pocket cover where most hunters least expect them to go.

Since those early forays into the deer woods I've boosted good bucks from thickets no larger than a small brushpile, and I've bounced them from low spots with high grass in rolling hills. They've been rousted from thick swamps an acre in size, cattail marshes and tag alder swales, but one fact is true with deer near farmland—they seldom head for high ground but will hide in areas where few hunters tread and wise men fear to go.

Terrain becomes a major part in solving whitetail deer travel wherever they are found. It ranks in importance with knowing

Flat Western country often holds whitetails near arroyos or cottonwood creek bottoms, and a good spot to glass from is a high rocky knob that affords good coverage of the entire area.

preferred seasonal foods. However, terrain is easily assimilated once a hunter gives serious thought to where deer live, feed or hide.

Topographical maps are useful, but nothing beats walking the area on foot. Some hunters of my acquaintance will walk almost every inch of their proposed hunting area, and make their own map that

This man is studying a detailed topo map, looking for likely deer hangouts. Such maps often show land contours, ridges, swamps, water sources, lakes, streams, swamps and other features that are important to hunters looking for deer hunting hotspots.

shows recognizable terrain features. Many use a Global Positioning System to mark key points and routes to get out of the woods safely.

These hunters look for key areas like where deer bed and feed, trails to and from those sites, and they scrutinize the terrain for rubs and scrapes from rutting deer. They learn where bucks move along escape trails if the hunting pressure increases, and they learn the terrain from a hunter's viewpoint . . . from the ground up.

It is this intimate knowledge of terrain and their obvious and not-so-obvious features that will separate the men from the boys. This point is one which I still recall from my early and dismal failures. Good hunters, with a keen attention to detail, know where preferred wild foods are found and know where the shortest routes are to nearby farmlands. If they can locate these food sources, so can deer.

Only through thorough scouting of an area can a hunter learn enough about the terrain to make an accurate and well founded decision as to where deer will move. Deer, almost universally during the early seasons, begin moving about an hour before dusk from their bedding areas to a food site. The reverse occurs about an hour before sunup when deer begin moving along familiar trails toward their bedding areas. It's along these trails where hunters hope to intercept a nice buck.

Whether they do or don't depends, to a large degree, on how well they know the terrain. An area should be as familiar to the hunter as to the deer being hunted.

Deer are far easier to scout in edge cover or farmland than in large unbroken tracts of swamp or heavy timber. There are only so many places a deer can hide in urban, suburban or close-to-people rural areas. The key thing to remember about such locations is that thick cover is a relative thing.

If a field is planted to soybeans, as an example, there is nowhere to hide in a bean field. That casual but pointed observation would then indicate the animals must be living in nearby thicker cover.

Glassing flat terrain with binoculars is a good scouting method if the hunter can get high enough to gain visibility of the area. The important thing is to take the terrain apart visually by thoroughly checking out all available nearby cover.

Heavy cover may be a huge mile-square cornfield or an overgrown railroad right-of-way. It could be a cattail marsh, sumac swale or abandoned fruit orchard grown over to briers and brambles. Often small or fairly large woodlots, drainage ditches, low brushy tangles in the middle of an open field are excellent possibilities. An island in the middle or a large stream or lake is a good bet because few hunters suspect such areas will offer a safe harbor for deer.

Remember one important fact: Deer will seldom travel more than a mile to feed on farm grown crops. They may munch on wild forage near bedding sites, and they may feed for days in a clump of mast-bearing oaks, but they will rarely travel long distances to feed in a farmer's soybean or winter wheat field. Often, deer that graze farm crops will bed down anywhere from 100 yards to a quarter-mile from this preferred food site.

Whitetails, like many people except you and me, are basically lazy and seem reasonably content with their lot in life. If this fact is understood, we can better understand why so many prime deer bedding locations are found close to food.

If local deer favor buckwheat, and the nearest buckwheat patch is three miles away, the animals will find a substitute far closer to home. Deer as a rule will not travel far to feed unless they are run out by hunting pressure, dogs or a lack of food.

If the main forage base during a hunting season is acorns, for instance, it wouldn't make sense to look for nearby bedding whitetails and their travel route to and from bedding sites near a cornfield if visual observation shows few fresh deer tracks. Hunters must hunt near areas where deer feed on a daily basis.

The ability to match food and terrain can be learned once you get the hang of it. Deer usually go to the best (and closest) foods for the season near a bedding site, and they follow certain terrain features to reach the food source. If sportsmen can keep that thought in mind it becomes the logical second step in finding key hunting locations.

100 PERCENT FARMLAND

There are very few spots where 100 percent of the whitetail habitat is made up entirely of farmland or truck crops. A mile-square cornfield with roads bordering all four sides would qualify, and deer can and will use such areas to satisfy their three basic needs—food, cover and water.

Huge cornfields are a pain to hunt. I know because I've done it many times with less than spectacular success although smaller cornfields are a snap to hunt. The problem with a big cornfield is its size: It is difficult to stalk a buck or move the animals when they don't want to leave heavy cover. The hunter, even on snow, will continue to play hide-and-seek all day. A buck may make a mistake but don't bet big money on it.

Take it from one who knows: trying to move a buck from a huge cornfield and into bow or firearm range is about as much fun as wrestling Mr. Perfect (Kurt Hennig), a strapping giant of a man whom I've hunted with on occasion. All the hunter will do in either case is get beat up, tired and frazzled from the exertion, and meanwhile, the buck will crawl into another corn row nearby and get away.

I remember once when two hunting buddies and I watched a tremendous buck drift agilely across a dirt road and into a large cornfield at noon as we headed in for a quick burger. The buck was so fat his belly jiggled like Jello, and his rack numbered at least 12 heavy points. The antlers looked more like a hat rack than a normal deer rack.

Larry Jacobson and Marv Whitcomb, two longtime friends, were with me. I figured that fat old boy would be a piece of cake, and that hunting him would be a walk in the park. That's what thinking did for me.

"I'll take the track," I said. "You guys spread out, and one cut to the north and find a good trail leading out of the corn and the other do the same thing on the east side. This buck doesn't have any cover on the south or west sides, and he should head toward one of you."

How naive I was to think an old rutting buck would perform in such a manner. Clueless might be a better description of this fiasco.

I quickly jumped on the buck's track in four inches of snow after giving my friends 15 minutes to get into position to ambush the animal. The snow deadened my approach, and I ghosted along as quietly as a hunting owl.

The buck entered the cornfield, traveled only 50 yards, meandered back and forth through the corn rows and laid down. Unfortunately, I didn't get a chance to shoot him in his bed. He got up from his bed as I entered the corn, moved several rows to one side of my travel path, and continued to lead me in a circle for four hours.

I eventually worked out of the corn, found Jacobson, and asked: "Have you seen any sign of the buck?"

"No," he said. "Marv walked down here an hour ago and he hasn't seen the buck. Where did he go?"

The truth was that without an army or several battalions of hunters it would have been impossible to move that buck from the cornfield. He stayed just far enough ahead of me to jump off to one side and backtrack to avoid any contact. On several occasions I found where he stood only 10 feet away and watched me blunder along his trail.

Darkness fell and we didn't get that buck, and we never saw him again. This points out the futility of hunting areas with huge amounts of tall crops like corn. There are just too many places for a buck to hide and only a mistake on the buck's part plus some luck on the hunter's part, will work.

It would have been a much wiser decision to take up positions along game trails as I should have suggested, and wait for him to walk out just before dark. But we were certain he would bed down and then run in panicked flight for heavy cover to the north or east. He did just the opposite; the buck hid in the corn, and watched me get tired.

Huge tracts of tall and thick cropland like that cornfield will hold deer, but only in times of danger. Frequently, deer will bed down in heavy cover and move after dark.

The ideal solution is to scout the immediate area and determine which trails are used to enter or leave the corn. Look for deer trails to follow brushy fencerows, ditches that drain croplands, narrow fingers of woods that connect with adjacent woodlots or any other terrain feature which affords cover during daylight hours.

SMALL WOODLOTS

Some of my fondest deer hunting memories are of small woodlots. This type of terrain is common in most suburban or rural areas where deer are found. A parcel of woods from one to 10 acres, and preferably longer than wide on the upwind side is a good bet. Wind direction is important to hunters, but the prevailing wind must coincide with the land and its terrain features.

I like small woodlots; you know the kind, all grown over to briers which tear hell out of fashion jeans and hunting pants alike. Often there are forgotten bits of timber and berry bushes . . . and at odd times, deer.

Many woodlots on farms are posted. This makes it all the better for a deer hunter with permission to hunt because whitetails often hole up where not every dude with a blaze-orange vest will hunt.

This terrain is common through most of the whitetail's range, and big bucks thrive in such locations. The woodlot offers cover, access to nearby heavier cover and food if they wish. Such locations are easy to find; getting permission can be hard.

What a deer hunter needs to know is how bucks (does are deer, too) travel in the area and how they leave it. Tracks in soft earth near croplands or along roadside edges plus sign of rubs or scrapes will reveal the deer's presence.

Find woodlots with some type of inside cover which leads to nearby heavier cover. Again, a narrow finger of woods, a wooded funnel or drainage ditch that connects a small woodlot with a larger one is an ideal location for a trophy buck.

John McKenzie, of Millington, Michigan, and I used to team up on deer in small woodlots, and we seldom went past the second

Look for deer sign. This hunter points to a single deer track along a little used trail near bedding cover. It was probably made by a buck. Tracks tell the story of where deer travel, and it's up to the hunter to know enough about local terrain features to determine hunting hotspots. Photo courtesy of Paul Kerby.

day of the 16-day firearm season without hanging our tag on two nice bucks. We worked hard at scouting, developed special techniques (covered in a later chapter) and scored when deer decided the pressure was too hot for them and chose to move on to an area with less hunter traffic.

One thing we learned is that many deer hunters bypass woodlots which are not visible from one side to the other. They usually pass up a good chance at a buck by doing so. We learned, early in the game, to allow brush busters to move deer to our select locations and we often shot the bucks they hoped to find.

Wind direction is important, and it's doubly so when gunning whitetails in small woodlots. A puff of wind from the wrong quarter once blew a chance for one of my buddies. He had been on stand for two hours, and the wind was in his face and blowing from a nearby heavy covert where he expected deer to be holding. He was watching an area downwind near an adjacent woodlot where the bucks were expected to head once the opening-day pressure became intense.

"I'd been there for two hours, and felt that any minute a buck would slip out of the bigger woodlot, cross the field into my woods and try to sneak out across the road into a big swamp," he said. "I sat tight, and several sportsmen tried a noisy drive on the big woods about 10 a.m. in hopes of pushing out an antlered deer.

"Five minutes later a buck slipped from heavy cover, ran along a fencerow for 100 yards and then dashed across an open field toward me. He entered my woodlot and two minutes later was moving my way, but was still screened by thick brush.

"The wind had been in my face all morning, but once the buck closed the gap I felt the telltale cooling of neck hairs and knew the game was over. He slammed to a stop, tested the wind and knew exactly where I was posted. He vamoosed out one side of the tiny woodlot, and the last thing I saw was his tail disappearing over a fence 200 yards away. He never came back, and I'll never forgive that wind change. It cost me a shot at a good buck."

This anecdote points out two important points; farmland deer are as savvy as whitetails anywhere, and they pay attention to what their noses tell them. The second point is that deer will follow desired cover whenever possible, but will not think twice about abandoning a specific route if danger is present and they feel threatened.

The ideal woodlot, in my opinion, is 100 to 200 yards long and 30 to 60 yards wide. It should be bordered on two or three sides by open fields with brush-choked fencerows leading into or out of heavy cover. Look for woodlots with tangles of heavy briers, brush or undergrowth inside the woods and croplands surrounding it.

Choice wooded areas are abundant and found wherever most whitetails live. They dot the countryside, and often can be seen from main highways, side roads and two-track trails, and many are

Fencerows offer a great travel route for farmland bucks, and this animal chose the wrong fencerow to travel. He found this hunter waiting nearby. One shot did the job.

found within 100 yards of a house. They all have one common denominator: They almost always connect with a fencerow, finger of woods or other heavy cover that leads to another woodlot. They may not be big tracts of land, but are relatively small. Size means little when one judges it for deer habitat potential.

Ignore clear-cut woods or other cover where most of the trees and undergrowth have been removed. Forget about those where it's possible to see from end to end or side to side, and ignore those that border fallow fields or land without food crops. Instead, look for wooded locations with food on two or three sides where visibility inside the woods is good, and where whitetails have an avenue or two which can be used to escape danger.

HILL COUNTRY

Hilly or rolling terrain offers exciting hunting possibilities, but it places an extra burden on sportsmen to know when, where and how deer travel for food or to bed down. If a hunting area is hilly, and has farmland nearby, it probably qualifies.

One important reminder: If the land is hilly, it must have corresponding gullies or ravines as well. One way to recognize and learn to hunt hill-country terrain is to understand that untroubled deer often cross open hillsides as a matter of course just as they often follow the bottom or sides of a gully. It's what they do during times of danger that can spell their downfall.

Many hills in or near farmland country are rather open although I've seen spots in Idaho, Montana and other western states where the terrain is fairly rugged for a whitetail deer. Most such hills near farmland may have a copse of trees along the sides or on top, but open visibility is a key factor. If a hunter can spot a buck 400 yards away it is equally likely that he can spot a sportsman as well.

Almost every hilly area I've hunted will have small depressions ringing the edge where deer can travel without being seen. Whitetails often travel these minor ridges or gullies during daylight hours although they will move through the more open country after dark.

My old bud, the guy who stuck me on a hill as a teenager, was partially right about whitetails but not in the area he placed me. He thought deer would swarm around me like flies over freshly dropped road apples, but he was wrong. He was on target where the terrain is almost entirely made up of hills, and where deer must travel or circumvent those hills to move from bedding to feeding areas and back again. My friend had both oars in the water, but unfortunately they weren't in sync with each other.

Glassing from high ridges in open country can be a perfect way to locate where deer are found and where they travel. Good binoculars are a key to studying terrain from afar.

It's very important to find high-country trails being used at dawn and dusk. Look for droppings, hair caught on barbed-wire fences and tracks in low, wet spots. Learn where deer travel, and look for a nearby ambush spot. A nearby hill that overlooks such areas offers a superb location for a pit blind, and since most of the hunter is below ground it can be a fine spot to waylay a buck on opening day. The trick is to find the best spot that overlooks active trails.

Hill country can be fascinating hunting territory for deer hunters, but a sportsman must learn to see those areas where deer travel and know where each trail leads. The best way to collect a hill-country buck is to watch a specific location for a week or two before deer season opens and learn where and when they travel. Make plans to be there ahead of the animals, and be ready. My Bushnell spotting scope has helped me locate moving deer many times, and good binoculars are an asset.

ABANDONED FARM ORCHARDS

Bucks survive by hanging out in some very unorthodox locations, and these areas are commonly spots where few hunters go. They've learned to identify nasty cover that humans often avoid, and they head for it like a homeless person heading for a hot and free meal.

An abandoned farm orchard that grows up to tangles of forgotten berry bushes is a great example. Such orchards often are found on old homesteads where the dwelling has caved in and the land has reverted back to heavy cover.

Many of these buck hotspots look better suited to cottontail rabbits than deer, and this is one reason many sportsmen bypass them in search of easier terrain. They often blow them off with a statement like "the hell with it. It's too thick in there for deer, and we'll rip our clothes apart looking for tracks. Let's move on."

They do, and the buck watches them walk away. Chances are good a buck was sitting tight within 50 yards. I've seen this scenario play itself out many times, but a tangle where a beagle would find rough going is just perfect for a farmland buck.

Bucks with the heaviest antlers live longer because they have learned to go to ground when near humans. They are savvy, and know how to avoid human contact.

I believe it is impossible for an abandoned orchard to be too thick for a big whitetail. I once saw a pretty 8-pointer jump a fence when hounded by hunters, and he jumped into an old orchard with reckless abandon. It was so thick two fleas would have had trouble trying to start a family. The tangle was a mix of blackberry and red raspberry bushes, and if you've tried walking through those thorny jaspers you know what I mean. They are so mean that canvas-faced bird hunting pants are ripped by the little thorny bushes, but a buck seems to slide through like he is covered with graphite powder. Once he hit the brambles, he didn't slow down until he was 50 yards inside it.

The hunters saw him go in, but there wasn't a man among the bunch with enough testosterone to try rooting him out. They all thought he went through the orchard and out the other side, and it was true . . . but not right then. Two hours later he moved out in front of me, and I was ready and waiting for him.

I was sitting near a crossing on the downwind side hoping for a shot if he decided to move before shooting time ended. He did, and I did.

I chose not to hunt that orchard, but knew the buck would move out sooner or later. The trick wasn't in shooting that buck but knowing enough about the terrain and his travel routes to be there, ready and waiting, when he arrived. It was an easy shot.

David Hale of Kentucky checks for scrapes. This is the beginning of a scrape, and knowing how terrain features lead from bedding to feeding areas will help him take a buck during bow season.

DRAINAGE DITCHES

Drainage ditches in agricultural lands are deer magnets. Here's why.

Wherever cultivation and farm crops are grown will be ditches that drain excess water from the land and carry it to nearby creeks or rivers. These ditches, in many cases, have been in place since the land was first tilled.

The amazing thing about ditches is that more people don't hunt them. They often traverse a field from one woodlot to another or from one swamp to a stand of thick brush. They are highways for deer travel just as an expressway moves hunters to where deer live. The only difference is highways are built on the land, and these ditches are below ground level.

Some ditches are only three or four feet deep and some can be 10 to 12 feet deep. The depth isn't as important as the fact that deer can reduce or eliminate being seen by traveling through them. One of the Michigan areas I hunt has a small ditch that is dry most years, and it drains a small parcel of low brushy cover.

What makes it important to me is it connects with a nearby swamp and stream at one end and an open clover field at the other. A deer can move out of the swamp an hour before dark, meander down the ditch and arrive at the chow line at dusk. The deer are virtually invisible to highway traffic less than 200 yards away, and tall marsh grass along the banks provides additional cover.

Many ditches or creek bottoms have additional cover as well. Some are loaded with brush, small tag alders and other low-growing trees and bushes. Many may be dry except during rainy weather but deer will follow drainage ditches for long distances to avoid contact with hunters.

The trick to hunting drainage ditches is to recognize them for what they really are. They are more than a way to drain farm fields;

they serve deer well as a secure way to enter or exit a food source without being seen.

TWO-BIT SWALES

A two-bit swale is seemingly no bigger around than a quarter, but I've seen them produce some nice whitetails. Picture a big open field that contains a tiny alder or sumac swale without any other cover for hundreds of yards.

The wee postage stamp-sized swale stands out like a wart on Aunt Agatha's nose. It's as obvious as a sucker punch, but few people recognize it as whitetail cover.

One year I was hunting ringneck pheasants with my German shorthair and two other people. We covered that field like a blanket without seeing a bird.

"Let's try that little swale," I said to my friends. They looked at me like I was a bit tetched but agreed to give it a try.

We had nothing to lose because my car was over a hill on the other side of the swale. I sicced my dog ahead, and took the middle while my friends were evenly spaced on either side of me and my pooch.

Fritz, my sure-as-death-and-taxes bird dog, was acting a bit strange. He didn't act birdy as if a pheasant was nearby. He acted as if he was doing something wrong like moving in on a rabbit, skunk or turtle. He had that look that bird dogs develop when they know they are doing something wrong.

I moved in ahead of the other hunters. We wanted pheasants, not rabbits.

We looked over that swale like we were searching for a lost wallet. We didn't see a thing until we reached the end of the swale and a whitetail buck burst out of the cover only six feet away. It had been hiding, and we almost stepped on him before he burst out with that dignified grace that only nice bucks seem to possess.

Rivers that run through thick cover as is found along both sides of this stream offer canoers a chance to get into and hunt pockets of cover normally not available any other way. Small points like the one shown on the river's right side allow hunters to drive or still-hunt toward the river and keep deer in front of them at all times.

It pays to hunt tiny pockets of cover. Small swales are a good bet, and they should never be overlooked. Hunt them as if hunting larger cover, and be ever mindful of the prevailing wind direction and your approach.

One thing about two-bit swales: they produce only on occasion, but more than one trophy buck has met his fate from such tiny areas. Swales are common wherever farmland is found, and it really doesn't take much more cover to hide deer than rabbits.

A swale usually is lower than the surrounding terrain but it can be slightly higher. I've found some two-bit swales in hollows on top of hills, and such locations attract bucks like movement and sweat attract spring blackflies. Treat each swale with respect because it just may produce the buck of a lifetime.

SWAMPS

When the average deer hunter thinks of a swamp he sees a sprawling area of cedar with more of it under water than above. Those types of swamps are commonly found across the northern tier of states and such areas are often found near farmland.

A swamp is a swamp, and two factors are the presence of thick cover and water. I've waded Alabama's water logged palmetto swamps and Great Lakes cattail swamps.

The most common swamps near farmland are much smaller in size. Many may range in size from one to 10 acres. They are dense, difficult to walk through and they feature standing water or boot-sucking mud. Alder, balsam, cedar, spruce or tamarack are usually found nearby.

There is a swamp not far from where I live, and as cedar swamps go it's a small one. But, it is a wet and wild tangle inside and deer hunters passionately avoid it because of persistent rumors of quicksand and rattlesnakes.

I know all about the rumors, and they aren't true simply because my friends have been responsible for spreading the falsehoods. They are trying to protect one small portion of mini-wilderness in a sea of farm country. The swamp does offer good deer hunting, and it isn't overrun by sportsmen. We hope to keep it that way so our children will have good deer hunting near home in the years to come.

The rumors have been spread in many ways. One time we were sitting in a diner before our afternoon hunt. A coffee-drinking customer sitting nearby was togged out in camouflage clothing, and he saw our similar clothing and posed the question.

"Are you from around here?" he asked. "Do you bowhunt?"

We nodded that we were and we did, and he continued, "What can you tell me about that little swamp three miles north of town?"

That was our prime hunting spot, and my partner didn't need much time to launch into his wild-eyed save-the-swamp spiel. Each one is a bit different because he adjusts it to match what he perceives as the mental make-up of his questioner.

Lee looked up, a terrified look in his eyes as he rubbed his scruffy beard, and began his spellbinding story. The stranger didn't stand a chance.

"That swamp is one bad spot," he said. "I tried hunting it four years ago, and although I get around well in the woods I didn't think I'd ever get out of there. There are bogs of boot-sucking mud, and I hear there are patches of quicksand scattered around. It's very tough to hunt, and I never plan to go back.

"I was lost almost from the moment I walked into the swamp, and after wandering around for five hours trying to get my bearings I sat down under a cedar tree. I dozed off, and then woke up with the feeling something was looking at me. I looked around but the feeling was too strong to ignore. Something was watching me.

"Then, only five feet from my boots I spotted a Massasauga rattler staring at me from a coiled position. I was scared, and didn't know what to do but when I moved I know I set a new world record for a sitting broad jump. I spent the night in that hellhole, and it wasn't until the next day the county sheriff and his posse spotted smoke from my campfire and led me out to safety.

"Yep, I know that swamp well, and I'll never go back into it."

His audience's eyes were as big as his coffee saucer when Lee ended his fabricated tale. He had touched all the bases: boot-sucking mud, quicksand, rattlesnakes, spending all night in an eerie swamp, a smoking campfire and the final irony of having a sheriff and posse root him out the next day. The sport didn't want any part of that tiny swamp so we sent him off to a good deer spot far away from us.

Swamps hold deer because few hunters really try to learn where the animals bed down or hide once hunting season begins. Such areas are made to order for the hunter with hip boots or chest-high waders, and the stamina needed to wade through mud, muck and water to find a good hunting spot.

It's not common knowledge, but under pressure a whitetail will stand for hours in chest-deep water. I once shot a little spikehorn which had been wounded by another hunter who failed to recover the wounded animal.

Firearm season had been open for several days, and Roger Kerby and Lee Blahnik were driving a thin strip of cedar swamp toward me. I heard a shot, another one and a lot of yelling.

"He's in the water and he's wounded," Kerby shouted.

The nearby lake was covered with skim ice, but I could see where the young buck had crashed through the ice. Try as I might it was impossible to see the little buck although I could see blood on the ice. The shoreline was searched, and then I saw what appeared to be a nostril sticking up from the water. I scoped the area and could barely see the buck's outline under the surface.

I yanked up my thigh-high boots, and waded out toward the deer thinking it was dead. The buck spooked from the water, and I quickly brought the iron sights of my Ruger .44 Magnum down behind the shoulders and shot him on dry ground.

That buck would have been lost had it not been for our efforts to recover a wounded animal. As sportsmen, we owe it to deer to recover each and every one.

Deer love swamps because few hunters go there. Here, Kay Richey and Steve Scott inspect a rub along a trail leading from boggy cover.

Swamps can be tough to hunt, and for many sportsmen, they choose to hunt the edges rather than the interior. Few people are willing to chance getting lost just for a deer, and that suits dedicated swamp hunters just fine.

There are other types of cover which hold deer and they will be mentioned in following chapters about hunting techniques. The trick is to remember that food and terrain are two major reasons why whitetails will be found in certain areas. The only other thing that will pull whitetails into another location is the rut, and here we go.

3

DEER DURING THE RUT

The wide-antlered buck tiptoed along like he was walking on egg shells. One second his nose was in the air with his upper lip curled back as he sniffed something he liked, and the next his nose was near the ground as he trailed a receptive doe.

It was the rut—that period when sexually mature whitetail bucks think more with their hindquarters than their heads. It was late autumn, just before the second full moon after the autumnal equinox, and this boy was ready for some action.

That was the scene when Roger Kerby arrived at one of his treestands. He guides deer hunters during Michigan's firearm season, but this was bow season. He entered his treestand with little time to spare. The buck, although 150 yards away, was closing the gap as Kerby scaled the tree like a squirrel, readied an arrow and dropped his camo face mask to cover glistening skin.

The buck was head-down and still coming, and he paid little attention to the camo-clad hunter high in the sugar maple. The buck moved past Kerby at a steady pace while grunting with every step.

"He was grunting like a barnyard oinker," Kerby said later. "I heard him coming for 100 yards, and just over the crest of the hill stood the waiting doe. It was a tense situation; if the doe saw any movement the game would be over before I could shoot."

His treestand was near the junction of three well-used deer trails, and the buck was heading for the intersection like an 18-wheeler rolling into a truck stop for hot coffee and a look at a pretty waitress. The massive buck passed within 10 yards of Kerby's stand, and as the deer continued merrily on his way the bowhunter came to full draw. He hesitated for a head pounding moment, and sent the arrow through the buck's chest.

"The buck kicked like a rodeo bull," Kerby said. "I knew I had full arrow penetration, and watched him run over the hill, still in hot pursuit of the doe. Fifty yards away he sagged to his knees, and fell within 10 seconds of arrow impact."

It was a clean kill. It wasn't just a buck but one for Pope & Young's record books.

Kerby's 9-pointer was big, and it scored nearly 140 points in the prestigious Pope & Young scoring charts. The score was more than enough to place it in the records, and it was taken during the rut when so many record-book bucks are taken by bow or firearm hunters.

I've been giving deer hunting seminars for more than 25 years. One question I always put to my audience is: When is the best time of year to shoot a whitetail buck?

Invariably, most hunters say the rut is the best time. I disagree entirely because the best time is the first day of bow season providing a hunter has conducted preseason scouting, found areas where bucks appear on a regular basis, and if the sportsman knows how to avoid the does that often precede bucks down deer trails.

This nice 8-point buck's neck is starting to swell as testosterone floods his system just before the rut begins.

The second best time, in my humble opinion, is the five days immediately preceding the onset of the rut. In northern latitudes, this almost always occurs within a week of the second full moon following the autumnal equinox.

The rut happens to be one of the most misunderstood facets of whitetail deer behavior. Rut rumors and old wives' tales have influenced countless hunters to believe their validity. Such tales would have wild-eyed bucks jumping from one doe to another like a game of musical chairs. Tales about rutting bucks often fall into the same category as Santa Claus, the Tooth Fairy and the Easter Bunny.

Mind you, some of this background on rutting bucks is true. However, much of what is commonly believed is as true as the belief that all politicians are honest. The fact is many hunters really know very little about the rut.

It's been my distinct pleasure to have spent time talking to and interviewing renowned deer researchers like Georgia's Larry Marchinton and Michigan's John Ozoga. Both men have many years of in-depth deer research under their belts, and they have forged new frontiers in the knowledge about rutting deer.

Ozoga also has authored four books on whitetails—*Whitetail Spring, Whitetail Summer, Whitetail Autumn* and *Whitetail Winter.* The complete set of four hardbound books, in a slipcase and author signed, sells for $105 postpaid from John J. Ozoga, N. 6383 Knox Street, Munising, MI 49862. These four books cover the four seasons of the whitetail deer, and any hunter will be able to learn from them.

What is the rut, when does it occur, what triggers it and what does it mean to deer hunters? Those questions can be answered fully based on research conducted by Marchinton, Ozoga, et al. It's important to realize that deer hunting, and hunting for big bucks, is a major business in North America.

There are continuing studies being conducted on bucks and does, mating habits, rutting characteristics and the like, and it may be many more years before biologists and scientists fully understand the whitetail rut. For now, the information that follows is based on scientific data and my personal observations of rutting whitetails over 40-plus years.

Hunters want to know how to shoot a rutting buck but it's important to know what the breeding period really means. So learn these things, and hunting will get easier.

There may be some hunters willing to poke holes in my logic, but suffice it to say that I'm in the deer woods an average of 85 days during Michigan's 90-day season. I also spend a few weeks in

Lee Blahnik shot this rutting 8-point buck while hunting near a pine plantation. He placed himself about 50 yards downwind from an active scrape and shot the buck as it checked its scrape in midafternoon.

September and January scouting prospective hunting locations for the upcoming or following season. Add to that the fact that I spend two or three weeks hunting in other states before or after our state seasons open or close, and it amounts to a great deal of time in the field studying whitetail deer.

Whitetail deer become sexually active in the autumn of their second year at the age of about 1½ years. Very few of these bucks will do any breeding unless the deer herd contains an excessively high number of does. It's sad but true that most of the deer taken during hunting seasons will be 1½-year-old bucks and does. Few deer reach the ripe age of five to seven years when their antler growth reaches its maximum growth potential. Deer management in many states is slanted to numbers, not trophies.

Doe breeding usually is done by dominant bucks, and these animals, depending on herd composition and location, will be 2½ to 4½ years old. In some locations where deer numbers are low, and hunting pressure is minimal, some bucks of 5½ to 7½ years will do all the breeding.

Young bucks are horny little rascals, and will try to breed any estrus doe they encounter, but more mature bucks will drive the youngsters off. However, in areas where doe numbers are high, some does will be bred by young bucks. In such cases, good genetics may be lost. The ideal situation is for does to be bred by the biggest and most dominant bucks in the area but it isn't always possible in every area.

Whitetail does become sexually mature at approximately 1½ years of age although a few early fawns may be bred late in their first season. Such does almost always throw single fawns or very little twin fawns.

It was once thought the rut was triggered by cold weather but if this were true many bucks in Alabama, Florida, Georgia, Louisiana and Texas would be frustrated and few would ever be bred. Actually, cold weather does not determine the rut.

The rut is triggered by a post-autumnal equinox phenomenon and by a changing photoperiod. The photoperiod occurs as the number of daylight hours and minutes diminish, and a whitetail undergoes behavioral changes which marks the onset of the rut. The rut, depending on location, can vary from late October and early November in northern states to mid-January or later in southern states.

The reason for a short but somewhat frantic rut in northern states is that does must be bred early and continue to fatten up before winter snows fall. This also allows fawns to be born in the spring when green vegetation is available. The southern rut is more prolonged because of reasonably abundant forage for fawns over a longer period of time.

Bucks are capable of breeding as soon as antler velvet falls off. They are ready two to three months before most does come into estrus. This early velvet shedding also allows bucks to establish dominance, and the most favorable buck to breed does is the healthiest, biggest animal with the best set of antlers. A buck must be prepared to defend himself, and the does, as the rut swings into full gear.

Decreasing hours of daylight result in a change in the function of the pituitary gland. Less sunlight makes the gland, whose primary purpose is to regulate body growth, function abnormally. The pituitary gland increases secretion of testosterone (a male sex hormone) in bucks and progesterone (a female sex hormone) in doe deer. The increased levels of testosterone in a buck can cause him to react in different ways.

The oldest bucks in the area are usually the ones which eventually will do the actual breeding, although some breeding will be accomplished by lesser animals if few or no trophy animals are present in the local deer herd. The biggest bucks are the top honchos in a herd's pecking order. Next in line are medium-aged bucks, and the little spikehorns and forkhorns are on the bottom rung of the breeding ladder.

Once testosterone begins building in a buck, antler velvet dries, antlers harden and velvet begins falling off. Bucks will paw at it with their hooves and rub their antlers against small bushes, saplings and trees. These functional movements are used to remove antler velvet, and to build neck muscle strength for possible later battles for dominant breeding rights.

Bachelor groups of three to six or more bucks may travel together in late summer and early fall. This changes two or three weeks before the rut begins.

The biggest, strongest and most fit bucks will have proven their dominance long before the first estrus doe is bred, and mate selection normally goes to the buck most fit for the job. This can and does change when few fully mature bucks are available, but the doe often will reject a young related buck.

Once a buck breaks away from the bachelor group, and does begin entering the earliest stages of the pre-rut period, the bucks begin traveling more in search of breedable does. This pre-rut phase is when most activity is seen near scrapes. Both does and bucks will check scrapes at any time of the day or night, but much of the actual breeding takes place after dark.

RUBS AND SCRAPES

A buck rub is a means by which whitetail bucks identify their boundaries (within reason) while notifying other bucks they are nearby. A rub will send a clear signal about the size and where they stand in the antlered hierarchy.

What rubs tell hunters is that at one point a buck passed through the area and rubbed his antlers on the tree. A buck, with certain exceptions, will rub a tree during one episode and never return.

Buck rubs do convey some information that hunters find informative. The size of the sapling or tree being rubbed will give a good indication of the buck's antler size.

Harold Knight checks a rubbed tree. The size of the tree indicates the rub was probably made by a young buck removing velvet from his first or second set of antlers.

A small sapling that is rubbed will frequently be used by a small antlered deer. Trees of an inch or two in diameter usually means a small buck is nearby. A tree measuring 2½ inches in diameter generally means a slightly older (2½ years) buck with a slightly larger rack that may measure from six to 10 inches from beam to beam. Rubs on trees measuring five or six inches in diameter are made by larger bucks in the 3½- to 5½-year class. Trees of eight to 10 inches in diameter are made by truly big and old bucks with heavy, large racks.

John Weiss, an Ohio outdoor writer and deer hunter of note, once told me: "Look for rubs on the largest diameter trees in the area; especially those from three to five inches in diameter and made on cedars, pines or smooth-barked trees. These rubs were made by the largest buck with the heaviest antlers in the area."

I agree, and have seen a few buck rubs on six- to 10-inch trees, and was fortunate enough to witness a 170-point buck rub a cedar tree about four feet off the ground in early September one year. That buck was working over a 10-inch diameter tree, and he literally ripped huge gouges out of the bark and raked the tree down to the cambium layer. Sadly, it was the last time I saw that animal.

Hunters can look for savaged trees or saplings once the rut begins. I've made mock scrapes that became active, and nearby trees were often ripped up by the frustrated deer. Some angry deer will destroy a tree while making a rub, and this is an important clue to look for when conducting a search for available food and proper terrain.

Scrapes offer other clues. Deer, like humans, mature at different rates and times. This single factor can help deer hunters account for good bucks early or late in the season. Nature has set up a schedule for does, but not all does will come into estrus at the same time because this timing factor makes it possible that the majority of does will be bred sometime during the rut.

The earliest estrus does often are the oldest ones in the herd. They will firmly establish which ground scrape will be used once the rut slides into full motion.

Here we tread on the slippery slope of controversy, but these early does pick the spot, and it remains the primary dating grounds until the rut ends. The buck may make the scrape, but I firmly

Archery Hall of Fame hunter Ann Clark of Cincinnati, Ohio, examines a buck scrape for sign of recent use.

believe the doe chooses which singles bar to hang around to await her future lover.

A scrape will vary in size from a small pawed area to something the size of a large dinner table. Satellite scrapes often are found nearby, but the big scrape usually gets most of the whitetail action.

Scrapes will appear like magic—similar to mushrooms after a spring rain—anytime from late September through January, depending on the latitude. Some writers and many hunters feel each scrape is a primary scrape and discount boundary, satellite or secondary scrapes as being made "by little guys." Small scrapes generally mean small bucks, and large scrapes often are made by large-racked bucks.

The average scrape will measure two by three or four feet, and is oval or egg-shaped. I've seen an active, primary scrape that measured five feet wide and 10 feet long. It was made by a huge buck that no one ever shot. He probably died of old age during the winter after I saw the scrape, but before he passed on, he spread his seed throughout the local deer herd.

I spent two weeks the following spring looking for his sheds or his skeleton. It was never found, and the animal may have moved into my hunting area from three or four miles away and left after breeding as many does as possible. He was a buck on his way downhill, and probably died during the heavy snows that year.

A whitetail scrape means very little by itself. It can mean that several bucks are using the area and staking out their claim to that terrain, or it can mean several lesser-antlered or immature bucks have passed through the site. More than one buck and often many does will visit a primary scrape during the pre-rut and rut periods.

If small bucks approach, swiftly drift in and out of the scrape after wetting it down with urine, then it probably means a larger and more dominant buck visits the site regularly or is waiting nearby for an estrus doe to pay a visit.

A scrape can offer clues to hunters. Once the chasing (pre-rut) and tending (rut) phases begin, it pays to examine a scrape thoroughly. My practice is to spray my rubber boots, clothing, hat and gloves with Scent Shield or Vanishing Hunter spray, and visually inspect the scrape without touching the overhead licking branch or the scrape and nearby vegetation.

Pay close attention to these clues. An active scrape will be wet and often smells of urine. Another way to think is to compare the smell of a filthy bathroom in a bus or gas station. You know the smell; a funky, lingering odor that permeates your nose and mouth and clothing. If a scrape smells like this, it is being used by deer.

The next thing to look at is the scrape itself. An active scrape will usually feature one or two hoof prints, antler tine marks and no debris. A buck will scrape the earth with its hooves to remove any fallen leaves or forest duff, and then urinate in it to leave his mark. The overhead licking branch may be frayed or chewed, and a nonsmoker often can smell a faint odor from the buck's preorbital glands.

The direction a buck travels can be determined by the scrape. A buck will paw the earth while freshening a scrap with urine and by pawing the ground.

Pay attention to the hoof prints and the pawing routine. If the earth is pawed toward a bedding area the buck is most likely visiting the scrape in late afternoon or early evening as he leaves a bedding site in heavy cover. However, if the scrape's dirt and forest duff is pawed out toward a feeding site, the chances are good the animal checks his scrape in the early morning on his way to bed down.

A buck will do many things while visiting a primary scrape at any time. The animal will paw the earth, rake it with his antler tines and urinate down his back legs and into the scrape.

Immature or frustrated bucks may masturbate and ejaculate into the scrape. This is often accompanied by checking out the overhead licking branch, and rubbing those branches with his preorbital

Theron Luft checks an overhead licking branch. Active scrapes always feature this branch, and it can be nibbled or chewed as a buck rubs its preorbital glands against the limb.

gland. Such young bucks often pant or grunt while visiting an active scrape.

Preseason scouting can give hunters knowledge of where scrapes may be found. Two scouting methods can lead a sportsman to an area where scrapes may be found. I often do my preliminary scouting from my car. I park where it's possible to see three-quarters of a mile, and use a window-mounted spotting scope to locate where deer enter a feeding site. Once these areas are established in several locations, further scouting is conducted on foot.

One woodlot I hunt is bordered by a long field planted to various crops. Crop rotation occurs each spring at planting time, and the food may be a cornfield, rye, beans or other edibles. The woods to the north (closest to the road) never has a scrape while the woods along the south edge will feature at least a dozen scrapes along its 150-yard border. Only one of these scrapes will be active during the rut, and it's here that several big bucks have been shot over the past 15 years.

Determining which of the dozen scrapes is the hotspot involves periodic watching during the pre-rut period. I usually put up a portable treestand and watch the area with binoculars. Does that linger overly long at the scrape or the presence of one or more bucks is a tip-off.

Many of the unused scrapes are boundary scrapes. They often mark the edge of a buck's domain, and are pawed once and seldom reopened. I've seen as many as 15 boundary scrapes within 100 yards along the edge of a woods, and they were made once by a buck during his nocturnal travels and never visited again. Almost all of these boundary scrapes lack an overhead licking branch.

Satellite scrapes are a different story. I'm a firm believer in making mock scrapes, and if it is tended properly and refreshed with a deer scent, it may become the primary active scrape in the area. John Ozoga agrees but amends his statement.

"I've made many mock scrapes while conducting deer research," he said, "but have learned that although a buck may visit a mock scrape, he often will make two or three satellite scrapes within 10 yards of the original. One of them will be the hotspot."

Years ago I felt that an overhead licking branch would be present over 85 percent of the active scrapes. That thought process has changed.

Over the past 15 years I've looked at hundreds of primary scrapes, and haven't found one without a licking branch. I've reconsidered my earlier thoughts, and now feel that if a frazzled licking branch isn't available, the bucks and does will go elsewhere.

Occasionally a buck will get really hacked off at a licking branch if it has been chewed and rubbed by another buck. I watched a nice 8-point mosey in, check the branch and scrape, and go into a fury unlike anything I've seen before. The animal reared up on his back legs, grabbed the branch with his teeth and thrashed the branch with his antlers. Ten minutes later after his temporary madness bled off excess adrenaline, the buck sauntered off.

I checked the branch, and it was gone. Totally and completely destroyed. I watched that scrape for three more days and no bucks or does came to the scrape. It was time to do something drastic.

I found a popple tree on the private land being hunted, and carefully sawed off a low limb. I carried it back to the scrape, tied it in place at the proper height, and crawled into my treestand. Just before dark the 8-point I had seen destroy the previous licking branch put in an appearance. He stopped in midstride about 20 yards from the scrape, walked slowly toward it, raised his head and began nibbling the branches and rubbing his forehead on the twigs. He freshened the scrape and returned often to it.

It's fun to watch a buck visit a scrape and work over the licking branch. They usually hold one end of the branch in their mouth, and rub the branch across the preorbital gland at the corner of their eye to deposit a waxy secretion on the wood.

I've watched year-and-a-half-old bucks stand for 15 or 20 minutes in a scrape as they urinate or masturbate, and check and rub the licking branch. One buck seemed to be in a trance during the entire visit, and would wander away only to return a few minutes later. Obviously, they get all worked up when all the conditions are right.

What isn't commonly known is the part a doe plays during this rutting procedure. A doe that is ready to be bred will advance on the scrape and leave her business card by urinating down her back legs

Find an active scrape, and your chances for a nice buck like this will improve considerably.

and occasionally defecating in the scrape. The urine carries traces of her estrus, and advertises through hormones in the urine and her vaginal tract that she is ready to be bred. All she is doing is waiting to be serviced by a buck although in some cases I've seen does seek out the buck when her time comes.

A buck may be an antsy guy and willing to take a ride on any doe in estrus, but he knows where the primary scrape is located and is never too far from the action. Does will signal their condition in the scrape, and I've seen them hang around for several minutes in hopes that a buck will appear. If he doesn't, she will track him down like a beagle on a hot bunny track.

Scrapes, during the rut, are a thing to marvel at because they are like highway billboards advertising who is doing what to whom. Hunters should watch for bucks that visit a scrape and find a doe's calling card.

And bucks do visit scrapes. In areas densely populated with deer a buck may visit a scrape three or four times daily. The reverse is true when whitetails are widely scattered—the buck may spend two or three days visiting other scrapes he has found during his journey.

A doe will remain in estrus for 24 to 28 hours, and then goes out if she isn't bred. These unbred deer are the ones that will come into estrus about 28 days later.

How prolific a sire is a mature buck? It's a good question, but in areas of heavy deer numbers a dominant buck may impregnate 30 does during the rut.

Another question I often hear is "when do bucks check their scrapes?" It's a difficult question to answer because of variables like size of the home range, number of does of breeding age available, and other factors. I've watched bucks visit primary scrapes in the morning, at noon, during the midday hours, in late afternoon and just before dark. Most of the breeding will take place after sundown.

One thing that few hunters realize is that bucks wind-check active scrapes from downwind. Almost always, a buck will make a slow deliberate circle so he can check for danger and for the presence of an estrus doe.

I've purposely sat in ground blinds or treestands to watch a scrape. There can be a deliberate parade of smaller bucks and does

Theron Luft has sprayed his clothing with Vanishing Hunter prior to kneeling near this scrape. The rutting scrape was located near one of the author's stands, and he saw a nice buck there two hours later.

visiting a scrape area, but a dominant buck—one four or five years old—is a pretty cagey animal. He's learned from early experience that charging directly into a scrape can bring a pile of trouble down on him. That's why he makes his move very slowly.

I watched half-hidden bucks stand motionless for 30 minutes or more, as immobile as a fine English pointer standing a bird for his master. They test the air, watch carefully for movement, and in many cases, are both alert and anticipating a doe moving to the scrape.

This is the moment of truth for a hunter. He can grow impatient and move, or remain motionless and wait for the animal to make his move. Of the two choices, a savvy hunter will bide his time without moving. Waiting out an approaching buck becomes a study in patience.

Bucks do wind-check scrapes from downwind. They may deliberately approach a scrape in fits and starts with long pauses, and a hunter must learn to wait them out. An important ingredient in this scrape-hunting scenario is knowing where to place a treestand to provide for the perfect shot, and it's an exercise that requires trial and error and the utmost patience.

A rutting buck will wind-check a scrape from downwind at a distance of 20 to 30 yards. Hunters who place a treestand 15 to 20 yards downwind of an active scrape may never see a trophy buck as it checks for danger. The reason is because he will move in slowly from downwind, encounter the hunter's scent, and disappear like a desert mirage. There is one way to foil a rutting buck.

Position your stand 30 to 40 yards downwind of the scrape. A cautious circling buck will make his final approach and be in position for a shot at 15 to 20 yards, about midway between your stand and the scrape.

Hunters must avoid wide-open terrain at all costs. A vast majority of the primary breeding scrapes will be in or very close to heavy cover. Bucks prefer to travel through thick cover, and often use it when approaching scrapes.

Leave enough open areas through which to shoot, but position yourself downwind of where you expect the buck to emerge at the scrape. Forget about the morning and evening hours that some writers say are the best times to hunt during the rut.

My friends and I have disproved that argument so many times it's a wonder anyone believes it these days. The truth is that bucks

The author uses a Puff Bottle that contains an unscented powder to determine wind direction. Where the wind blows will indicate to the hunter where a ground blind or tree-stand should be located. The hunter should always be downwind of an active scrape when hunting. The occasional squeeze of this bottle sends powder into the air, and it's easy to tell exactly where the wind is carrying human scent.

will tend a scrape at any hour of the day or night. We've shot rutting bucks at daybreak, 10 a.m., noon, 2 p.m. and just before dark. Of these time periods, I've had the poorest success at daybreak although I know several friends who have shot a nice buck at that time. One reason is that in many locations getting past other deer during the pre-dawn hours is difficult. The animals are spooky as they move to bed down, and the slightest noise, movement or human scent will wreck a hunter's best laid plans.

Bucks are more active during the rut than at any other time of year. Surging hormones keep them on the move, and I've had my most consistent rut-hunting success from 10 a.m. to 2 p.m., the time that many hunters find least attractive.

Here's why. A buck during the peak of the rut will breed most does during evening hours when the woods are silent and sportsmen are in bed. They often fade into heavy cover an hour before dawn, and rest for two or three hours.

I deliberately sleep in during the rut. Time permitting, I rise at 7 or 8 a.m., have breakfast, shower and am heading for my stand by 9 a.m. I have two quirks: I never approach a stand from the same direction two days in a row, and I never hunt the same stand on consecutive days. This avoids deer from patterning me. If anyone is going to be patterned, I want it to be the buck.

The trick is to ease into the stand from downwind or across wind from suspected bedding areas. Climb into the ground blind or treestand without a sound, get positioned and don't move for four hours.

It's easier said than done. I'll often use a small garden rake to softly clear a path of dry leaves and fallen sticks or twigs enroute to my stand. Any unusual noise like a twig snapping, especially on a calm day, can set alarm bells ringing in a buck's head.

The most overlooked thing a bow or firearm hunter can do is not have the bow or rifle ready when a buck appears. All too often it will be hanging from a limb or standing in the corner of a ground blind, and the buck steps into the open with every sense at full alert. Fumbling to retrieve a bow or firearm means movement and possible noise, and it has saved the lives of many rutting bucks. Follow the old Boy Scout motto of always being prepared.

I always wear rubber boots when hunting, and tuck my pant legs inside my boot. I'm right-handed, and stick the bottom limb of my Oneida Black Eagle bow into my left boot to relieve arm strain. When a buck shows up, my gator-jawed Pollington Pro Release is on the string with an arrow nocked.

My left hand holds the bow and since I always sit in a treestand it requires very little movement to raise and draw the bow. I watch the deer, wait until the buck turns or lowers his head, and then make my draw, aim and shoot.

An estrus doe is the most important item when hunting rutting bucks. A doe must eat to keep up her energy and weight in preparation for a lengthy winter pregnancy. A buck, on the other hand, eats little during the rut which accounts for the fact he can lose 25 to 30 percent of his body weight during the rut.

An old buck, fully intent on breeding every doe in the area, will lose weight and may perish during the rigors of winter. Does seldom have this problem although they can and will lose weight after conception and during winter months. In areas where hunting pressure is minimal, a good spot to ambush a buck is where doe and fawn trails enter or leave heavy cover adjacent to a food site.

Bucks know that food sites are great pick-up places to hustle the local doe population. Learn where those trails and food sites are located in each hunting area, and try to set up downwind from an active trail. The most important rule here is not to spook the does or fawns because their frantic flight will spook nearby bucks.

Knowledge of the rut and how it affects bucks and does is important. So too is the specific ways of hunting various types of terrain during the rut.

Once the first rut ends in northern states (usually in mid-November) the savvy hunter knows that 24 to 28 days later estrus does will come into season again. In many places snow is on the ground by then. It's important to hunt near doe concentrations and often the hunting will be done in thick cover.

A rut's peak and length varies according to latitude and somewhat because of longitude. The rut is much shorter in the north and a good bit longer in southern states.

Here are several last-minute tips about scrape hunting to remember.

LOCATE THE SCRAPES

The idea of hunting for rutting deer isn't worth a tinker's damn if the sportsman doesn't have a clue about scrape locations.

That means a great deal of walking, studying the ground and looking for active scrapes.

I once walked into a new area to hunt during the rut, and began walking the edge of a woods. Numerous scrapes were found but none were active.

My next step was to zigzag through heavy cover near bedding areas. It was a gusty day, and the leaves sounded like someone walking on corn flakes. I didn't hurry but would move a few feet, stop, look around and take several more steps before stopping to repeat my inspection.

It was late October and the rut had just begun. My path took me deeper into heavy cover, and three hours of scouting had produced several early scrapes but they were haphazardly spread around and none showed recent use.

The next patch of heavy cover had two heavy deer trails running into it, and I decided to see if they intersected. My pace slowed to that of a rapidly moving snail when I spotted the glint of sunlight on antlers. I stopped, checked the area with my binoculars and spotted a dandy 8-pointer pawing a scrape. He was 40 yards through heavy cover from me, and offered an impossible bow shot.

He continued nibbling and batting the overhead licking branch with his antlers, and whenever he made noise I took another two or three cautious steps forward. This was as much still-hunting as scrutinizing the ground for active scrapes.

The buck was quartering away from me and oblivious to my presence. He began raking a nearby tree with his antlers, and each step brought me closer to my objective—a fallen log 18 yards from the deer. The buck stopped, looked around and tested the breeze, and reentered the scrape to paw it again.

It took 20 minutes to reach the log without being seen. A doe approached the buck from one side, but didn't spot or smell me. He hooked at her with his antlers, and she ran off. He watched her go with his head turned away from me. The last few yards took 10 minutes, and I fully expected the buck to mosey on.

The buck was urinating down his legs while standing in the scrape. I eased to one knee, drew my bow and waited for him to turn slightly to offer a quartering-away shot. He did and I quickly aimed and shot. The buck folded up after a 50-yard run.

Find active scrapes and you'll find deer providing you are scent-free, and enter the area without being seen, heard or winded.

DETERMINE SCRAPE ACTIVITY

A scrape without continuous activity is a waste of time. Check scrapes for fresh urine, pawing, antler tine marks, hoof prints and nearby availability of a good tree for a stand. Determine travel direction of bucks using the scrape, and plan to sit 35 to 40 yards downwind to intercept the buck as it wind-checks the scrape from downwind.

SCRAPES MEAN MORE THAN ONE ANIMAL

Granted, a scrape may be used primarily by a big buck but it attracts other smaller bucks and does as well. I've seen up to seven bucks visit a scrape in one day.

A hot scrape is a magnet for every buck in the area. Let's face it: Not every hunter has the time and patience to wait out a big trophy. Many hunters will take the first antlered buck that comes to the scrape, and that is OK because it reduces the buck population and may make it easier to simplify the taking of a bigger buck if the hunter has more than one buck tag.

Always examine every buck that comes to a scrape. Nontypical racks are uncommon in my home hunting area but by studying what is available, it's possible to pattern a larger buck and learn when he visits a scrape.

This hunter checks a scrape along a wooded edge near a cornfield. It has been used by a buck recently.

WHEN TO HUNT A SCRAPE

A good hunter can tell when a buck comes to a hot scrape. Obviously the time to be there is an hour or so before he is scheduled to arrive. Bucks, by nature, are complex animals. One may check scrapes during the dark while another may make his rounds at noon. Some only come in that last 30 minutes between sundown and the end of legal shooting time.

The longer a hunter sits in a stand the more likely he is to move at the wrong time. If the timing is accurate, and the buck stays on schedule, the best time to hunt is when the sportsman knows he will be there. However, even a buck as regular as a dish of prunes in tending to his scrape duties may be off an hour or so either way.

The rut obviously doesn't last forever. Sportsmen will have a fairly intense two-week period in which to waylay a buck, and how they spend those 14 days may determine how much venison they will consume after hunting season ends.

BE ODOR-FREE

It's easy to lose track of things when hunting a rutting buck over the scrape. There are does and fawns passing through the area, and they may arrive before, during or after a buck moves to the scrape.

An odor-free hunter has a far better chance of shooting a buck near a scrape than one that fails to bathe, sit downwind or stink up the area by not taking scent precautions. I own a Scent-Lok suit and the new Scent-Blocker suit made by Robinson Laboratories. They are a tremendous aid to bowhunters, but I take being odor-free one or two steps further. I'm fanatical about being scent free. I even spray my bow, arrows, treestand, tree limbs and clothing with liberal amounts of Scent Shield or Vanishing Hunter.

I've had bucks, does and fawns approach from directly downwind, and can say that I haven't been winded by deer since taking these precautions. I once passed up 26 does and fawns feeding 18 yards directly downwind of me only to shoot the 27th deer that passed under my treestand. It was a buck and it fed in a winterwheat field with the does and fawns. Being odor-free can pay big dividends for any deer hunter.

Scrape hunting is great fun, and possibly the most fun a sportsman can have in a ground blind or treestand. With that, we move directly into the next chapter. Hopefully, my thoughts on ground blind or treestand hunting will shed some light on how, when and where to use each one during the hunting season.

4

GROUND BLINDS OR TREESTANDS?

B eing up in the air or on the ground is an issue deer hunters face whenever they hunt, and the debate about which is best is as volatile as a brushfire fueled by a heat-charged prairie wind.

Each side has strong views on the topic; every hunter has good and bad things to say about their choice, and choosing one is as personal as which color of morning toothbrush to use. The burning question is if one method is better than the other.

The truth is that both hunting methods—ground blinds or treestands—produce deer. Of major importance is determining which method is best suited for each person. It's important that hunters know the pros and cons of both, and then make a logical choice that will work for them.

Fueling the personal fire that burns within every deer hunter is a desire to take a good buck. Whether it is done from a treestand or from the ground is a matter of choice. The important thing is to forget the baggage many hunters carry with them.

This excess verbal baggage can take any number of forms, and often is based on personal views. Rarely do hunters consider anything other than their own beliefs, and in many cases, the verbiage is cloaked in misconceptions.

"Treestands are best because any breeze will blow human scent over or away from approaching deer," a hidebound tree climber may say. "Besides, a treestand hunter can see more of the area and watch deer movements, and deer seldom expect danger from above."

"Nuts," retorts ground hunters. "No one can be comfortable while worrying about falling from a tree. You squirm or fidget around too much for personal safety, and it's difficult to make a good shot from 20 feet in the air."

The arguments are all too familiar because I've been on both sides of the fence. It's like a writer arguing with an editor, and vice versa; misconceptions on both sides keep the argument fueled and burning.

I was once a confirmed ground blind hunter because at the time Michigan hunters couldn't hunt from a tree. I hunted many other states at the time where treestands were legal, and it made little difference whether I was bow or gun hunting. I didn't want any part of climbing trees. Trees, like horses, were two things I never learned to trust.

Tree limbs break at inopportune times, or winter numbed fingers release their grip at the wrong time, and I'd crashed down through branches on more than one occasion. I preferred having both feet on the ground.

It was Claude Pollington of Marion, Michigan, who lifted me off the ground and into one of his treestands. He had begged and pleaded with me for a month to try hunting from a tree, and I finally relented . . . against my better judgment.

An Alabama deer hunter sits in a ladder stand with his rifle to wait for a buck. Treestand hunters should wear a safety belt or harness whenever hunting off the ground.

"There's a nice 8-pointer coming in almost every evening to work that scrape at my son's stand," he cajoled. "It's a low stand, and even if you fall it is only 10 feet. You'll shoot a buck tonight if you can overcome your squeamishness about being off the ground and in a tree."

Everyone has a personal fear of falling. For me, it's more intense than with many people. If I stand on the roof of a house or a tall building and look down, I feel as if the ground is pulling at me. Perhaps it's the effects of gravity, but being off the ground disturbs me, and I make no bones about it.

He had worked on me for a year, and often I would almost give in before remembering treestands from other years. Bruises fade with time, but the gut-wrenching feeling in your stomach as you bounce down from limb to limb was something I no longer needed. Bruises, I felt, could become broken backs, necks or legs, and I felt my earlier falls may have used up all of my luck.

"C'mon," he begged. "Just be careful, don't slip and sit still. The buck will be within 20 feet. You can't miss."

"OK," I whined. I would try, but wasn't one bit happy about it.

Now, mind you, I wasn't overly afraid of height; it's just that I was petrified of falling. Over the years I've broken my back twice while bopping around the outdoors, and the thought of doing so again from a treestand wasn't very appealing.

It was an easy climb into the pine tree. The branches were evenly spaced, and a Summit treestand was firmly anchored. Heavy pine boughs stood out behind the stand to break my outline, and a well-used scrape was 20 feet down and to my left. It was made to order for a right-handed bowhunter.

After I'd climbed into position, sat down and readied my bow, I relaxed. The Oneida bow lay across my lap, an arrow nocked, my Pollington Pro-Release attached to the string, and the Patriot broadhead set at the proper angle on my arrow for perfect alignment. I flipped the camo face mask down over my face, leaned back against the tree trunk to wait for the buck to arrive.

"Hey, this isn't too bad," I thought. "The visibility is good, and the breeze is blowing my scent away from the scrape. If a rutting buck tries to circle to wind-check the scrape, and crosses the open area, he will pass within easy bow range."

Marty Pollington with a good-sized deer he took from his favorite treestand.

An hour passed, and I watched young whitetail bucks sparring 200 yards away in an open field. Does stood near the bucks like bored spectators at a bar fight, and I wondered if a buck would show up soon.

Dusk was rapidly settling over the land when I heard the unmistakable sound of soft and deliberate footsteps behind me. The sound stopped, and soon another footstep was heard. I couldn't risk turning for a look. I had been cautioned to wait for the buck to step into the open after checking for danger. Another long minute passed and the buck took another step, paused and stepped almost into the open.

All I could see was his nose, the 8-point rack, and three inches of neck. He needed to take another two or three steps before I could come to full draw, aim and shoot. The buck swiveled his head and stared over his rump in the direction from which he had come. I used that moment to lift my bow off my lap and prepare for a shot.

My fingers found the release aid, and I checked to see if the arrow was perfectly alined on the Bo-Doodle shoot-through arrow rest. It was and then my eyes focused on the buck, and I moved the bow only when his attention strayed from my tree. Each movement I made was a study in slowness; an inch at a time caused my left arm to straighten out as I lifted the bow into position to make my draw.

The buck stood motionless. His nostrils quivered, and his eyes seemed to bore through everything in sight. He was wary and in no hurry to make a mistake.

His neck was swollen with the rut and appeared grotesque. Inch by inch his rounded neck stretched forward like an uncoiling snake to sniff the scrape, but he still had to move four feet to give me a clear shot at the heart-lung area.

He apparently fell in love with what his sniffer told him. A pig-like grunt rumbled up from his chest and diaphragm, and he took two steps forward and into the scrape. His feet were a blur of movement as he savaged the ground, and then he stopped as suddenly as he started. With a slight head movement he began rubbing his pre-orbital gland across a nearby bush and then turned to the licking branch.

He worked himself into a full rutting frenzy as he tore into the licking branch. He chewed it, raked his antlers across the overhanging branch, and was oblivious to anything else. His testosterone levels must have been boosting hormones into his system, and he cared nothing about his surroundings as I made my move.

I came to full draw, locked the release against the corner of my mouth, steadied the lighted sight pin low behind his front shoulder, and shot. The release was smooth, and the arrow pegged the deer through the heart-lung area with a *thunk*.

The 8-pointer wheeled, smashed through the nearby tag alder swale, circled once behind it and headed for an open field 200 yards away. My Game Tracker string tracking device had line peeling out of it as if a big chinook salmon was taking line.

"Deer on!" I mumbled to myself to avoid scaring other deer while holding my bow aloft. That's just what it felt like when an arrow-shot deer runs off trailing string. I was elated because my jittery feeling over being up in a tree had paid off with a shot at a rutting buck at spitting distance.

Seconds later the string stuttered, stopped, and inched forward a few more feet before stopping for good. The deer was down, and all indications pointed to a dead buck.

The string made for easy following of the blood trail and I gathered it up as it wove through the tag alders. The 8-point with the swollen neck had traveled 75 yards with a neatly severed heart and had died on the run.

Pollington was as excited as I was. "See," he joked, "treestands aren't so bad after all. You've been missing out on great action for years."

I admit there is a time and place for treestands. But I'm also convinced ground blinds serve a useful purpose and wouldn't want hunters to think the foregoing anecdote is an all-out endorsement of treestands.

The trick to taking deer with something that approaches regularity is to know when and where to choose a ground blind over a treestand, and when an elevated stand could increase the chance of success. In some areas whitetails have been hunted so often from treestands they are spooky and will walk along with their nose in the air and eyes scanning nearby trees in an attempt to spot hunter movement.

Roger Kerby favors cedar or pine trees for his stands, and prefers to squat while waiting for a deer. The author prefers to shoot from a sitting position. Treestand hunting means different things to each person.

A familiarity with food sources and terrain features can help hunters make the decision easier when choosing between hunting at ground level or 10 to 20 feet up a tree. A hard-nosed sportsman who cannot or will not switch from ground level to a treestand, or in the opposite direction when hunting situations dictate, is stubborn and is reducing his odds of success.

Both ground blinds and treestands have something to offer bow or firearm hunters. We'll take a close look at both, and offer suggestions on when, where and how they can be utilized in most hunting situations.

GROUND BLINDS

The buck moved as quietly as drifting ground fog. He stopped every few feet to test the air, and each pause lasted a minute before the buck would move forward again.

I'd been watching him from my ground blind in southeast Tennessee as he eased from a soybean field. He would stop, look up and around in all directions before heading toward a finger of oak-filled woods along a brushy fencerow.

My ground-level surveillance was in order because this particular 9-pointer apparently had been hunted from treestands for so long he had forgotten his basic training. As he moseyed along he spent too much time looking up into trees and too little time scanning nearby ground areas.

The buck was nearly screened by thick brush along the fencerow, and was hard to see, but each step he took brought him closer to my hay-bale blind at the edge of a small woodlot. He was coming my way, and my hands perspired as they gripped the stock of my Remington .270.

The buck was overly curious and concerned about a weathered oak along the fencerow, and several times he would stop to stare up into the branches. Then it became obvious; the buck was looking at an old treestand instead of looking ahead and to either side for ground level danger. This heavily antlered three-year-old buck was clueless, and apparently had forgotten the lessons his mama taught him early in life.

The deer finally satisfied himself the treestand was unoccupied by a hunter, and made his move like a racehorse leaving the starting gate. He shot out into the open field within 25 yards of my ground blind, stopped and turned for a final look at the old treestand. It was a fatal mistake.

I raised the .270, slid the Bausch & Lomb's crosshairs low behind his front shoulder, and caressed the trigger. The shot seemed as loud as a cannon going off in the still autumn air, and the buck sank to his knees before rolling over on his side like a deflated balloon.

That Tennessee buck had tunnel vision. He had learned about the danger of treestands and hunters who bowhunted or gun hunted from elevated platforms, but had forgotten his early childhood training. He had forgotten about the dangers that lurk at ground level, and his carelessness cost him his life.

This incident happened in a heavily hunted area. A friend later told me that he had shot several bucks from that tree with a bow or firearm but had quit hunting the treestand because local deer had become accustomed to the potential danger of a hunter lurking 20 feet off the ground.

A Minnesota deer hunter of my acquaintance, while bowhunting daily near his home, has yet to bag a whitetail buck after six years of treestand hunting. Yet he bagged a buck the second day out while bowhunting from a makeshift ground blind so ugly it looked as if a hobo troop had used it for summer camp.

"I can't understand it," he told me before I suggested a switch to a ground blind. "I see bucks almost every day, but the steep angles and intervening brush make it difficult to obtain a clean killing shot. I either miss completely, a twig deflects my arrow or the buck seems to be aware of my presence and shies away far out of bow range."

It's a complaint heard each year. The solution is easy. Hunt from the ground.

Claude Pollington feels treestand hunting is the best thing to happen to bowhunting since the advent of the Michigan two-buck license. But, he hastens to add, that elevated platforms are not for everyone.

"The angles are totally different when shooting down from treestands 15 to 30 feet in the air," he said. "A straight-down shot is difficult for some bowhunters and too many people fear heights. Some cannot shoot accurately from any height, and others wiggle around so much with insecurity that a whitetail can spot the movement 100 yards away."

And that's what that Tennessee whitetail was looking for. The treestand he inspected for many minutes was 30 feet up the tree, and those who climbed that high to sit in it must have suffered the willies.

Me, I used to break out in cold sweats whenever I climbed into a treestand. I was as nervous as a teenager on his first date with that cute cheerleader, and I would ruin any hope for a shot by constantly fidgeting around or checking to see if my safety harness was properly fastened. My nerves were a wreck any time I was over six feet off terra firma, and it took years to conquer that fear.

It also took that 9-pointer on Pollington's land to make me see that there really is no need to climb 25 or 30 feet up a tree to shoot a whitetail. The lower heights work fine providing the hunter knows the score and how to safely hunt from treestands.

Many hunters, including me, are convinced that in heavily hunted deer areas, where countless treestands hold bow or gun hunters, whitetails have learned to look up.

Some deer spend more time now looking into trees than they do studying the terrain ahead of them. It's this inbred fear of danger from trees that can make ground hunting a pleasant and productive hunting technique. All the old arguments about elevated stands concealing movement, circulating human scent far from the area and allowing for better shots are not as valid as they were 20 years ago.

The old saw about deer never looking up has been disproved so often it's a wonder anyone still believes it. Deer do look up, and as surely as does drop spring fawns, these newborns will learn to look up. It's in their inherited genes.

There are ground blinds and there are others which to the uninitiated may pass for ground blinds. Some are abominable creations which look more like windowed outhouses than a place from which to hunt deer, and yet some are genuine works of art although they are not pretty.

Two years ago I hunted from an eight-sided metal blind with a flat floor. Each of the eight sides had a jalousie-type window that could be opened for a shot. It sat in place along an Alabama clover field, and deer soon became accustomed to seeing it. The windows opened silently for a shot, and the windows were made of smoked Plexiglass. Hunters could see out but the deer couldn't see in, and it was a consistent deer producer for the landowner.

A ground blind need not be as fancy as that one, but it must be functional. To be functional it must blend in with the surroundings, offer a clear lane for shot, and break the hunter's outline. Anything less is a waste of time and effort.

My ground blinds may not be pretty like steak and cake, but they are functional and in tune with nature. I favor simple cornstalk blinds when hunting in or near standing corn; a hay-bale blind where hay bales are common make a perfect ground blind. Pit blinds are possibly the best of all.

These blinds blend in well with their surroundings, and are located at ground level where shoulder-height shots are the rule rather than the exception. A ground hunter does not have to turn himself into a human corkscrew to take a shot as a treestand hunter often does. He only has to rise to one knee, or shoot sitting down, to make a direct hit into the vital chest area.

Hunters have hunted from ground blinds for generations. Early Native Americans as well as modern hunters have picked a spot according to the prevailing wind direction and positioned a blind

Hay bale blinds are perfect for hunting in farm country where hay bales are common. Determine where deer travel, and place two round bales at a 45-degree angler and sit back in the shadows. Such ground blinds are warm, and wind isn't much of a factor.

downwind from where the animal is expected to appear. Early and modern hunters often chose the wrong spot more often than not but experience is a good teacher when choosing a blind site.

From the day it hits the ground as a gangly, long-legged, spotted fawn to the day it dies, a whitetail is high strung and nervous. It is as explosive as a keg of dynamite, and it will spook easily. Many hunters have seen does shy from a bird flying overhead and I've watched bucks and does bolt at the sight of a squirrel running across a limb or on the ground. Every deer sense is alert for danger.

Good ground blinds must be positioned properly and never used on a daily basis to prevent the deer from patterning hunters rather than the other way around. Preseason scouting is essential to locate the wild foods and agricultural crops that deer thrive on. The next step is to learn where deer bed down, where they feed and how they move to and from bedding or feeding sites. Further scouting will reveal those little-used escape trails bucks often follow when danger threatens.

In each hunting area, note the prevailing wind direction, and watch deer to see how they travel under various wind conditions.

Camouflage is important whether hunting on the ground or from a treestand. Kathy Marchetta applies camo face paint to hands and face, and uses the side-view mirror of a car to make sure all areas are covered to avoid shiny skin from giving away her location.

Try to locate a ground hide downwind from where you expect deer to come from, and this often will vary from morning to evening.

Much of what I've learned about ground blinds over the last 30 years has come from hunting with other people in Michigan and some 25 other states with sizable deer populations. The more one hunts, and the more exposure to other people's methods, the more a hunter can learn. It's easy to pick up a technique from another sportsman and adapt it to your personal hunting area.

Pollington now owns 1,500 acres under a 10-foot fenced enclosure. But years ago when I hunted frequently with him, there was no fence. Most of his ground blinds were positioned near truck crops like winter wheat, buckwheat, corn, Imperial whitetail clover and alfalfa. The deer often traveled from west to east in the evening and east to west in the morning, regardless of wind direction. One peculiarity of the deer movements, before the fence was installed, was to travel in those directions daily. I often saw deer moving downwind rather than into the wind.

"One of the finest ground blinds in the world where hay is grown is several rectangular hay bales placed downwind of where deer feed or travel to a bedding or feeding location," Pollington said. "Whitetails are accustomed to seeing hay bales in farm country, and the natural odor of hay can help offset human scent if an unexpected wind switch takes place. Position hay bales out to 20 yards downwind from the trail for bowhunters and approximately 50 yards away for firearm hunters."

Such hay-bale blinds are hotspots near feeding areas if they are left in place during a late-season bowhunt. Second-cutting hay is avidly consumed by deer.

Once I was trying to fill my doe tag in mid-December and found that the deer were eating my blind with me inside it. They never picked up my scent because I was seated inside the hay, and I later shot a doe at six feet as she walked past the opening of my blind. That, my friends, is close shooting.

Pit blinds are a chore to prepare, and even more of a challenge to hunt from, but they are so productive that it's a wonder they aren't used more often. A good pit blind can be open or enclosed with short sides and a roof for bow or firearm hunting. These dug-out pits can be placed downwind from trails in wooded areas, near the edges of swales or swamps, in the middle or along the edges of open agricultural fields or wherever deer move. The trick is to find the proper area, and to dig them in such a manner that bow or firearm hunters can comfortably shoot. Too many pit blinds are too small, and the hunter frequently is skylighted and easily spotted by approaching deer. Use the following instructions for pit size and shape for best results.

Dig a pit approximately three to three-and-a-half feet deep, and at least four feet wide (from front to back) and four to five feet wide from side to side. Dig the back of the pit down 24 to 30 inches, pack it down firmly and use it as a seat. The balance of the pit should be dug to the proper depth for feet and legs, and ample room is needed. Position it with brush, cornstalks or trees behind the pit so they will break up the human silhouette, and remove much of the brush or vegetation in front of the pit blind that could interfere with a shot.

One of the finest pit blinds I've used was along a cornfield in North Carolina. The late Merle Decker made it for me and left a few cornstalks standing in front of my blind, and wove a heavy webbing of cornstalks together behind me. Corn grew on both sides of the pit blind, and deer moved through the crops to feed each evening.

One afternoon just before dusk a doe and two evenly matched bucks entered a nearby soybean field adjacent to the corn. I watched them from a distance of 60 yards . . . much too far for my bow. Then another buck entered the soybean field, took one look at the other bucks and scattered them like a tornado scatters cheap aluminum house trailers.

The doe wasn't keen on playing rutting games with him so she hied herself into the corn away from the bully. He pranced around, all full of himself, and looked tough while trying to con one of the lit-

24″–30″

18″–22″

3′–3½′

4′–5′

The proper dimensions of a pit blind. The best ones are dug in front of cornstalks or tree limbs which break up the hunter's silhouette.

tle bucks into a scrap. I wanted him, but was trying to keep one eye on the doe that was feeding and moving down the corn toward me.

I kept one eye on the jumbo buck, and the other on the doe, and was getting cross-eyed trying to watch both animals. It was a toss-up which one would get to me first.

The buck seemed to stand his ground, but the doe kept feeding toward me at a steady pace. She was 20 yards away in the corn, and rapidly feeding in my direction. She had absolutely no idea that there were any humans within 100 miles.

The buck made his move to intercept her, and I slowly raised my camouflaged Oneida bow for a possible shot. I'd shoot if he approached within 25 yards before the doe reached my pit blind. Unfortunately, she fed right up to my blind, poked her nose through the corn stalks and got a snout full of human scent. She nearly blew my cap off with her snort, and then blew out of there in a major hurry. Of course, the buck disappeared in the middle of this fracas, never to be seen again.

Needless to say I didn't shoot a deer that night. However, the incident proves just how completely deer can be fooled by a well positioned pit blind.

Pit blinds are deadly when properly placed in heavy cover. Bucks, in particular, are cautious about entering open fields but will

During the firearms season, dig pit blinds downwind from an active deer trail in thick, heavy cover. Use brush to break up your silhouette.

move through heavy cover in a more casual manner. A trick a New York buddy uses is to locate a well-used buck trail. Once he knows a buck is using the trail he determines the wind direction, digs a pit near a toppled tree or brush pile, and then walks away from it for two months.

He doesn't set foot in the pit again until opening day of the New York firearms season. He then circles around downwind, walks upwind to the pit, and climbs in with everything he needs to spend the day. Most years he gets a nice buck, often before lunch. However, his hunting technique needs additional definition.

His pit blind is always located in heavy cover, and along seldom-used trails. He feels once the firearms of opening day start barking any buck in the area will head for heavy cover. Those bucks in his area sneak along through thick brush, and eventually one will pass within shooting range.

Stump blinds are common in parts of Canada, northern Wisconsin, northern Michigan, and northern Minnesota, and throughout Maine and other heavily timbered states. Stumps, usually from cut cedar trees that burned over years ago in forest fires, make fantastic ground blinds when properly positioned.

Place stump blinds (these stumps can be knocked apart and repositioned in ideal spots) where a bow or firearm hunter can watch a good area. An Ontario area I once hunted had been burned over years before, and the blackened stumps dotted the edge of an alfalfa field. Deer fed in the alfalfa during early morning hours and again just before dark, and this stump blind blended in with the surrounding environment. It stood there for years, and the deer (and bears) didn't seem to mind it. Each year my friend who owns the land will shoot a buck and a bear from the same stump blind.

One of the newest hunting sensations is the one-man or two-man pop-up camouflage tent. These blinds can fit in anywhere, and can be installed in less than two minutes. Some come with a detachable top and some have a built-in top, and two, three or four shooting windows allow adequate coverage of a hunting area.

Pat Marino of Williamsburg, Michigan is a big fan of the pop-up tent, and uses his almost daily when ground hunting. The tent has helped him shoot many bucks.

"The most important thing about using pop-up tents is to choose a camo pattern that blends in with the hunting area," Marino said. "I have brown, brown and green, and grey patterned camo and they provide the perfect cover for a bow or firearm hunter who wants a quick place to hide."

He advises hunters to keep all windows closed to prevent a swirling breeze from carrying unwanted human scent to approaching deer. He always positions his tents downwind of where deer will appear but a wind switch can ruin a hunt if too many windows are kept open. He packs a folding camp chair with a back rest in to his hunting area, sets up the tent, places the chair inside, and adds available local dead vegetation like swamp grass, fallen branches or pine boughs to help conceal the tent.

"I've had bucks, does and fawns walk right up to my tent," he said. "Deer can be very curious animals if they see something they've never seen before and if the wind is in the hunter's favor. I just sit tight, and don't move, and take bucks every year from my three pop-up tents."

One more thing before we move on to treestands. A hunter in a ground blind will usually get a closer shot at a whitetail than a tree hunter. I remember countless bucks and does I've taken from ground blinds at distances of 10 yards or less, and the hunter often has much better cover and is less visible. Hunters are not seen as readily providing they sit still and the wind is in their favor.

Pop-up tents like Game Tracker's Apex, Carbon Cabin, Carbon Pop-Up or Quick-Set Eagle or Ameristep's pop-up blinds are lightweight and easy to use.

A ground blind doesn't need to be elaborate. With proper camo clothing, a winter hunter can sit with his back to a tree and downwind of a deer trail and wait for a deer to come along. This hunter blends in with the snow and trees.

TREESTANDS

One oft-asked question is why hunt whitetails from a tree. One reason is because the prevailing wind at 15 to 20 feet above ground will, to a certain extent, distribute human scent over a wider area and above the predominant ground-level air currents. This will place a portion or all of the human odor above a whitetail at close range, but it doesn't negate the fact that any deer approaching from downwind will probably pick up some human scent at 100 or 150 yards.

This means that hunter-savvy deer may be spooked. It also can mean the animal doesn't get enough human scent to become alarmed but it may be enough to make it jumpy.

Another reason hunters prefer elevated stands is because it gives them a greater visibility over a larger hunting area. One objection is, just how much area does a hunter need to cover? Is it necessary to see deer movement at 100 or 200 yards in all directions? I think not.

The argument for greater visibility is invalid for bowhunters. I feel the only area a bow or firearm hunter must be able to see is nearby, i.e., that range in which the sportsman can effectively shoot and kill a deer with bow or firearm. Anything more is a waste because unless the animal is in effective range, a shot is improbable.

If a hunter is 30 feet up a popple tree and 75 yards from a deer, or facing the wrong direction in a wide-open birch tree 10 yards away, the buck might just as well be on Mars as where it is. If you can't shoot, you can't, and it's your fault and problem.

The third reason some deer hunters choose a treestand is because it allows them to hunt brushy areas where there are varying wind patterns. Such locations offer too many hassles for a ground hunter, and many times such areas are rejected in favor of a better and easier-to-hunt location.

This is an Eagle bow or firearm blind and positioned so it will provide extra cover for a bow or firearm hunter. It works best when hunting from a bare tree after the leaf drop. A hunter would stick out like a sore thumb without some form of camouflage. These types of blinds also reduce human scent a bit but hunters still should remain downwind of an active deer trail.

Heavy cover, such as the edge of a cattail swamp, is another. Southern pin oak flats covered with water demands treestand use. Wherever a sportsman lives, whitetails often will inhabit areas where it's impossible to see through, and even more difficult to thread an arrow or bullet through.

It's taken years, but I've overcome my fear of falling. I'm still not nuts about hunting from great heights, but if a treestand is positioned 20 feet or less off the ground I can get comfortable, and with luck and skill, shoot a passing buck.

Treestands come in all shapes and sizes, and can be positioned at different heights off the ground. I've sat in willow trees that sway five feet in either direction when the wind blows, and I've stood in other stands in dead popple trees which I felt would topple if an ant sneezed near its base. Dead or swaying trees are not my cup of tea, and as I grow older, I find less fascination in sitting in them regardless of how good the deer area happens to be.

Years ago one of my friends had a permanent stand high in a dead popple. It overlooked a hole in a property line fence, and deer always moved through the hole rather than jumping the fence. I climbed into position one evening to wait for deer to move, and the old popple seemed creaky and wobbly.

Enough cover surrounded the nearby area that the only shot possible was when a buck darted through the hole. Once he began to move through I would shoot, and it always resulted in a dead buck.

This night was different. Cold weather was approaching and I was contemplating how long the popple would last. As I considered the possibilities, two does, three fawns and a 6-point buck headed for the hole in the fence.

My Carbon Express arrow was nocked in place, and my bow was up and ready to be drawn. The does and fawns jumped through the fence hole and turned away from me while the buck stood on the other side to watch them walk off.

He stepped to the hole, leaned forward and made a move but not the right one. My bow was at full draw, and when he made the false start I released the arrow. In place of the head fake so common with whitetails, this buck gave me a full-body juke that faked me out. The arrow hit the ground near where his heart and lungs should have been if he had continued moving, and the buck stared at the quivering arrow in wonder. I knew the feeling; I was amazed at the buck's action.

He turned and walked back the way he came. It was the last buck I saw from that creaky popple tree. I climbed down when shooting time ended, and the tree seemed to be listing a bit to one side like a foundering ship in rough seas.

That night the wind blew, and the next day the fence-hole treestand was laying on the ground. If this proves anything, it is: never trust old, dead trees; use common sense when choosing a tree for a stand, and trust your gut feelings about a tree.

Some treestands are elaborate with railings, padded seats and sturdy construction with positive locking features that hold it securely to a tree. Other stands are cheap, made of inexpensive and unsafe aluminum, and there are many stands around I wouldn't let my worst enemy sit in.

Many treestand makers, especially those that have been in business for years, subscribe to an industry standard for workmanship, construction, safety features, and those who subscribe to it and pass, bear a seal of approval on the stand. Any stand that doesn't follow industry standards that are checked yearly by insurance companies, are not stands I want to trust.

Many hunters believe a good treestand will allow them to shoot to all points of the compass should a buck wander past. In reality, a good stand should be able to safely support a hunter, provide some cover from below (deer do look up), and it should blend well with the tree it hangs on while allowing some hunter movement

Permanent blinds made from poles buried in cement about four feet in the ground are commonly used by Michigan deer hunters on private land.

when deer are at close range. The best treestands are relatively simple with narrow ranges of fire.

Let's face it. A treestand will offer shots in only one or two directions. If the stand is properly positioned, and downwind of the deer, a hunter needs to consider only one direction. It's simply impossible to cover everything within 360 degrees of a stand.

Look for treestand locations downwind from where deer travel. Trails leading to and from bedding or feeding areas are good bets, but don't overlook trails leading to an active scrape or watering area.

Bucks often follow a major or minor travel route until they get within 100 yards of a fresh and active scrape, and then begin to circle to check downwind for deer or human activity. A stand located downwind of the point where bucks veer off and begin circling can be a big-buck hotspot.

A question frequently heard is: How high should a treestand be? Years ago when Bill Jordan of Realtree camo fame first began his business I had several opportunities to hunt with him in Georgia. Bill is tall and long-legged, and I'm not.

I couldn't climb into his treestands. Jordan often hunted 30 feet or higher, and his treestand steps were too far apart for me to comfortably climb. I'm surprised he didn't get nose bleeds or suffer fainting spells from breathing such rarified air.

Jordan did shoot bucks, and several very impressive animals from such heights. Me, I've learned that such extreme heights give me the jitters just looking at them from the ground, and thinking of such narrow-angled shots has deterred me from hunting at excessive heights. Which brings us back to the question of how high to hunt.

My thoughts are that the ideal treestand height for accomplished bowhunters is about 15 feet. Accomplished means just what it says: The hunter must be able to shoot accurately, remain motionless while deer approach shooting range, and be comfortable enough with his equipment to feel secure.

Some of my hunting buddies have shot good bucks from stands only eight feet off the ground, and others sit perched on a stand at 18 or 20 feet.

A major key to success for bowhunters is cover. I admit a partiality to evergreen trees. They offer abundant cover, create shadows

Drawing on a deer is good practice but it's important to make sure the hunter has enough elbow room to come to full draw. This hunter placed his stand 15 feet off the ground, and has just enough room to draw.

even in December when northern hardwood trees are as bare as people in a nudist colony, and they give off some scent.

The lower the stand, the less of a shooting angle there is for bowhunters. If the deer is close, the hunter will have a sharper angle to shoot at and it can increase the chance of missing or wounding an animal. The farther away a deer is, the more the angle decreases, regardless of stand height and the easier (within reason) the shot will be.

A common fault of many treestand hunters is they snuggle up so close to a deer trail that incoming or outgoing deer can spot their movements as they prepare to shoot. It's better to position a stand 20 yards from an active trail, and select a tree with nearby trees to act as camouflage for your position.

A Missouri buddy sits in a clump of five trees (he calls his stand the Five Sisters) that grow from a single trunk. He must turn his body slightly to shoot around one or the other of the five tree trunks, but the heavy screening prevents deer from spotting him. He nails his buck each year, and never has to find another treestand site.

Wide open or bushy trees? It's another common treestand question, and one that bears investigation.

All things being equal, most veteran tree hunters prefer a bushy tree over an open one. Open treestand sites offer unlimited visibility, adequate maneuverability and a clean field of fire. But one wonders if that is what a deer hunter really needs, and I don't believe it is.

It's my belief and that of many expert hunters that bushy trees are best if the hunter removes just enough foliage or limbs to offer a clear shot at deer moving through the area. Never deface a tree, and do not remove all limbs even on private property, but judiciously prune away a few offenders so a bow can be drawn or rifle lifted into shooting position. Maintain the tree's integrity, and keep it full and natural looking to prevent deer from spotting any slight movement.

A common fault is that hunters pick trees they feel "look good." They tend to overlook trees that are available nearby and offer better features.

My course of action is to look for the perfect tree in the perfect spot. They are hard to find because the tree must have a natural opening at the proper height for a stand and it must have the opening in the proper spot for a right or left-handed hunter.

A treestand must be positioned so a right-handed hunter can swing left to shoot, or a southpaw can swing right to shoot. Little nubs, limbs or twigs can be removed to prevent making noise as a bow or firearm is raised into position for a shot.

Many good looking trees have tumors or a growth exactly where the stand must be placed, and if a hunter does so, it can reduce the stand's stability. That item is enough to cause me to look elsewhere.

A treestand must be comfortable. If not, the hunter finds himself in an awkward position, and that increases the possibility of a sore back, neck or lower extremities. An uncomfortable hunter must move to relieve the stress on his body, and movement has saved the life of many a grand buck.

A comfortable treestand means more than a stable platform. Many hunters choose a stand with a firm and comfortable seat that allows the back to rest against the tree trunk without being poked by a small stub or broken branch. The hunter's feet should always be firmly planted on the treestand floor or grating.

My motto when buying a treestand is to follow the four Ss. No, it doesn't mean "shoot, shovel, swear and shut up." It means safety, stability, strength, and sturdy construction. Such stands are easily put in place, and allow sportsmen the maximum comfort while relieving strain on back and legs.

An acquaintance of mine likes portable stands that can be clamped to the tree, and Bob always sat where his feet should be. He complained continuously about his legs going to sleep, but when I pointed out that he sat with his legs dangling over the stand's edge, he soon figured out that this uncomfortable position cut the blood flow to his legs. It didn't take him long to figure out that numb, tingly, gone-to-sleep legs were hazardous to his health when climb-

This Super Starr Deluxe Ladder Stand is safe, stable, strong and sturdy.

ing down from a stand. He also decided that such a position made it virtually impossible to shoot when a buck passed his stand.

It seems every treestand manufacturer has brochures that picture a hunter standing, leaning out into thin air while drawing his bow to shoot at a deer. I've fought this image with a passion for many years and for various reasons.

A standing hunter, even if he wears a safety belt or harness, is in an unstable and precarious position. Anyone who has vertigo should never stand in a tree, and I've learned to shoot sitting down. It's comfortable, safe and allows for accurate shots.

Sitting down to shoot eliminates excess movement that comes with standing up, changing position or drawing a bow. It's true that most hunters can't pull as much bow weight while sitting as while standing, but very high poundage or draw weights have advantages and disadvantages. I'd rather be safe and stable in a sitting position, and draw 60 pounds than be unstable while moving too much trying to draw 70 pounds.

Besides, I'm convinced that a sitting hunter is much less conspicuous to a deer than one that stands upright in a treestand. I wear high rubber boots, and stick the lower limb of my Oneida bow in the top of my left boot. When a buck shows up, it requires little movement to lift the bow free, draw, aim and shoot.

Treestand safety is of major importance to anyone who climbs a tree to shoot a deer. Most accidents occur when climbing into, sitting or standing in one or climbing down from a treestand. Any brief mental lapse can result in a fall.

Safety belts are the bare minimum, and a full body harness is much better. I wear a Game Tracker full body harness and climbing system that has adjustable shoulder, waist and leg straps to ensure proper fit. A quick attach/detach design secures the hunter in seconds, and triangular climbing rings allow the attachment of a safety rope for secure climbing. The full body harness transfers weight to legs so the shock load is focused on the thighs and away from the abdomen. The main harness connecting strap has break-away, sewn-in folds to slow a hunter's descent in a fall.

I fell once from 12 feet when my hand got tangled in my hunting coat. I fell, bounced off a limb with my back and hit the ground. I was scared but not hurt.

Since then, I always wear my full body harness and climbing system. The climbing system attaches to climbing rings on the waist band of the harness to lock a hunter in place and frees up the use of both hands to install tree steps or a stand.

Too many hunters have been crippled for life or been killed in treestand accidents. The use of a safety belt or harness should be mandatory for any hunter who takes to an elevated stand to hunt.

Safety belts and harnesses are not just another way to get hunters to part with their money. Simply put, they can save a hunter's life.

Another common fault of many hunters is they wish to sit at the edge of a field or huge feeding area where deer can be seen in all directions. This enables the hunter to see deer daily, but it precludes the opportunity for many shots.

For optimum performance, a treestand should be positioned inside the wooded area through which whitetails move to reach the food site. How far inside is anyone's guess, but a minimum of 50 yards appears best. One hundred yards is even better if the hunter can position the stand downwind of approaching deer.

Deer often move from bedding to feeding area via different routes, and these trails can resemble the frayed ends of a rope. But, they often meet to form one or two main trails leading from heavy cover to the dinner table. The best spot for a treestand will be 20 to 25 yards downwind from where the minor trails converge into a major trail that most of the deer eventually wind up using. Pre-season scouting can find where minor trails feed into the major ones, and that is where you should be.

Hunters often want to know what treestand to buy. There are any number of good stands on the market, and choosing one is like choosing the paint job on a new car. It's purely subjective but the bottom line should never be price but the construction, stability and safety of the stand.

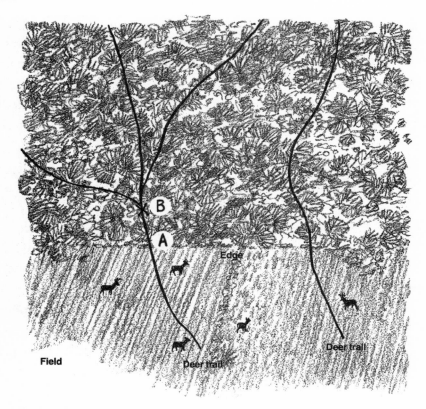

Position treestands away from the end or edges of a field. You'll see more deer from a field-edge stand (A), but you'll shoot more deer from a position in a wooded area where two or more trails converge (B).

Stands come in many types such as climbing, ladder and portable models. As these words are written I have hunted deer for 45 years, and at age 61, my choice is a quality made ladder stand. They are easy to attach to a tree, easy to climb and descend, and are very stable when properly attached.

Treestands I've used include Game Tracker's Gorilla Silverback Magnum, King Kong and Gorilla Deluxe ladder stand. Other manufacturers with excellent climbing or ladder stands include Ameristep, API Grand Slam, Eagle Bow & Gun Blind, Lok-On, Old Man, Summit, and Super Starr Deluxe Ladder Stand.

Close-up of a Summit treestand.

Strap-on climbing sticks have become very popular because they can be quickly and quietly attached to a tree. Many treestands attach to a tree with a chain and turnbuckle or a ratchet strap. Hunters should check a treestand and chain or strap integrity every time before using it, and it's wise to remove stands at the end of the season to prevent theft and to make sure the chain or strap doesn't bite into the tree or make them impossible to remove. The same safety inspection should be applied to the steps of a ladder stand or climbing sticks.

Much has been made of being downwind of a deer trail. It's a basic fact of setting up a ground blind or treestand, but hunters must realize that by doing so it may place them upwind of another trail. If an animal on a trail downwind of your stand gets your scent, there will be a great ruckus created by blowing and snorting deer. Any buck within hearing distance will spook, and it's safe to say that your current stand site is blown for the day. Deer occasionally return after being spooked, but often do so by an entirely different route.

Hunters must constantly work around shifting air currents. Even when the prevailing wind is from one direction, a storm front moving in can cause the wind to swirl or change directions. The savvy treestand hunter should have two or three alternative sites in mind to cope with wind-direction changes.

In hilly or mountainous terrain hunters must cope with air thermals during morning and evening hours in addition to wind direction. Warming air in mountainous areas moves uphill in the morning and will carry human scent with it, and the reverse is true in the late afternoon and early evening as cooling air forces the scent back down the hill or mountain.

Treestand hunters in such areas learn to anticipate these daily changes, and place their stands above or below deer runways to prevent being winded. A Puff Bottle of unscented powder is handy to carry, and a little squirt will indicate wind direction and thermal movements.

Ground blind or treestand? Each can be extremely productive for deer hunters but the misuse of either method can ruin a hunt. Both can be prime spots to ambush a buck, and that is the topic of our next chapter.

5

TEN AMBUSH SITES FOR BUCKS

Show me a whitetail buck, regardless of age, and I'll show you an animal that can be taken by a skilled hunter. The operative word here is "skilled," because there is a huge difference between being skilled and being lucky.

True, a hunter may shuffle out into the corner cornfield, choose a spot that looks good, stand around thinking about a late breakfast and kill a buck with trophy antlers. This peculiar set of circumstances happens every year, but it doesn't occur often enough for many of us to develop a friendly, long-term relationship with Lady Luck. A knowledge of deer foods, habitat, terrain and hunting techniques are far better tools for the bow or firearm deer hunter.

Inside the heart of every deer hunter beats a desire to learn how and where to ambush deer—to find a spot where success is a sure thing, and where year after year they can take a nice buck.

Such locations exist, but a hunter must learn how to hunt each one. No book can fully explain precisely the minute differences between your funnel area and mine. Each one of the 10 ambush sites are different, and their size and/or variation may be as different as boys and girls. It's up to hunters to learn the differences in local areas, and decide how best to hunt them.

This chapter will point out 10 key ambush sites where big-racked bucks can be taken with regularity—year after year after year. A buck a year is possible from each of these spots providing hunter pressure doesn't chase the animals off, food sources do not change or the habitat and terrain features are not altered by clear-cut coniferous or hardwood stands, buildings erected in the middle of the cover or any one of many other factors that can cause extensive habitat change.

The locations are not magical places where bucks stand in place, apparently oblivious to everything around them, as a hunter blazes away. They are common in farmland areas, near urban and suburban locations, and in rural countrysides. Such areas exist wherever farmland and woodland create edge cover and where food is plentiful enough to attract deer. The key is to find them.

Another key factor with each location is that all necessary ingredients, as with good soup, must be present before they become genuine hotspots.

It falls on each hunter's shoulders to determine whether all necessary factors are present before the hunt begins. Hunters must study all available data on the area long before the season opens.

I'm a firm believer that nothing exceeds a farmland whitetail buck for survival savvy. They are born and raised near humans, and those animals that have survived two or more years are crafty. They know how to avoid human contact, and their life depends on instinctive reactions to danger.

The following hotspots only work if a hunter understands enough about whitetails to know when and why they use such locations. The

Whitetail bucks often hide out in small woodlots. Such areas often are grown over with berry bushes, briers and thick covers. Many hunters overlook such areas, and miss out on good bucks like this 10-pointer. Blink and you'll miss seeing this buck as it pussyfoots away from your stand.

areas discussed are survival hotspots; places where a buck will go when hunting pressure gets heavy. They produce because we must depend on other hunters to force the buck to be there when you want him to show up.

Bucks grow big and old by being a tad bit luckier than their cousins, and by learning valuable lessons early in life. Increased noise on opening day (even before daybreak) is enough to send wall-hangers heading for cover long before the first pink blush of dawn creases the eastern horizon.

Hunters, unfortunately, are their own worst enemy. They are gregarious by nature, and babble away when they get out of the car. Doors slam and flashlights wink as they stumble through the woods to a blind built the day before. Will a whitetail buck hang around to see what all the opening-day hoopla is about? Not likely. They hide and venture out only after dark to feed near remote bedding locations.

Noise, human conversation and scent disturb deer. It makes them move early, and bed down in a safe thicket where few hunters ever go. It's a matter of survival for them, and if the tables were turned, humans would adopt similar behavioral patterns.

Hunters need to know where bucks will go when danger threatens, and use the wind to their advantage while allowing other sportsmen to move deer in your direction. It requires footwork and common sense to determine whether each of the following hunting locations offer what you need, and what a big buck needs, and it also means leaving loud-mouthed hunting buddies behind.

Solitary hunting doesn't seem to appeal to many whitetail hunters for reasons I never understood. Robert Ruark's famous Old Man once said: "One boy is all boy, two boys is half a boy and three boys is no boy at all." Think about that statement, and compare it to hunting with your friends.

One person is quiet. Two people talk and yell back and forth, and when a third person (or more) enter the picture, the noise level and disturbance increases to the point where no self-respecting buck would be found within a half-mile of the commotion. Two hunters generate twice as much scent in a hunting area, and most ambush sites are made to order for just one person. A second hunter makes noise, makes twice as much movement, and the result is fewer buck sightings.

Ruark's Old Man was talking about teenage boys goofin' off instead of working, and I'm talking about deer hunters. To paraphrase his statement: One hunter is all hunter, two hunters is half a hunter and three hunters is no hunter at all.

Gregariousness is fine at church, family reunions, weddings and work but it falls short when a hunter is working an ambush site.

Learn the joys of solitary hunting, and become more dependent on your own actions and judgments. Take leave of hunting buddies, or work with them on other hunting techniques where a larger group of warm bodies is needed, but hunt ambush sites alone. It may sound difficult, but the results are worth the effort.

One specific hunt became a turning point in my deer-hunting career. It taught me the wisdom and value of solitary hunting, and I learned the importance of knowing how and where to locate one-man ambush sites.

It was the fifth day of Michigan's 16-day firearms deer season, and many hunters had given up and gone home. I'd been busy the first four days helping friends and relatives get their bucks, and now the woods seemed as empty of whitetails as my freezer was of venison.

Two days earlier I had watched a nice 8-pointer sneak through the brush in an area I'd never hunted. The brush was a narrow finger of gray dogwood leading into a thick cedar swamp where whitetails bedded down. It was logical that the faint trail was an escape route used only in times of danger. The trail wasn't bold and wide like other deer trails I'd seen, and it obviously wasn't an area frequented by large numbers of deer. On close examination, it turned out to be an escape route used by just one buck, and only when he was pressured to seek heavy cover to avoid the numerous hunters who tried to drive the nearby swamp.

Bright and early the next day I took a position 50 yards downwind from the faint trail. Two hours passed without sign of a deer. I was daydreaming of coffee and a hot Danish when the clatter and racket of car doors slamming drifted downwind on the freshening breeze.

It sounded like a small-scale riot in progress. It was five days into the season, and a group of hunters was planning a drive in hopes of moving a buck past someone. Earlier thoughts of coffee and pastry slipped away as the hunters began noisily moving my way.

Several does and fawns squirted out ahead of the hunters as the animals headed for the security of the cedar swamp. The drivers had posted two standers near the swamp, but they overlooked the tiny sliver of thick cover entering the swamp. That was fine with me because I had it covered, and they didn't know another hunter was in the vicinity. Neither did the buck I'd been looking for.

The buck was cool in the face of danger. He didn't panic and run headlong for cover before studying the terrain in front of him. He came slinking along like an antlered snake through the thick dogwood tangle moving slowly with his head held low in a semi-crouch.

He would take a few steps, pause to look back at the approaching drivers before moving again. Each step was a study in animal concentration. He used the cover to his advantage, and evidently had used this escape route before and had never encountered a problem. He wasn't expecting me as he closed to within 50 yards.

The wind was blowing from him to me, and since my position in the fencerow provided cover the buck didn't know I had him in my sights. I settled the Bushnell's crosshairs low behind his front shoulder, and admired him briefly before taking a shot.

As the rifle roared the buck stumbled, caught his balance and continued at a dead run along the dogwood for 50 yards before his legs quit working and he folded up. I was punching my firearms tag before tying it to his antlers when one of the deer drivers approached. He wanted to know why I'd been sitting there.

"Bucks always head directly into the cedar swamp," he said. "This is the first time I've seen one move along this dogwood swale."

"It may be the first time you've seen deer move through here," I responded, "but that's because you've fallen into a rut of driving the area the same way. Each year you push this spot, and each time a buck slips out ahead of the drivers and no one gets a shot."

I told him that many bucks, particularly large animals, often have escape routes they use in times of danger. The big bucks seldom follow the lead doe and her fawns or smaller bucks, but prefer to use a little-known trail off to one side which enables them to work into heavy cover without being exposed to hunters.

That ol' boy shook his head, muttered something about "luck," and wandered off to join his buddies. He didn't take time to study the escape route, and didn't learn from the experience. The next year I shot another buck in the same location, and the drive again contained the same hunter.

"You again, huh?" he muttered as I field dressed my buck.

"Yep."

"Got lucky again, eh?"

"Yep."

I'm a man of few words when hunters won't listen to reason. Trying to educate people who don't want or resent the offer makes me a bit testy. Sadly, all too many hunters go through their deer hunting careers without ever learning anything except that one

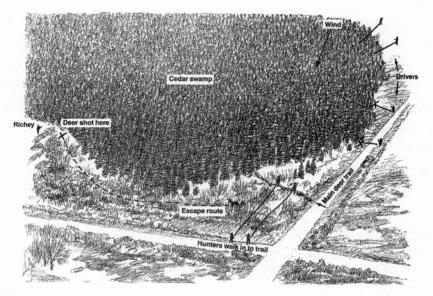

The drivers had posted two standers near the swamp. I took my stand in a tiny sliver of thick cover at the entrance. Unwittingly, the drivers pushed the buck straight toward me along an escape route that led into the swamp.

method and one area that once produced a buck for them. It's called hunting memories.

The following pages should generate some thoughts on ambush sites. It should stir up memories and questions. Some folks have spent a lifetime studying whitetail deer, and they can often spot an ambush site just like a professional photographer can spot a perfect picture.

Ambush sites fall into 10 categories, and here's the first one.

ESCAPE ROUTES

Escape routes, those little-used deer trails favored by big bucks when the going gets tough, are hard to find. In many cases they will parallel a heavily used game trail, but often will be found in thicker cover. A bent blade of grass, a broken twig or an occasional footprint may be the only clue to their existence.

The key to finding these trails is to know where deer bed during the day and where they move to feed. Escape routes often are found nearby, and it requires looking to find them. Hands-and-knees examination of the ground is the only way.

One trail I found was 50 yards off to one side of a main trail, and it didn't reveal itself until one hand and a knee were in the middle of the indistinct path. A fall mushroom was growing there, and I studied it for a moment before everything started clicking into focus. There, beside the mushroom, was the splayed track of a big deer. I inched forward, looked in the direction of travel, and spotted a bracken fern sharply indented from a deer's hoof. Five feet farther along I saw another faint track, but a hunter would have to be really looking hard to spot the trail. It didn't look like it had been used for weeks, but it was an escape route through heavy cover.

I followed the trail on hands and knees, and it led through a narrow sumac thicket while the main deer trail skirted the tangle. Fifty yards farther on it sneaked through a seemingly impenetrable

This hunter was working a pine plantation with some patches of heavy brush. He had seen this buck enter and leave the plantation before opening day of the firearms season. He waited downwind from the trail the buck used, and when it passed by him, he shot.

wall of dogwood and on into a tiny stub of thick cedar swamp that connected with the larger cedar swamp.

This is it, I thought excitedly. This is where a buck can be shot. The escape route is the key because it offers heavy cover for a nervous buck to use between feeding and bedding areas, and it should produce on opening day.

I stood up and surveyed the terrain. I lowered my profile to a level used by a buck and looked again. The animal would be hidden from view of hunters guarding the main trail 50 yards away, and the buck could pass through to the swamp without being seen.

Now came the hard part. I had to figure out where to sit in order to ambush the buck on opening day.

I had to study the wind. Fortunately, I knew the prevailing wind direction in the area. I then had to find an area which would be downwind and within shooting range of the escape route. After spending three hours scouting the area, only one spot showed promise. The tiny wedge of tangled cedars that connected to the main body of the swamp was my logical choice because it offered a place to hide. A cedar had fallen in a storm, and the maze of roots provided a backrest and concealment behind me. It looked perfect but I wanted to be sure a moving deer would be visible.

I placed a dead tree limb horizontally three feet above ground between two cedars. This would be the approximate height of a buck's back as he ambled down the escape route. I paced off the distance from the trail to the cedar roots, and it was only 35 yards away.

Good, good. Now it was necessary to sit with my back to the roots and see if the limb could be seen.

No, dammit, other cedars blocked my view of the trail. I moved the limb 10 feet down the trail and tried again. No dice.

I moved the dead limb halfway between the first and second locations, sat down and looked. The limb was barely visible through the wall of cedar trees.

I had my spot.

The next time I saw that trail was two months later. Opening-day hunters were all around me, but were evenly spaced along the well-used trail leading into the swamp. I entered from downwind an hour before sunup, sat down quietly with my knees up in front of me. My old Ruger .44 Magnum was braced against my right shoulder with the fore-end resting across my knees.

I knew there would be time only for a quick shot, and I wanted a heavy bullet with tremendous shocking power for the short-range shot. When and if a buck appeared he would be visible for only an instant, and I suspected he wouldn't show until several minutes after shooting began along the main trail. It was my belief that he would hold back, allow other deer to filter down the trail and bump into the hunters.

My judgment was dead-on. Ten minutes after daybreak a small group of young bucks and does came along the main trail, and the shooting started. Then the yelling began in earnest.

"Get one, Joe?" someone yelled 100 yards away.

"I hit him, and he ran toward you," came the reply.

It was followed by two more shots, and the noise of a hunter moving through the heavy brush. Another shot, and then just the faint murmur of happy conversation. Someone had taken a small buck.

The shots and conversation registered on my brain but I kept my attention riveted to the escape route. If a decent buck was coming he'd be along any moment.

Long, white antler tines showed like the winking of headlights far away on a dark night as the buck pussyfooted through heavy cover along his escape route. I could see the antlers for a second, and then they disappeared as he stepped behind another cedar tree.

I raised the .44 Magnum carbine slowly off my knees, and resting my cheek against the cold wood stock, stared at the dead limb

The author hunted this buck for five weeks with a bow before missing a shot. Herb Boldt sat on a small hill in the area, and shot this handsome buck with a .35 Remington as it snuck down an escape trail on opening day of firearms season.

which was still in place. Within moments the buck would be in position for an easy shot, and I had to be ready to punch the safety off. Two or three seconds was all I would have before the animal would be screened from view again.

126

First the nose and then an eye and antlers came into view. The buck paused, looked away at the unheard commotion apparently going on as the other hunters relived the kill. The buck then made his move.

I flicked the safety off without conscious thought, and as the buck's neck came into view I stroked the trigger. The 9-pointer went down in a heap and never got up.

I didn't move for 60 minutes. The other hunters had heard the shot, but I didn't want them to know where I had been sitting or where the escape route was located. It's just one way of keeping your hunting area intact.

Never tell and never draw attention to the location of your hunting position along an escape route. Sneak in and out, and if necessary, tag the deer, walk to the car, drop off your firearm, and return for the buck after dark. The anecdote at the beginning of this chapter proves it's not always possible to keep the area a secret, but in many cases other hunters will just feel you were lucky to be in the right place at the right time. It pays to never discourage that feeling.

Escape routes are never easy to find, but look for them in thick cover up to 50 yards to one side of a main trail. Once you've found one, guard that information with your life.

SNOW-COVERED CORNFIELDS

Earlier in this book I described a hunt for a big buck in a snow-covered cornfield. We didn't shoot that buck, but since then I've learned how and when to hunt small, medium and large tracts of planted corn.

The trick is fundamental, but it often eludes many hunters in northern climes where tracking snow conditions are as much a part of the hunt as fluorescent-orange clothing. Whitetail deer in farm-land areas eat corn once snow covers other food, and a standing cornfield is a late-season magnet for them.

The one thing to remember is that does and fawns generally are the first deer to come to feed. Bucks follow later, and move to

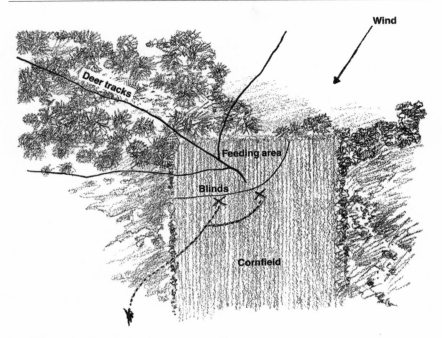

Construct a cornstalk blind downwind from the general feeding area where whitetails congregate. This ambush site is one of the best, provided the hunter can walk to his blind without disturbing the area.

the corn during the last minutes of daylight. If legal shooting time in your hunting ends an hour before dark . . . well, ignore this tip and proceed to the next one.

Of utmost importance when hunting corn is knowing when the animals feed. A cornfield may be a mile square, but deer generally will feed in one small area rather than grazing everywhere. They will feed there until food runs out, and then move to another nearby location that may be only 50 to 100 yards away.

Finding where deer feed is easy when snow covers the ground. Countless deer tracks are congregated in a relatively small area, and cornstalks are broken down and the cobs are chewed heavily to remove the kernels.

Find the feeding site, and construct a natural blind from corn-stalks. Make it small, keep it natural and make sure it is downwind of the feeding area.

Check the proposed blind area for deer tracks in the snow; it doesn't pay to construct a cornstalk blind only to learn that white-tails are moving upwind into your scent stream. Police the area well, and select a downwind location where deer do not travel. It may be slightly farther from the feeding zone than a hunter may desire, but there it is. We all have to make concessions to common sense.

Ideally, the blind should be within 50 yards of the food site. Break down a few cornstalks to provide a shooting lane, and enter the blind from downwind. Keep the wind in your face at all times.

Late-season cornfield hunting can be cold, but gunning corn-fields places a heavy emphasis on being able to sit still. Several hunters I know hunt the corn each year during gun season, and each one manages to tag a nice buck.

"But, it can be colder than hell," states a hunting buddy.

"It also means being able to sit motionless for two or three hours," another corn hunter told me. "If cold and immobility are two things you can't handle then you're better off moving through the woods with other hunters."

Then he snickered because he knew these hunters would push deer to him for a close shot as animals leave thick cover to feed at dusk.

Whitetails feed in standing corn during late fall and through the winter because it offers a good food supply and ideal cover. It's not uncommon to watch deer filter into the corn along a maze of trails, but these trails almost always lead to the dinner table. A down-wind blind along a trail is an alternate selection but being winded is possible.

One hint of human scent, and the hunt will end for the day. And rest assured that on subsequent days the deer will remember your position, and be ever cautious during their approach. The deer almost always arrive with the last light, and once spooked, they may wait a bit longer to head for the corn. Frightened deer may not make it to the corn until after legal shooting time ends.

The same philosophy works for bowhunters as well. The only difference is the blind must be positioned somewhat closer to the feeding areas. Properly positioned, a late-season bowhunt can produce tasty venison and a close shot.

DRAINAGE DITCHES

A drainage ditch, dry creekbed, or any deep, narrow depression in farmland country can be an excellent place to harvest a buck during hunting season. Bucks, and to a lesser degree does and fawns, travel these natural terrain corridors whenever danger is near. Some hunters have learned their value, but many have not.

One year I was hunting red foxes in southern Michigan farmland. The Walker hounds jumped a fox in a slashing, and hazed the animal back and forth through a large woodlot for 30 minutes.

I knew red foxes often travel the drainage ditch that cut diagonally across the section. The ditch was six feet deep, and a tiny trickle of farmland drainage water flowed through it during warm weather. It was ice-covered and slippery now, but on many occasions I had killed a dog (male) fox in midwinter as he tried to escape the hounds by running down ditch ice.

I took up a station 50 yards from the woodlot and waited just around a tiny bend in the ditch. The hounds were pounding my way, boo-hooing at full volume, and I felt Big Red would soon come scooting into sight.

My jaw dropped open when a buck with one remaining antler skidded around the corner, spotted me and slid to jerky stop 10 yards away. He crawled and scampered up from the ditch, and was last seen taking a hasty exit to a nearby field.

A drainage ditch crossed an open farm field and almost touched this small woodlot. Rich Millhouse took up a stand near the edge of the woodlot, and when late-season bowhunters made too much noise, they pushed this 8-pointer into the ditch. It fled for safety only to bump into Millhouse and offer an easy bow shot.

Deer season was over, and deer-running hounds are worthless to fox hunters. I grabbed a hefty stick and scared off the dogs when they came yodeling around the bend.

That incident was a big tip-off. It proved that under stress bucks will use drainage ditches or creekbeds for travel when hunter pressure backs them against the wall.

A ditch or creekbed should have some cover. Barren, wide-open ditches are seldom used by bucks because they offer little protection for a moving animal and spooky bucks will choose other escape routes. Ideally, a ditch will have some cattails, tag alders, or sumac growing inside it, and it will not have much water. A jump-across stream is just right.

The ditch should have heavy cover within 200 yards on either side, and it must be thick and located near the ditch. A hard-pressed buck like the one chased by our foxhounds took to the open fields once he spotted me but had I been located elsewhere he would have ran another 100 yards and exited into an adjoining woodlot.

Adjoining woodlots, swales, marshes or other heavy cover should have immediate access from the ditch. Look for a tiny sliver of woods which leaves a woodlot and enters the drainage ditch, and check any brushy fencerow that connects the ditch with other nearby cover.

A buck will generally leave a woodlot at the first hint of danger, jump into a drainage ditch and proceed until he comes to an exit where he has enough available cover to conceal his movements. Deer then filter into or through the new cover until they feel safe from any danger.

Each drainage ditch or creekbed is different, and they must be hunted with common sense. Choose a site downwind from any thick cover which enters or leaves the ditch. Never sit fully exposed at the top of the ditch unless some nearby cover offers concealment, but sit down in the ditch near the junction where the fencerow or finger of woods meets the drainage ditch. A buck will work through the cover until he reaches the comparative safety of the ditch, pause for a moment and continue on his way.

If a creekbed or ditch is long and straight, but has one little kink or turn in it, sit on the downwind side of the bend and listen closely. A deer's hooves will clatter on the ice or the hunter will hear the thudding of hoofbeats as the deer moves closer. Be ready for a close shot.

My favorite firearm for this hunting is a 12 gauge 3-inch Magnum shotgun with No. 4 buckshot. A fast-pointing .44 Magnum carbine is another excellent choice.

EVERGREEN PLANTATIONS/ CHRISTMAS TREE FARMS

Sportsmen who hunt in the northern tier of states have long known that evergreen plantations or Christmas tree farms are hotspots for snowshoe hares. The white hares find food, cover and protection from overhead predation in such dense thickets. Whitetail bucks also seek protection from the elements and from hunting pressure, and they hole up in such cover.

Evergreen plantations are incredibly thick, and nearly impenetrable in some locations. The trees often are planted in rows and close together, and once the trees reach maturity, they form an overhead canopy as thick as the Amazon jungle.

The thicker and more difficult they are for hunters to move through, the more attractive they are to bucks. Mind you, a big expansive tract in not necessarily better for deer hunting. A small, compact 10-acre plantation is plenty big enough to harbor a trophy whitetail buck.

Christmas tree plantations are a different story. Unlike evergreen plantations, a Christmas tree farm is much different. The trees aren't as big, and modern growers often string high fences around them to keep deer out during winter months when food supplies are short. Note too that most Christmas tree plantations are cut down every seven to eight years, the stumps turned up and the fields replanted. Deer will use an unprotected tree farm for occasional cover but not like a big evergreen plantation.

This bowhunter set up downwind of a trail leading out of a small pine plantation. He knew this buck was close, and when it decided to move, it should come toward him. It did.

Never confuse Scotch pine, spruce and balsam plantations with a cedar swamp. Swamps are low-lying areas while most evergreen plots are located high and dry on somewhat sandy soil.

The ideal location for a plantation hunting site is where the evergreens connect with a swamp on one side via some type of brushy cover and croplands or upland hardwoods on another. Nearby food is important, and a spillover of deer often occurs between the swamp and the plantation.

Does, fawns and lesser bucks will hole up in the swamp when firearm hunters arrive, but a smart buck will disappear into a plantation when hunters start moving around. Once inside, a big buck is tough to find and harder to hunt, and doing so is a bit like hunting huge cornfields.

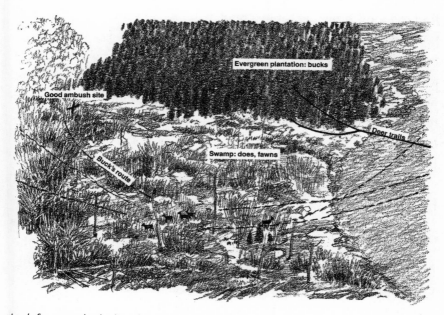

Look for an ambush site where an evergreen plantation butts up against a cedar swamp, feeding area and hardwoods. The best spot is any thick brush that connects the evergreens with a feeding area.

Bucks are difficult to move during a drive because they can dodge behind an evergreen 20 feet away and never be seen. Hunters can try still-hunting, moving a step at a time, and spend more time looking than walking, but that age-old technique seldom works with these deer.

Few whitetail bucks move into an evergreen plot until after hunting season opens. Once hunters are on the move, and noise or pressure from bowhunters increases, a buck will head for cover like a woodchuck jumping into his meadow hole. A big buck can be as happy with 10 acres of evergreens providing him with all the cover he needs. The more snow that falls, the happier a buck is if farmland is found nearby. Snow on boughs acts as a deterrent to many hunters.

Hunters who aren't afraid to get bushels of snow dumped down their necks from brushing against snow-laded evergreen boughs must find the most probable route a buck will take to gain safety. This can be accomplished long before hunting season opens. Look for brushy fencerows leading from nearby food sites or adjacent woodlots into the evergreens. Find a natural depression like a gully or dry creekbed between two rolling hills which contacts the plantation. Look for any terrain feature that can offer cover to a moving buck as he seeks sanctuary in the pines, and areas leading from feeding or wooded sites to heavy cover are seldom used except on opening day.

After scouting the area, and locating the main travel lanes used by a buck seeking a hidey-hole, a hunter must find the best place to ambush him. Mature bucks generally approach a pine plantation upwind to wind-check the area before committing themselves to the move. This means a hunter must be downwind from the probable entrance site.

The ideal ambush site will be inside the pine plantation, and downwind from the buck's route when he decides to take up temporary residence. Such areas generally have thick cover which means short shots, and those who traditionally hunt such areas often take

His technique is simple, and beats hell out of wading through a swamp. Hip boots or chest waders are a must if the swamp is filled with water, but a canoe should be used whenever possible to work into the interior. A buck may jump or swim a small stream, but canoe travel allows for silent, odor-free travel.

Find the ideal swamp, use a canoe to travel into the middle of it, find a nearby bedding area and be ready to shoot. It's easy providing the hunter doesn't get spooked by solitary travel where the only other living creatures are birds and deer.

SMALL WOODLOTS

A teeny-tiny woodlot in a farmer's back forty will often serve as a hideout for farmland deer. It often seems too small to harbor deer, and that is one reason why many such small timber stands may go unhunted. Hunters should check out these locations with bow or firearm.

Many years ago, John McKenzie and I would scout small woodlots in early October. We didn't realize it then, but we were passing up some fine bowhunting opportunities. Our objective was to scout bucks prior to Michigan's 16-day firearms season which traditionally opens November 15.

We looked for buck rubs, scrapes, tracks in soft earth near croplands, and we looked for and found bedding areas. We put all the puzzle pieces together to form what we called The Game Plan for implementation on opening day.

At the time we were hunting in southern Michigan which had a very low deer population when compared to that of today. We knew the area had few bucks, and they were like circuit-riding preachers 150 years ago. The bucks would be in one place today, four miles away the next, and three miles away on the third day and back home again on the fourth.

We learned that regardless of which mile-square section a buck may be haunting today, he would move that evening to another spot as much as four miles away. These farmland bucks moved day and night whenever the mood struck them, and we had to learn where they crossed dirt roads and which woodlot would appeal to their sense of safety.

Our method was simple but time consuming. We drove our own cars, met early in the morning, and decided how and where each one would travel to find tracks crossing back roads. We did our homework every day for 45 days before the season opener, and by the time November 15 rolled around, we knew exactly where the deer would be on that day.

John would head in one direction and I would travel another. We each carried a stiff broom with us, and drove slowly and noted where fresh deer tracks were found. We would mark each location on a map, brush out the tracks with the broom, and continue on until we had made a full circuit.

We would meet again, compare notes, and once we learned whether the deer were on a two-day, three-day or four-day schedule, it didn't take a calculator to determine which sections would hold deer on the opener.

We would then scout the sections destined to hold deer on opening day, and look at everything in them. We began by walking the edges of farm fields, and paid particular attention to corn, soybean and winter wheat fields. We would note the tracks, their direction of travel, and number of animals in the area.

In many cases, a tangle of low-growing berry bushes would serve as a bedding spot for the buck, and almost every time the buck would be in his bed long before daybreak arrived. Our plan, once the big day rolled around, was simple.

We knew where the buck bedded, and would silently position one hunter downwind from the bedding area along a trail the deer would use to flee the area. This hunter would be in place an hour before the other man circled around and began to walk downwind

This nice buck is coming out of a bedding area, heading toward a patch of heavy cover.

through the woodlot cover. The plan was to execute a sneak-drive, and allow the wind to wash hunter scent downwind to the bedding buck.

Seldom would the sneak-driver see the buck as it ghosted from its bed. The deer would hear and smell the hunter moving downwind, leave the safety of its bedding area, and begin a dignified retreat along a trail which would lead to another patch of heavy cover.

If we guessed right, which we did 95 percent of the time, the buck would walk right up to the standing hunter for an easy shot. Every buck we killed for many years (with only one exception) was in heavy cover and bedded down long before sun-up.

FUNNELS OR NARROW FINGERS OF WOODS

Everyone knows what a funnel is. It is wider at one end than the other, and it is used to channel liquids from one receptacle to another. A funnel in deer country serves the same purpose; it funnels deer from a big area to a much smaller one.

In this case, a funnel channels deer movement into areas that are much easier for a sportsman to cover. Narrow fingers of woods are a perfect example.

Farmland deer near heavy cover often feed in farm fields or along acorn ridges. That much is obvious to most deer hunters, but one factor they often overlook is how deer move when danger threatens. The second part of the equation is also easy; they move into and through heavy cover.

The big question then is where do they go in heavy cover. Does, fawns and young bucks may skip across a field like first-graders heading outdoors for recess, but large and more mature bucks with heavy antlers choose to use whatever cover they can find to mask their movements.

A narrow finger of woods which connects a woodlot with another thicker brier-choked orchard, cedar swamp or woodlot attracts whitetail bucks. These funnel-like narrow fingers of woods are found everywhere.

Deer may get caught feeding in farm fields when opening day rolls around. The smaller immature deer may dart across open fields in an attempt to gain safety, but big bucks are not as foolish. They head for safety along routes which offer some cover and protection.

A finger of woods that connects with heavy cover in two or more directions is a natural. Bucks move slowly through the thick cover, check ahead for any hunter presence, and if all goes well they reach safety without being seen.

Many such funnels or woody fingers are brushy and difficult to walk through, and they offer excellent concealment for a buck doing a disappearing act.

Avoid woodlot fingers that are open and offer little cover. Instead, choose those with heavy cover. A buck may use these areas on opening day and then not use them again until late in the season when deer drives take place. Intense preseason scouting will inform

Matt Pollington poses with a terrific 13-pointer taken on opening day of the Michigan bow season. This buck moved down a narrow finger of woods (funnel) between two woodlots.

hunters which narrow woodlot fingers deer will use, and old tracks, droppings, rubs and scrapes will alert hunters to the best ones to hunt.

Select a natural ground blind or treestand site long before the season opens. Position it downwind from the travel lane, and stay away from it until opening day. Avoid leaving human scent in the area because it can and will spook bucks.

I've seen wooded fingers that are a half-mile wide and I avoid them like they are filled with poison ivy. The best ones are so narrow you may have to sit with your back to an open field in order to be away from the trail. This will work providing you are not silhouetted against a barren field.

I once hunted a brush-choked wooded finger that connected two woodlots, and it was so narrow I had to sit in an adjacent corn-field. Several cornstalks pulled down around me acted as natural camouflage, and the 9-point buck I nailed that year came sneaking along the trail on the second day of the season. He never suspected I was there until my No. 4 buckshot caught him in the ribs at 30 yards.

A hunter isn't bound by law to sit within the finger of woods, and common sense told me that if I tried to squeeze into it I would spook the deer. I moved to the cornfield, and the result was an easy shot at a nice antlered buck.

The best blind for these narrow areas is a natural blind although a pop-up tent will work under the right circumstances. Just remember that narrow connections between woods, or between woods and swamps, are natural avenues for travel, and should never be ignored. To do so is to possibly miss out on the buck of a lifetime.

FENCEROWS

Whitetail bucks like thick and brushy fencerows, and the only reason I can determine is because they offer some concealment. Often a fence may be down in places, and more often than not it will be grown over with dogwood, sumac or some other thick cover. Gaps or gates in the fence and low-growing cover will provide areas a buck can move through as he travels from one patch of thick cover to another.

It's these natural breaks in a fencerow which offer attractive hunting sites. A buck under pressure often will follow a thick fencerow, and often the fences will traverse open fields and this

Nancy Kerby took this spike while it followed an overgrown fencerow (seen in the background). Bucks often choose such routes when they provide the only decent cover between open fields.

allows a buck to scan the terrain ahead for any sign of danger while being screened by brush.

A buck will move in fits and starts, and will often pause to look over or through a thick fencerow to view the countryside on the opposite side. They often move into the wind, but that isn't something a hunter can always count on, and they often stop just before a break in the fence or at an open gate to check for danger before proceeding.

A hunting buddy kills a buck each year during Ontario's gun season, and he does it along a brush-choked split-rail fence that meanders through an open field between two slashings.

"Each year a buck will move cautiously along that split-rail fence, take a peeky-boo through a wee gap in the fence and then press on for the slashing," he said. "I sit downwind of the gap where I can watch both sides of the field in a little hide of broken split rails, and each year on opening day a buck will travel along the fencerow on the side away from other hunters and walk right up to me."

He seldom has to take long shots at bucks crossing through the opening because years of experience have taught him to sit tight and wait for a buck to appear in the fence's gap.

"There have been times when the buck was within 20 meters of me before I saw it, but almost always they hesitate before going through the gap," he said. "I raise my rifle and shoot as they check out distant fields. It's so easy it should be illegal."

Bucks that travel along fencerows seldom jump the fence unless a hunter shoots and misses. They usually follow the fence, be it split-rail, stone, or wire, until they come to a natural opening. These openings act as a funnel for deer and deer hunters. Pick a stand downwind of a fence opening. Usually, but not always, deer will move through such openings near heavy cover. They seldom move through a fencerow in the middle of an open field; instead, they prefer being close to a swamp or woodlot before they make their move.

Look for fencerow breaks within 30 yards of heavy cover. A stand can often be built inside the woodlot, and this vantage point will offer concealment and a clear view of the area. It allows hunters to pick a spot to shoot long before a buck gets to them.

Whitetail does often follow fencerows as well. The hunter should be far enough downwind from where the fencerow connects with the swamp or woods to allow does to pass unmolested. Does, fawns and lesser bucks often precede a large buck down a fencerow, and if these animals catch your scent or spot movement the buck may try to escape across an open field. Sit still, look sharp and be prepared to pass up lesser bucks for a chance at a nice rack.

HILLTOPS IN OPEN FIELDS

There's an open field in Kansas, and each year one of my buddies takes a nice buck from the hilltop in the middle of the field. There are other hills nearby, but this one produces season after season.

What would make one hilltop more productive than another? This particular hill happens to be a bit higher than the others, and it offers a brushy fencerow 100 yards away in one direction and a narrow finger of woods 100 yards away in the opposite direction. A farm lane cuts across the base of the hill, and these natural travel trails are within easy rifle range.

The nearby hills offer roughly the same options to a hunter but they seldom produce. This hill, as my friend can attest, delivers shots at whitetail bucks hoofing it for heavy cover on opening day. Each year he shoots one of the largest bucks taken in the area, and each time the animal is shot at 40 to 100 yards.

Why? We don't know and we've pondered the question countless times. And really, who cares? If it's not broke, don't try to fix it.

His hilltop overlooks a main road 500 yards away, several open fields and semi-open brushlands within 200 yards. Feeding areas are found within 200 yards, and the rest of the terrain is wide open. Yet, each year my Kansas buddy kills a buck.

The basic question is: Although bucks travel open terrain on opening day under heavy hunter pressure, why do they often travel near the base of high hills?

I've seen this phenomenon in many other states, and it seems bucks often skirt the highest hill in the area. My friend's hill rises a scant 200 feet above the mean level of the surrounding terrain but bucks are attracted to the hill as an escape route, and that is good enough for me and him.

Another friend, Paul Kerby, used to hunt a similar hill within a mile of where these words are being written, and years ago he constructed a tiny blind on top of it. It wasn't an elaborate blind, and not as pretty as fresh-cut flowers, but it always produced for him until the land was sold to a person who dislikes hunters.

"I knew that when the sun came up, and shooting began nearby, sooner or later a buck would come charging across the open field and pass within 100 yards of my hilltop blind," Kerby said. "The shots were never easy, and often were at running bucks, but if I missed the first buck another would come along later."

Open hilltops offer superb views of the immediate area. A spotting scope can be helpful in determining whether distant animals carry antlers or not, but if they are so far away a scope is needed, they are too far away to shoot. The important factor in hunting open hilltops is to remain motionless and keep a low profile.

"It took me four years of trial and error before I found the perfect hilltop," Kerby said, fondly recalling his lost hilltop. "I tried several, and watched deer at a distance but seldom had a shot. Picking the right hilltop is a lesson in futility at first, but once I made the right choice it was easy to take a buck every year but I sure do miss that spot."

Whitetails can and will travel near some hilltops and avoid others. There seems to be no logical reason for this behavior, and it may sound as if an ambush site on a hilltop is a hit-or-miss proposition. And so it is, for a year or two, but once the proper location is found it can become your private shooting gallery.

Pit blinds are good for hilltop use although an elevated blind may provide greater visibility and give a hunter more time to spot a buck and get ready for a shot. My old friend Claude Pollington had

Herb Boldt sits with his back to a tree on a high hill, watching a trail below him. Such tactics can produce quality bucks.

the perfect hilltop for a stand, and he had a pit blind in it. He called it Execution Knob for good reason. He and his friends killed numerous bucks off that knob for many years.

His pit blind on the knob reduced his profile and offered a rock-solid shooting platform. Long shots can be a rule for hilltop hunters, and the more stable your shooting position, the better chance one has of collecting venison.

This is one ambush site where hunting with others can be productive. If four hilltops are found within a quarter- or half-mile area it behooves hunters to spread out—one on top of each hill—and learn which spot is best.

Small hilltops can hold only one hunter, and he must know where bucks come from. They often move at dawn, and a hilltop usually doesn't pay off later in the day.

Flat-shooting rifles and light, fast-stepping bullets are used on hilltops. A rifle should be sighted in to shoot three inches high at 100 yards, and should hit at point of aim at 250 yards. Just remember when shooting down at a deer that the tendency is to shoot high. Plan on this, and you'll connect every time if you are familiar with the rifle.

This year, if hilltops are a part of your local terrain, try hunting one. Just don't be discouraged if your neighbor takes a nice buck a quarter-mile from your stand; it just may be that he knows which hilltop is best. All you can hope for is that he gets sick the next year and can't hunt on opening day. Then, you'll have it to yourself.

CATTAIL MARSHES

One year I was hunting ducks in a marsh along Michigan's Saginaw Bay. The area was a maze of tiny potholes surrounded by knee-deep water and cattails. It was a bluebird day, and even the bluebirds weren't flying.

I decided to take a hike through the cattails in hopes of jump shooting a black duck or mallard before the evening flight occurred. It was hot, and the air was so still I could hear myself sweat. I stumbled over invisible muskrat tunnels, slipped and nearly fell while tripping on underwater hummocks, and never saw a duck.

I was about to chuck the whole mess as a waste of time and energy when a lone drake mallard vaulted from the cattails in a burst of feathers. I swung ahead and above the climbing bird, yanked the trigger and caught the drake with a charge of high-brass 6s. Down he came, head over curly tail, into a nearby tangle of cattails and algae-dappled water.

I waded over to retrieve my bird, and paused to listen to the sound of something big wading away from me. I hurried that way, scooped up the drake mallard enroute and wondered whether someone else was hunting the cattail marsh. I'd seen no other hunters, heard no shots and thought I had the marsh to myself.

The sloshing sound of something wading through the water became louder, and as I rounded a thick wall of cattails I came almost face to face with a nice buck. The animal was in waist-deep water, and appeared to be having some difficulty moving over the mucky bottom.

He studied me, recognized me for what I was and immediately started heaving himself through the water. He blasted through the cattails, and within seconds was out of sight although the sounds of his hasty progress could be heard for several minutes.

Since that day I've run into several bucks using cattail marshes for secret getaway spots. Bow season was in progress at the time of my first encounter, and I suspect the buck had a narrow escape with a bowman. The animal had taken refuge in a swamp atop a muskrat house, and had I not shot and retrieved the mallard, the buck would have stayed put in relative safety and without a care in the world.

I've had several people tell me about shooting nice bucks coming to cattail marshes. One man said a buck had been pushed into the marsh with other deer by hunter pressure, and he spotted their movement after listening to the noise they made in the water. He and his friend made a short stalk and both shot nice bucks as the deer stepped out of the marsh and onto dry ground.

Playing tag with a buck in a thick marsh is tough work, and it can lead to heat exhaustion unless the hunter follows a few simple rules.

Deer trails leading to a cattail marsh are the places to start. If sign shows recent travel, and wet entrances or exits have deer tracks, it's logical to assume deer are using the marsh for a sanctuary. Take up a downwind stand in the cattails about 20 yards from the trail. If the marsh bottom is firm, a short stepladder can keep you out of the water while providing an elevated shooting platform. Just use caution to stay back in the cattails, and don't move.

Allow moving deer to approach the cattails before taking a shot. Laws vary from state to state, and many prohibit shooting deer in the water. This would place a deer in an unfair position, but no state I know prohibits shooting a buck as it approaches the water.

Others tell me that a skilled hunter can stalk a buck by hunting from muskrat house to muskrat house during hunting season. The trick is to move from one area to another and into the wind. Gaps in cattail tops often reveal small potholes ahead, and muskrat houses often dot the water. Since tiny muskrat houses are essentially dry ground, the deer is not shot in the water . . . or so they say. It sounds like a gray area to me, and although it may be legal, it smacks of taking unfair advantage of a fine buck.

These 10 ambush sites are some of the finest areas in which to waylay a buck. With a little original thinking all can be adapted for use during bow season. Some require preseason scouting; all demand a hunting position downwind from where deer should appear; and others require the use of other equipment. But nothing offers the magical excitement of ambushing a buck on his own turf except possibly stalking him.

And that, my friends, is the next chapter.

6

STALKING TACTICS

Whitetail deer are reasonably easy to stalk. Note I said "reasonably;" nowhere are they a leadpipe cinch, and one successful stalk in five is a great average because the animals are cautious, spooky and fearful of human movement and scent.

A whitetail can be successfully stalked if the hunter selects suitable terrain, spots the buck before he sees you, uses the wind to his advantage, and lets natural sounds cover human noise.

Bear in mind, however, that many things can go wrong— even during a perfect stalk—and the hunter winds up with lots of exercise but no venison. Shifting wind currents, a movement at the wrong time, noises unrelated to the stalk (like a barking dog or another unknown and unseen hunter moving about) and countless other problems can evolve as a stalk unfolds. One of the most

This hunter moved slowly and quietly, stopped often, and finally worked within range of this buck. It is standing, looking back over its backtrail and has its nose in the breeze searching for danger.

common problems is bumping into an unseen deer while staying too focused on the buck being stalked.

A stalk can be a one- or two-man effort, and of the two I prefer the two-man stalk only because one hunter stays behind and signals to the moving hunter when it's clear to move again. A one-man stalk offers as much enjoyment as a medium-rare steak and a sundowner after a long day afield, but it is much more difficult to bring to fruition than stalking with a partner.

My twin brother, George, and I once teamed up to stalk a nice buck, and it worked. We had tried stalking on other occasions, and had met with good and bad success. One thing about this method of hunting whitetails: It's never easy, but the suspense is enough to keep your adrenaline flowing for long periods of time.

It was late November, and the morning sun rose cold and egg-yolk yellow in the eastern sky, and the last soft snowflakes drifted lazily down to form an inch of fresh powder on the ground. The conditions were perfect for a late-season stalk on a buck I'd been watching for several days.

I cruised toward George's house and glassed open fields for sign of the buck. My eyes scoped brushy draws and side hills for sign of the animal. The buck had a distinctive track, and apparently an old wound caused him to limp and drag his left hind leg.

Several deer tracks crossed the side road on the way to his house, and I checked each one. A few were does with fawns, and one may have been a buck traveling alone, but he didn't walk with the pronounced limp that made our quarry's trail so easy to recognize.

We wanted that gimpy-legged buck because I felt he may have trouble making it through the winter. His rack wasn't great, but his injury made him crafty. It would be a contest to take on this buck on his own turf, and injury or not, it wouldn't be easy.

I cut a smoking-hot deer track near the section where George lived. Previous sightings of the animal caused me to suspect the buck bedded down in a small swale near an adjacent swamp. I examined the track and learned it was Ol' Gimp-Along. The buck's track looked like he was cutting corners and would cross George's road on the way to his secluded bedding area. It was a hunch on my part, but I felt I was close to the animal at the time.

I slowed my pickup truck briefly and watched as the slew-foot buck cut across the road 100 yards away. I was convinced this ol' boy would be hanging on our buckpole long before the day was done. We were confident we knew where he would hole up, and it was just a matter of our making all the right moves. Our knowledge of the terrain and the buck's habits gave us all we needed to pull off a classic stalk.

"This is going to be too easy," I thought as my truck wheeled into his driveway a quarter-mile from the buck crossing. It had all the makings of a quick and easy stalk, and since George hadn't filled his tag the buck would be his if we scored.

I told George of spotting the buck and we began second-guessing where he would cross another road, and where I thought he would bed down. We drank hot coffee as he stuffed four .44 Magnum hollowpoints into his Ruger carbine. He grabbed his Bushnell 8 × 40 binoculars, donned a blaze-orange vest and we were off.

I pulled my binoculars from the truck, and we eased down the side road to where the buck had crossed. My travel down George's road had not bothered the animal. Since the earlier heavy hunting pressure had dwindled to nothing, evidently this buck wasn't too worried about hunters. I saw the buck dawdle 100 yards into the field off the road, and he walked 50 yards in one direction and doubled back. Then he headed toward a hill behind George's barn.

"He's looking for a spot to bed down," George said, as we took up the track. The wind was in our faces, and we knew once the buck laid down it would be in a spot where he could smell danger upwind and still watch his backtrail.

The tracks led over the hill. My brother recalled seeing other bucks bed down in a tiny swale behind the barn, and he wanted to check it out. It never pays to ignore any cover, regardless of size.

"I'll belly up to the crest of the hill and check the swale with my binoculars," he said. "We don't want to go crashing in on the buck, and spook him into the next county."

He bellied down in the snow and wormed his way up to the crest. He studied the swale 50 yards away with his binoculars for several minutes before sliding back down to my position.

"The tracks went into the swale," he whispered. "They also go out the other side. From the crest I could see the entire swale, and the buck isn't there. I glassed each stump pile and overturned log, and finally spotted his track heading out. He's still moving at a steady pace in front of us."

We bellied up to the crest of the hill and glassed a standing cornfield 100 yards away. A moving buck, once the rut has ended, will often gobble down a last-minute snack before packing it in for the day. The standing corn was sparse and in a small field, and had the buck been in the corn we could have seen him. This deer apparently wasn't hungry. We finally picked up his tracks heading through the corn and into a brushy fencerow.

Farmland bucks often bed where they can watch their backtrail and where the prevailing breeze will carry the scent of approaching hunters to them. Favorite bedding locations are in slashings, berry patches in thick woodlots, drainage ditches, small swales and other heavy cover. Occasionally they will bed on a small knob of brushy land slightly higher than the surrounding landscape, a position that gives them a distinct advantage over hunters or predators.

We hunkered down, and one by one we crossed the field to the far edge of the corn. The tracks were strung out in a neat, dark line against the new snow and they headed right for the fencerow. So far, so good.

Bucks like this one often bed down during midday with their noses into the breeze and occasionally checking their backtrail. It's not impossible to get this close to a bedded whitetail but it is tricky.

We followed the general direction of the tracks to the fencerow with our binoculars, and couldn't be certain which way the buck went once he reached the fence. He could have turned north toward a sumac thicket 100 yards away, turned south toward a brushy swale or jumped the fencerow and continued straight across another open field toward a nearby swamp.

"Which way did he go?" George asked. "Think he headed for the sumac?"

"I've never seen a buck or doe use that sumac clump," I said. "It's too open and exposed, and too close to that fencerow. If I were a buck I'd probably jump the fence or go south toward the swale.

"Let's sneak over to the fence and find out. We'll take it one step at a time. Watch me for hand signals. If I see the buck I'll motion for you to stay down. We don't want to blow the stalk now, and we're only 30 minutes behind the buck."

We crossed to the fencerow without incident and began circling to sort out the buck's track. The animal had moved north along the fence, turned around and headed south, and then doubled back to duck through a brushy gap in the overgrown fencerow. The tracks continued toward the swamp.

One thing that slows down a deer stalk on fresh snow is sorting out the tracks. In this case it wasn't too bad, but at other times it can be time consuming as the stalked buck mixes with other deer.

More stalks are blown because a hunter barges right in on a buck without checking first to determine the animal's location. It's critical to spot the buck before it spots you, and this can only be done by proceeding with utmost caution and checking the terrain from afar.

We kept a low rise of ground between us and the swamp 400 yards away, and worked into a position to check for sign in front of us. There we saw the buck's shake-a-leg tracks heading straight across the field toward the swamp, and the field turned into a weed field just before it entered the swamp.

Open fields require diligent glassing. A buck can bed down in a tiny hollow in the weeds, and unless it moves, an animal becomes almost invisible. A deer can bed inside the weeds, along its edges or may continue on through. Only time-consuming glassing with good binoculars will tell the story, and it's no time to press ahead recklessly without checking first.

We glassed the field for 20 minutes and picked it apart inch by inch, spending lengthy periods on suspect areas. There was no sign of the buck.

"Let's circle the field as much as possible," I suggested. "We'll cover the downwind and cross-downwind sides first."

We checked the cross-downwind field edges, and then slid directly downwind to look it over. The field was nearly bare outside the weed field, and we felt as exposed as a germ under a microscope.

I was wishing for my snow-white camouflage clothing, and was about to mention to George that the buck had to be inside the weed field, when we spotted his tracks heading back away from the swamp and over a small knoll. The tiny ridge barely concealed a small ice-covered ditch and another adjoining weed field.

Our spirits soared because we knew the buck was still ahead of us, and he didn't have the first clue we were dogging his trail. His tracks were unhurried, and by now the animal had at least 60 minutes headstart on us.

That buck led us through that field and wound in and out of another sumac swale without stopping. We circled the last sumac clump, and suddenly a rooster pheasant flushed 300 yards ahead of us.

We thought it strange a ringneck would cackle into the air for no reason, and then we considered the bird may have flushed ahead of the deer. We circled wide around the field, glassed it thoroughly and intercepted the buck's tracks again.

We knew the buck was still on the move, and was slanting slightly away from us. We also knew we were reasonably close, and would have to double our efforts to avoid closing on the animal. We knew we had to slow down and make a special effort to keep the deer from spotting our movements or getting our scent.

"There are some fallen trees along the edge of the upcoming woods," George said, pointing ahead. "The buck may be there or he may continue through the woods and lay up next to the lake."

We carefully but swiftly followed the dragging hoofprints through the new snow and stopped just below the crest of a small rise. We glassed the next weed field while standing near a towering oak but couldn't see the deer. We were getting ready to move out along the tracks when I happened to catch the sight of sunlight glinting off antlers in a tiny fencerow near the downed trees. I couldn't be sure, but it looked like a deer's body with its antlers silhouetted against the morning sun.

"Hold it," I whispered urgently. "I think I see his antlers."

I focused my 7 × 35 Bausch & Lomb binoculars on the animal, found myself looking at the buck's twitching ear and his polished antlers. Although it was a heavy-bodied deer, the rack wasn't terribly big, but if we could pull off this stalk it would be a good buck that anyone would be proud to claim.

The buck's tail was switching back and forth, and his head was swiveled around so he could watch his backtrail. The deer was much too far away for George's .44 Magnum. If we had topped the hill instead of pausing just below the crest, the buck would have seen us and been long gone.

"There he is," I told George. "He looks like he'd bedded in that tiny fencerow leading down to the woodlot near those fallen trees. If he stays there we'll have good cover most of the way for a stalk. Let's not rush the last part of this stalk."

He agreed, and then scamped up the hill and cautiously eased his eyes over the crest and quickly picked out the buck holed up in the fencerow. What he saw caused even more excitement.

"What a spot," he said. "Hey, wait a minute. He just stood up, took a few steps and laid down in the thick brush and appears to be looking the other way."

I took a peek and confirmed his suspicions. The buck was facing away from us, a lucky break. We'd have to move while his head was turned from us. Fortunately, the wind was still in our face.

We quickly worked out a set of hand signals, and took just enough time to double check the buck's position again. We timed his movements, and about once a minute he would leisurely turn around to check his backtrail.

"We'll move out, one by one, as soon as his head turns away from us," George said. "I'll go first, and once I've crossed the open field you come along the next time he turns away."

Our hand signals were simple. If the spotter held up one hand it meant the other hunter should stop—immediately. If the spotter gave a rapid back-and-forth hand wave, the other would move out fast, run low to the ground and keep his progress as silent as possible.

The buck's head turned around to study his backtrail, and he turned his nose back into the wind. George moved out and crossed the open weed field. Our first goal was to gain the thick cover of the fallen trees without being spotted, and this would put us within 100 yards of the deer.

George made it with little problem and now it was my turn. I had to freeze twice while crossing the open field as the buck lifted his head for a look around. Each time George caught the motion of the buck lifting his head, and since I wasn't watching the deer but was watching him I caught the hands-up motion and stopped. Both times the buck looked the other way, and then settled back for a bit of rest.

I crossed the finish line, fell in beside my brother near a jumble of wind-tossed trees and breathed a sigh of relief. We were close now, but George had discovered another obstacle to overcome—an old farmer's fence.

"What are we going to do about the fence?" I whispered.

"Beats me," he said. "Let's get to the fence first without being spotted and then we'll try to figure something out. We're within 100 yards now, and it looks like we'll have to be within 50 yards before I can get a clean shot at him. There is just too much brush between us right now for an accurate, killing shot."

We bellied down along the fence and with heads and butts down, we wormed our way for 25 yards without being seen. It was slow going as we looked for a break in the old fence. We didn't want squeaky fence wires to spook the buck now.

We had covered another 10 yards when a solitary crow flew over. Its loud caw sounded like a death knell on our stalk, and we froze in place as the buck lifted his head and stared our way. The deer looked at the crow, back to the ground near our semi-concealed location, and then went back to checking the wind. George was relieved when the crow continued on its way.

We quickly took turns closing the distance to the fence's junction with another line fence. This could prove to be the turning point in our stalk, and either way we went George had to be on the other side of the fence or we would have to give up.

The early sun was up even with the treetops, and less than a quarter-mile away we could hear the muffled jabber of kids waiting for the school bus. A thought came to mind: The buck probably bedded down in the same general area each day and was accustomed to hearing the school bus clatter down the bumpy dirt road.

Our plan swiftly developed and was one of simple logic. We'd time George's progress over, through or under the fence with the noise of the passing school bus. It seemed crazy enough to work, and any sound he made may be covered by the kids or the bus as it bounced down the washboard road.

We talked it over briefly, and he felt it might work.

"Sounds a bit far-fetched but it's just crazy enough to work," he whispered. "We had better find a crossing spot in this fence within the next few minutes or we'll miss out on the bus noise."

He slipped off down the fenceline while I watched the buck. It continued to study its backtrail every minute or so, and seemed to spend the rest of the time checking the wind and terrain ahead of the brushy fencerow. George waved me down the fenceline to him, and within a minute I pulled up beside him.

He put his lips to my ear and whispered: "We're in luck. Here's a spot where I can crawl under the fence. I hope I can make it through when the bus comes along."

No sooner were the words out than we heard the rumble and noisy clatter of the bus battering its way down the lumpy road. We looked at the buck, now only 60 yards away but still concealed by the brushy fencerow, its attention riveted on the noisy bus. We were nearly broadside to the buck now, and since it was listening to the approaching bus George prepared to slide under the fence.

"Try not to make it squeak," I warned. "That buck is antsy enough right now, and although he's listening to the bus, a squeak from this direction may ruin everything."

He took one more look at the buck, nodded his head in agreement and wiggled under the fence like a rattler burrowing under a warm rock. The fence didn't make a sound. I chose to stay where I was while George bellied down in thin weeds and made his way to an old piece of rusting farm machinery just 20 yards from the buck. He made it while the buck stared at the sound of the departing school bus.

The buck's head was nearly invisible from my vantage point, but his snow-white antlers stood out in marked contrast from the brushy fencerow. He apparently had listened to the school bus daily, and seemed curious about the sounds. The bus stopped, kids piled aboard with noisy conversation, and the bus moved down the road.

The buck turned his head around and wind-checked the surroundings. He shot a quick glance at his backtrail, and as he did George shifted sideways along the farm machinery and into position for a shot. He knelt next to the rusting equipment, slowly raised his .44 Magnum and savored the moment. This, the end of a stalk, is the epitome of excitement; the kill is anticlimactic. I knew George had the buck dead to rights, and I knew he'd take the shot as the buck turned to study his backtrail. But for now, he wanted to enjoy the moment.

Nearly a minute passed, and then the buck turned his head slowly to check the trail he'd made walking to his bedding area.

George centered the iron sights on the buck's neck and slowly squeezed the trigger. The buck lurched once and rolled over.

To be truthful, not all stalks end like this. Many are blown when a buck spots a moving hunter, or when too much noise or an errant breeze carries scent to the deer.

Stalking deer is moderately difficult, but not impossible. Let's look at the ingredients that go into a successful stalk, and what hunters can do to tip the scales in their favor. Six factors, when pulled together, can lead to a successful stalk.

KNOW THE WIND

Whitetails are scent conscious and use the wind when traveling from food sites to bedding areas and back, and at every other time of the day and night. Hunters who stalk deer must play the wind and keep it in their face as much as possible. Working a bit crosswind is fine providing it won't blow human odor to the deer.

There are any number of ways to check the wind. For years, smokers have used cigar or cigarette smoke to test wind direction and velocity. A bottle of unscented Puff Powder is great; a single squeeze of the plastic bottle can reveal wind direction in an instant.

Hunters who stalk deer must constantly check the wind. It is the No. 1 problem they face, and it's wise to understand that when a breeze hits a woodlot, the wind can shear slightly to one side or another. More stalks fall apart because of the wind than for any other reason except being spotted.

Develop the habit of checking the wind whenever you stop to glass ahead for a buck. It becomes even more critical once you've

This shotgun hunter used a short-barreled 3-inch magnum 12-gauge shotgun with No. 4 buckshot to take this small buck. Working into the wind was a key factor in his success.

closed to within 100 yards of an animal, and it is every bit as crucial to success as watching the bedding buck when each movement is made.

A stalk can be made crosswind if the hunter stays on the cross-downwind side of the deer. A stalk made across and upwind from a buck is destined for failure.

Only an ignorant or foolhardy hunter will try to stalk a bedded buck when his scent is being carried downwind to the animal.

Bucks almost always bed down where they can view their back-trail and where they can check the prevailing breeze. Calm days are best for a stalk, although I've had limited success on extremely windy days when the breeze is steady from one quarter. Never stalk deer when the wind switches constantly from one quarter to another.

KNOW THE TERRAIN

An in-depth knowledge of local terrain is very important when stalking deer. It does little good to know a buck has holed up in a specific location only to learn it is impossible to stalk close enough for a shot.

Chapter 2 discussed learning terrain features. A solid under-standing of the countryside where a stalk will be made is especially important when deer hunting. Study terrain features during spring, summer and fall, and learn what it looks like when snow covers the ground in northern areas.

Deer stalkers also must recognize that farmers rotate crops. What crop was planted last year may have been replaced by some-thing else this season. What provided good cover for a stalker last hunting season may be an open winter wheat field that will provide little or no hunter cover.

Learn where fencerows lead and where they originate; know the locations of tiny swales, swamps, sumac clumps, and brushy

Roger Kerby stalked to within 75 yards of this buck as it bedded down in northern pine trees. One shot, and the buck ran a short distance before collapsing in the open. Kerby had scouted the area before the season.

areas; know the configuration of swamps or cattail marshes; learn how rolling hills and brushy creek bottoms or woodlots tie in with other terrain features—in other words, know your hunting area well and study it as often as possible until all features are indelibly imprinted in your mind.

Learn to anticipate how a moving buck will follow certain terrain features. Bucks often fall into one of two categories—open field travelers or heavy-cover movers. If a buck crosses a road through a wooded funnel he probably always moves through heavy cover. If the buck, like the one recounted at the beginning of this chapter, crosses an open field he'll probably stick to open areas until he beds down. Whitetail bucks are creatures of habit, and like humans they resist change.

I once blew a stalk on a fine 8-pointer because I didn't have a firm knowledge of the terrain. That busted stalk taught me a valuable lesson.

A buck had crossed a road during the night along a tiny brushy creekbed and continued along the ditch through heavy cover. "Aha," I thought, reading sign in the fresh snow, "a brush traveler."

This was many years ago, and I figured I was as savvy as Daniel Boone when it came to unraveling buck tracks. What I hadn't learned was that bucks know where they will bed, and it's usually where they can see and/or smell approaching danger.

I didn't know the lay of the land, and 30 minutes into the stalk I topped a rise in plain view of the world, fifty yards away from a low-lying swale bordered by sumac and brush. The buck was facing into the wind, watching his backtrail.

As I topped the rise the buck slammed out of the swale. He took three long bounds, placing a wall of brush and a small hill between us before I could raise the rifle to my shoulder, aim and shoot.

I had clumsily blundered into that buck at close range, and it was gone. I felt dejected. I had hiked into the area without knowing the terrain, and it had cost me a shot at a nice buck. Had I known the countryside I would have realized a swale lay just over the hill, and would have circled around on its downwind side and checked everything before committing myself. Instead, I boosted that buck into a blind, panicked flight without ever getting a shot.

This is, however, the manner in which hard lessons are learned.

Don't just learn the terrain, but really study it like graduating from high school with all your class boils down to passing a geography test. Know where deer travel, and where they bed down or feed. Learn terrain lessons well, and you'll be on the right track when the time comes to stalk deer in brushy or open country.

SPOT THE BUCK FIRST

This portion of stalking whitetail bucks is so elementary many will wonder why it is mentioned. Unfortunately, I know many hunters who have blown a stalk within the first few minutes by being seen by the deer. Learn to see deer before they see you.

Good binoculars are indispensable when stalking deer. A quality spotting scope is an asset, but can be clumsy and cumbersome to tote along when moving along the trail of a nice buck. It's good for open-field glassing, but is nearly useless when tracking a buck in heavily wooded cover. Stick to quality-made binoculars.

Mountain hunters have long known the secret of finding a comfortable spot and glassing faraway slopes. Deer hunters should take a tip from the mountain hunters and learn to use binoculars to check the terrain.

I hunted whitetails several years ago in western Idaho between the Salmon and Snake rivers. It was reasonably high country, and deer moved just before dark from heavy timber or cottonwood draws into the open to feed. Walking all over the mountain didn't pay off, but sitting in one place with binoculars allowed me to take a very nice 8-point with one shot from a .243. My guide thought I was undergunned, offered me his 7mm Magnum but I declined.

"These bucks are tough," he said. "You'll never kill one of our mountain deer with a .243. Use my gun, it's plenty big enough to knock down a big whitetail.

"If I had wanted to shoot a 7mm Mag I would have brought my own," I told him. "Shooting deer isn't a matter of big or small calibers and bullets but where you put the bullet."

I spotted the buck with my Swarovski binoculars as it eased up the mountain toward us. I quietly informed the guide that the buck was within 100 yards, and I was going to shoot. He again offered me his 7mm Mag, and I again refused.

I held the crosshairs of the Swarovski 1.5-6× scope on the white patch of the buck's throat, steadied my aim and shot. The buck went down and never moved.

The point of this whole exercise is to spot the buck before it has a chance to see you. Always ease up to the crest of a hill, and slowly inch your head over. Use nearby cover to break up your outline. Glass tracks in sand or snow, and check as far ahead as possible for sign of the buck. Do not, as I did on my busted stalk, stumble over a hill thinking the buck may be a long distance away. He can be, and often may be, very close.

Bring your knowledge of terrain and wind direction into play. Ask yourself where would I bed down so I can smell the wind and still be able to watch my backtrail.

Answer this question, and you'll be a leg-up on other deer stalkers. Learn to anticipate deer movements, and learn to use binoculars to study the terrain.

Binocular use is a studied and practiced art. Learn to pick the terrain apart, and to look for horizontal shadows or lines in an otherwise vertical landscape. Become accustomed to taking a field, woods, fencerow or weed field apart inch by inch, and don't look for

Billy McCoy inspects a rub on a fair-sized tree in a palmetto swamp in central Alabama. Successful hunters know the terrain.

a whole animal but for the glint of sunlight on antlers or the flick of an ear or tail. Never look for a calendar photo of a buck, but instead look for movement or something that appears out of place in the surrounding environment.

Even when a buck beds down he is in motion. Ears flick, a tail moves, the body moves and the head turns. Look for a glimpse of movement to reveal an unseen buck bedded down before committing to a stalk through new terrain.

Never hurry a glassing job. Learn to glass ahead, and do so from cover. Never move unless you are 100 percent sure the animal is not present, and then never take a whitetail buck for granted. I've seen bucks move through an area and then double back in a moment of indecision. Know, too, that bucks and all whitetails are spooky and often do the unexpected. That's what keeps good bucks alive.

WHITETAIL NERVOUSNESS

It's impossible to overemphasize that whitetail deer are a spooky lot. They are frightened of their own shadow, unknown noises, hints of danger from unknown sources and have been known to flee when instinct seems to tell them to go. It takes very little to frighten deer. If a hunter bears this in mind he can make a successful stalk.

Simply remember that whitetails are cautious and smart. Always be cognizant that a buck (or doe) will spook at any noise it can't immediately identify, and will probably run for several hundred yards if frightened by a strange movement.

Whitetail nervousness should be foremost in a hunter's mind when he begins a stalk. Look for the animal to lay up in unexpected locations, and realize that deer are on pins and needles throughout their bedding, feeding and travel periods. Never take them for granted, but instead learn to anticipate this nervousness and use it to your advantage.

WHITETAIL CURIOSITY

I've watched deer spot hunter movements in a hay-bale blind, and have been amazed many times to see them take cautious, inching steps forward in an effort to determine just what caught their attention. Other times, I've seen bucks curious about the sounds of passing vehicles or children's voices.

If the preceding paragraph and the preceding portion about deer nervousness seem at odds, so be it. Deer are curious and they are nervous, and what will spook one buck may make another deer eager to learn what they saw. Both traits can work to a stalker's advantage.

I once shot a nice buck along Michigan's busy interstate I-94. The buck had bedded down in thick cover near the highway fenceline, and was intently watching cars and trucks whizzing by on the freeway.

I had stalked the buck for a quarter-mile, and knew whitetails often bed near highway fences. A big 18-wheeler came burping down the road with loud backfires from a faulty engine. The buck seemed fascinated by the strange sounds, and didn't hear my final approach.

Lennie Rezner employed his stalking skills to get within range of a northern buck in brushy cover. He prefers to kneel when taking a shot.

In fact, the last thing he heard was my shotgun coughing up a lethal dose of two one-ounce 12-gauge shotgun slugs. One heavy slug caught the buck in the neck, the other behind the shoulder, and he died probably thinking the loud noises were backfires from the truck.

Curiosity is only found in whitetails that are not overly spooked by heavy hunter pressure. If the animal feels safe, and has no reason to suspect human intrusion into the area, deer may become curious about strange noises or movements. But don't bet the family fortune that deer won't bolt once they satisfy themselves that the movement or noise may mean a threat to them.

Deer may be curious but they are spookier than many animals. You can bet on it.

USE EVERYDAY NOISES

A whitetail deer, in reasonably relaxed situations such as when bedded down tend to view everyday noises with mixed reactions. The sounds of a squirrel scurrying through pin oaks is common, and the cawing of a crow a quarter-mile away is another example of everyday sounds deer are used to hearing.

However, a squirrel scolding a stalking hunter 50 yards away is enough to put a buck on Red Alert. A crow that spots hunter movement and circles overhead as he calls to his brethren for reinforcements offers another threat to a buck's well-being. A frightened blue-jay once spooked a buck for me when I was within 50 yards of the animal, and the last I saw of the buck was his white flag disappearing into a swamp.

Learn to use everyday noises to your advantage. School buses travel on regular schedules, and homeowners leave for work at certain times, and these sounds are commonplace for rural deer. Use them as often as possible when hunting.

The clatter of a school bus can cover the sound of a squeaking fence, and the rustle of a squirrel digging acorns can mask the sound of a hunter traveling through noisy leaves or weeds.

As long as a sound is not foreign it will not spook deer providing it doesn't come from an unexpected direction. Be prepared to listen for and identify natural sounds, and be ready to make them work for you.

7

DRIVES THAT WORK

The cold November wind was blowing tiny BB-sized chunks of sleet into my face as I leaned against a tall oak and strained my eyes for the first sign of an approaching deer. My hunting buddy and I had been on stand for 30 minutes as the two drivers circled upwind around the 10-acre woodlot before beginning their downwind mini-drive.

Suddenly, a buck materialized through the storm like a wraith and began mincing toward me along the woodlot's brushy edge. He would stop for 10 or 15 seconds and stand motionless, looking around. Twice he stared my way only to swivel his head around to study the sounds of drivers zigzagging downwind toward him.

This buck wasn't a grizzled old veteran of the deer wars, but he was cagey and not fond of being pressured into moving in this direction. He was being crowded, and knew it. The buck didn't have anywhere else to go except straight downwind, and I remained motionless because the animal would soon be in my lap.

He was partially screened by heavy berry bushes and brush and he moved gingerly. Each step was studied deliberation. Within seconds the deer disappeared from sight between two large oak trees.

I used the opportunity to shoulder my Remington 12-gauge pump shotgun and get ready. I knew the buck would soon be within range. He appeared again from behind a thin screening of trees and brush, and studied the terrain ahead. He wasn't taking any chances, but being upwind of me he had no way of knowing I'd set up camp in his backyard.

The buck apparently satisfied himself about an absence of danger, and turned my way. As he bounded across a clearing 10 yards in front of me, I held on his shoulder and touched off the shot. The 3-inch magnum load of 41 No. 4 buckshot caught him in the shoulder, chest and neck, and he covered only 15 yards before toppling.

The 5-point buck was the third buck our four-man team of hunters had taken in two days using a system we call the mini-drive. One buck was a massive 9-pointer with heavy beams and long, thick points. The other was a trophy 11-pointer, and we had become used to seeing bucks almost every day with this deer driving technique.

Driving deer is an old-time hunting method with roots buried in antiquity, and it can be a productive way to hunt. Unfortunately, the drive techniques used by many hunters leave too many holes for deer to escape through, but the trick is to turn those holes into dead-end alleys watched over by hunters.

A knowledge of deer movements and terrain features is of paramount importance to the success of a deer drive. It does little good to push deer in the desired direction unless the animal knows he has easy access to heavy cover along the way.

Roger Kerby (right) points to an area to be driven and tells his assistant how they will drive the area downwind. Kerby relies on downwind drives, and although he has several types in his repertoire, most are a variation of the mini-drive through long and narrow cover.

Most deer drives fail because hunters attack a cover with a shotgun approach. They make too much noise, advertise their presence and hit the cover from first one direction and then another. A drive should be orchestrated, and one man with intimate knowledge of the area must be the conductor. His job is to place drivers and standers where they will be most effective.

I often hunt whitetails during the firearm season with Roger Kerby of Honor, Michigan, who happens to be one of the best deer drivers I've met. For many years our success rate with bucks averaged about 80 to 85 percent, and in a state like Michigan where the statewide hunter ratio is about 25 to 35 percent, our score is indeed high. Many of Kerby's tactics will be explained later.

Strict attention must be paid to details. Little things that often are overlooked can offer avenues of escape to a driven buck. Errors in judgment seldom produce bucks on deer drives. An error can send a good buck into panicked flight that makes the animal more difficult to hit, and the deer may run long distances before stopping again.

An important point to remember when driving deer is to concentrate your efforts on small covers. We've all seen those massive deer drives where literally dozens of hunters mill around jabbering like monkeys picking fleas while they try to hammer out a decisive course of action on how to push a particular piece of hunting turf. Chances are good the conversation will take place within hearing distance of the cover to be driven, and then everyone splits up into groups of drivers and standers. More chatter, more noise, and no one seems to realize that whitetails have excellent hearing. Is it any wonder that a self-respecting buck will have used all this confusion and noise to vacate the area?

"Hey Joe, you go over by that dead elm and stand still," one hunter may say.

"Which dead elm?"

"That big one by the swamp."

The words are yelled back and forth as if any deer in the area were wearing ear plugs, and Joe heads off in the general direction of an elm tree to watch the swamp's edge. Meanwhile, up and down the line a herd of vocal hunters align themselves near the cover to be driven in hopes a buck will come to them and offer something other than a fleeting shot. In the meantime the drivers are going through similar noisy movements at the other end of the cover. They ready their pots, pans, whistles and other noisemakers, and the drive finally begins.

Everyone, according to deer-driving dogma, must walk side by side. In practice, the faster walkers forge ahead of their buddies, and holes open up between drivers.

The hole between fast-walking and slow moving drivers grows larger as the distance between them grows. Soon a hole large enough to drive a battalion of Sherman tanks through exists. Any guess where remaining whitetails will head?

They will lie low as the noisy drivers filter by, and then calmly get up and escape through the gaping hole. The drivers, intent on making an unholy racket which they believe will move deer ahead of them, seldom see deer because they are too engrossed in trying to keep the line tight and to make more noise.

Such drives usually fail. And the fault lies with the drivers and standers.

I participated in only one such drive and thought putting up storm windows would be more fun. Cleaning the garage would probably produce more deer.

Such drives have several strikes against them before the action begins. The drives often take place in a large area where it's impossible for drivers to keep track of each other, and often in dense cover, drivers get themselves turned around and drive back in the same direction they just covered. Another problem, even if the drivers manage to stay somewhat near each other, is the noise. Too much noise allows deer to pinpoint drivers.

Deer guide Roger Kerby said, "The secret of success when driving deer is to make silent downwind drives after standers have silently moved into position. We choose small parcels of cover to drive, and then comb them in a systematic manner.

Roger Kerby (right) and one of his assistants study a diagram drawn in the snow. It silently tells each one where they should be during the drive.

"We make no noise, never talk and we push deer in the direction they want to go. We don't try to drive deer upwind, and we don't try to push deer in such a way that they resort to headlong flight. We keep 'em moving slowly ahead of us to the standers."

Make no mistake about it. Kerby is the drivemaster. He often discusses specific covers to be driven with his brother Paul, but he makes the decisions and it's clear who is in charge. Kerby is the main man because he knows the terrain, knows where bucks usually bed down in the cover to be driven, and knows where they will head when a slow-moving driver approaches. He knows the best ambush spots for standers, and he's as ugly as a grizzly bear with a toothache if someone messes up. His knowledge of the hunted terrain is incredible. Invariably he will choose an isolated bit of cover that often is passed over by other hunters, and it's in these spots where we score on hefty whitetail bucks.

The game plan is the same, cover after cover. We'll gather at our hunting vehicles at least one-half mile or more from the area to be hunted, and quietly make our plans.

"OK gang, we're going to drive the sidehill," Kerby announces as a small cheer goes up from those of us who have been in on buck kills at that location.

"Dave," Kerby says, pointing at me, "you know where the bucks come out. You take two standers, and put one at the top of the sidehill where it pinches down and the other where the little gully comes up out of the hill. No talking from now on, hear?"

I nod in agreement because I know I'll be sitting on top of a little knob overlooking a field, and any conversation once we near the sidehill stands can spook wary bucks. My presence serves as a stop-gap in case a buck sneaks out past one of the other standers and tries to gain his freedom across the open field.

We move silently into position after I caution my two standers to be motionless and quiet. I station them, and if they've never hunted the area I'll lead them by the hand to the proper location. They are cautioned not to move until we come for them, and I point out where the buck will generally appear. This is accomplished by sign language without uttering a word. Then I'll ease out of the area and climb my hill. It then becomes a waiting game.

The covers we drive are chosen with care. Each offers known buck escape routes, and each cover is longer than it is wide. Many driven covers may be 100 to 300 yards long, but no more than 100 yards in width. Some spots are only 30 to 50 yards wide.

One sidehill we drive is some 300 yards in length, but is less than 50 yards wide at its widest point. The cover is thick, and this is why few hunters venture inside. It offers superb bedding cover for whitetails, and two or three good escape routes at the downwind end. It's along these routes that bucks head when the pressure is put on them, but we always have a hunter there to greet the deer.

The Kerby brothers generally drive the sidehill. Actually, one man can do it as well as two providing he moves back and forth from one side of the cover to the other. They make no noise, and on more than one occasion Roger has shot a buck in its bed while the deer watches Paul passing nearby. It frequently takes them one hour to circle around to the upwind end and begin the downwind drive. This gives standers plenty of time to get into position and get comfortable before the drive kicks off.

The standers are positioned in such locations that they can see approaching deer and spot the drivers coming along behind. The only danger in driving deer occurs when a stander shoots at an approaching buck without knowing where the drivers are. Kerby has standers positioned where they can look down on the action, and spot the deer and drivers at the same time. In over 20 years of driving deer we've never had an accident or a near miss.

"I try to work the cover so slowly that bucks slowly ooze out in front of the standers," Kerby said. "Push them too fast and hard, and they will squirt out the sides in nervous flight and no one gets a decent shot."

Mind you, not all deer drives work. If they did, everyone would adopt this hunting strategy. But drives will work if each piece of cover is hazed in the proper manner.

Kerby's success rate is about one buck for each three or four driven covers. We've had times when we would take three bucks from one cover. We've also had times when we've driven eight or 10 covers in a day without seeing a buck.

That's why they call it deer hunting.

Driving deer is a hunting method compatible with much of North America's farmland areas. Whitetail habitat usually is a series of heavy cover pockets surrounded by open fields, croplands or woods.

Brothers Paul (left) and Roger Kerby work together to make deer drives successful. This buck taken by one of their hunters isn't a big-racked buck, but some hunters are happy with any buck. And that makes the Kerby brothers happy too.

It's a mix of heavy and sparse cover, creekbeds, drainage ditches, clumps of swamp or marsh, etc. It's in these tiny pockets where bucks hole up, and it's here deer drivers can find action if they do it right.

Here is a brief look at the elements needed to drive deer, and the various types of covers likely to be encountered.

PICK SMALL COVERS

Small covers mean just that. Choose a cover long and narrow, and with brushy terrain inside. The downwind end should be narrower than the upwind end. This turns the cover into a downwind funnel, and it directs deer to waiting standers.

Cover to be driven should be no more than 150 yards wide, but 50 to 100 yards wide is ideal. Forget about wide, extremely long covers and pick something from 100 to 300 yards in length.

Choose covers that other hunters ignore for one reason or another. Many of our favorite covers are filled with dense cedars, tag alders, swamps or very heavy vegetation where it is tough for drivers to move in an upright position. Some spots are driven on hands and knees because it is almost impossible to walk upright. Find a spot where you are constantly stumbling over and around deadfalls or through thick brush, and spend more time climbing over and under thick cover, and you'll have found an ideal spot providing it meets the length and width parameters.

THE SOUNDS OF SILENCE

Simon and Garfunkel made this a popular song, and Kerby has made it a hallmark of his drives. Leave police whistles and pots and pans at home, and forget about yelling like a demented soul. I've heard drivers crashing through the brush like rhinos, and whooping like hound dogs on a hot track, but all that noise pinpoints the hunter's position for the deer.

Standers must be in position long before the drivers start moving through the cover. Standers must move into position as noiselessly as possible, and this means no talking at any time. Try to avoid stepping on dead branches, raking hard fabric clothing against trees and brush, and once in place, don't move.

Never drive vehicles directly to the hunting area, and even if cars and trucks are parked a half-mile away do not slam vehicle doors. Ease them shut quietly, and make no more noise than necessary to load firearms and to walk to the stand.

Refrain from making any disturbance on stand. Silently brush all dried leaves from underfoot, and clear debris away so you can pivot silently for a shot at a passing buck. Then, learn how to sit or stand still; do not move or make noise.

CHOOSE FIREARMS CAREFULLY

We choose our firearms with care; where we will stand dictates our choice of firearm. If we are driving we'll use a 12-gauge shotgun loaded with No. 4 buckshot or a Ruger .44 Magnum although a semi .308 is good in close cover.

If we plan to stand, and the cover is extremely thick we'll often choose a shotgun loaded with buckshot or slugs. The key determining factor is the distance from stander to where the deer will appear, and if it's inside of 30 yards we'll choose a buckshot-loaded 3-inch magnum 12-gauge every time.

If the cover is reasonably open, and the distance from stander to driver is from 30 to 100 yards, any rifle will serve the purpose providing the hunter is accustomed to the firearm. Standers who wait on hilltops or near fences overlooking wide-open spaces would do well to arm themselves with a flat-shooting rifle. A 4× scope or even a variable power scope can help the hunter pick a spot if the deer is wearing antlers.

This information is merely the basics, and must be interpreted according to the terrain and the hunter's needs in each area. Judge for yourself what type of firearm is needed, and adapt these policies as they meet personal needs.

Years ago, when Kerby and I hunted every day of the firearm season together, my vehicle was like an arsenal. I had a wide choice of firearms to match my needs, and on any given day I might choose any one, or all, of five different firearms depending on the cover being hunted and my role on how it is hunted.

I always carried my Remington 870 3-inch Magnum 12-gauge shotgun and No. 4 buckshot for close shots. In another gun case was my pre-1964 Winchester Model 70 in .264 Winchester Magnum with a 2–10× Swarovski scope for long distance shots. If I knew I would be driving thick cover I had an Ithaca Model 37 3-inch Magnum 12-gauge with an 18½-inch barrel stoked with buckshot for those inevitable shots at 10 yards. I also carried a scoped Ruger .270 for more open shots through wooded terrain, and for anything between 30 and 80 yards I would pack a Ruger .44 Magnum carbine. One of these would work regardless of the terrain hunted, and I often found myself loaning a rifle or shotgun to a hunter who brought a .338 Winchester Magnum that he was afraid to shoot. My arsenal always came in handy.

The following deer-drive techniques work. Each will produce the best results if practiced in similar areas as described below. All can be adapted somewhat to fit the needs of local terrain, but the orchestrated movements of drivers and standers must be tightly followed if a hunter would like to be successful. Never be afraid to improvise, but do so cautiously after first learning how each method is supposed to work.

THE MINI-DRIVE

The mini-drive is one of my favorites because it has produced many bucks for me over the last 35 years. It is so named because it can be used by three or four hunters working as a team, and it can be specifically adapted for two men in certain types of cover.

Terrain must be chosen carefully if only two or three hunters are used, and depending on the size and shape of the cover either one or two men can serve as drivers or one or two hunters can be standers with only one driver.

This drive is probably the most successful of all. Its very success, however, depends on a downwind movement of the driver(s) and utmost silence of standers as they approach their posted spot. It also counts on the hunters knowing the exact location of one or two escape routes or active deer trails leading to nearby heavy cover along the downwind side, and it means choosing a suitable ambush site nearby.

The hunters, above all, must approach the hunting area to be driven by walking upwind quietly. This approach will prevent deer from becoming aware of your presence until it is too late for them to leave the cover safely. A spoken word, twig snapping or the creak of a farmer's fence can spook big bucks from heavy cover long before drivers and standers are properly positioned and ready to shoot.

Standers must move into their appointed position without making a sound. Often a buck will lay up within 25 yards, and since mini-drives work best on long, narrow covers, any sounds made can easily be heard by a buck.

Clear the area of dead tree branches, dry leaves and twigs from underfoot. Understand that standers may be in position for as much as an hour and this is the maximum amount of time needed to conduct a mini-drive. Many drives in this type of cover start and end within 15 minutes, and this is all the time needed to shoot a buck if everything goes as planned.

Choose a stand with nothing in front to impede the swing of a rifle or shotgun. The stand site must be downwind of the escape route or active deer trail, and ideally it should be within 20 yards of where the deer should appear.

The perfect stand will have a tree or bush behind to break up the human outline. Kneel or sit to reduce your silhouette, and stand only when absolutely necessary. Standing hunters tend to move more than a comfortable, sitting hunter.

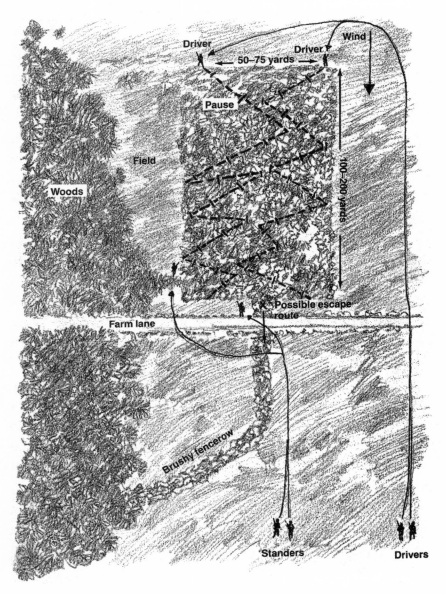

In the mini-drive, drivers walk upwind quietly. Standers move into position on the downwind side 30 minutes before the drivers circle around the woodlot and begin the drive.

The mini-drive works simply because the driver(s) scent drifts downwind toward the deer. The animal smells the slowly approaching hunters, and will move slowly away from them. This means a properly executed mini-drive will place a deer where you want him, not where he may wish to go.

This is based on the premise that deer—especially bucks—will move away from a hunter while traveling downwind. If the hunter is on the left side of the driven cover the buck will almost always slide to the right to avoid coming into contact with a human. If the hunter suddenly shifts position to the right the buck will cross to the left. A group of hunters can use this knowledge, and the ability to shift randomly and often, to stay upwind of the deer and opposite the animal when they approach the end of the driven cover. This should place the buck directly in front of a stander.

Two drivers have a much better chance of hazing deer where they want than does a single driver. Two drivers can synchronize their movements to cover the entire area while keeping each other in sight at all times while watching ahead for the buck.

A mini-drive must be executed slowly and quietly. Noise must be kept to a bare minimum, and should consist only of that made by two drivers moving downwind as silently as possible as they drift back and forth.

We've learned after many years of experience that the perfect mini-drive means taking four or five steps, and then stopping for 10 to 15 seconds. A deer will often panic when we stop, and then bust out ahead and in front of waiting standers. After we take a brief pause, we take several more steps, stop again and look all around. This drive is very similar to still-hunting.

A zigzag pattern of moving downwind prevents deer from staying in one spot and allowing hunters to walk past. The stop-and-go and zigzag turns will move deer.

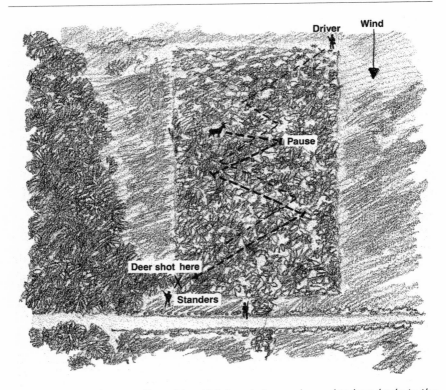

Bucks move away from a solitary driver. This knowledge can be used to haze bucks to the stander. Deer slide to the side opposite the driver, and are forced into exiting the woodlot where expected.

If two hunters are driving the cover, one moves toward the other as he moves toward the edge of cover and then they move back toward the middle. This means, by stopping and starting and zigzagging, two hunters can cover a small area and prevent deer from circling around behind them. The best strategy is for one driver to be slightly ahead of the other.

A single driver should start at the corner upwind and opposite the downwind stander. He moves slowly from one side of the cover to the other with sudden stops to study the upcoming cover. Once he reaches a point where the cover edge is visible ahead, he should stop and then move the opposite way at a 45-degree angle toward the opposite edge.

It's the frequent stops and starts and sudden changes of direction that send whitetail bucks into a panic. Just time your direction changes so you'll be opposite the stander at the end of a drive. This eliminates any possibility of being in the line of fire when a stander shoots.

A trick we occasionally use is to carry a few small rocks. As we near thick brush on a drive we'll lob a rock or two ahead to spook hiding deer. Sometimes it causes hesitant deer to start moving.

We try to make small noises once we approach within gunshot range of standers. The *caw-aww* of a crow, or a bird whistle, will alert standers to your presence and does not frighten deer. Use calls sparingly, and keep it low. Move after each call so deer won't pinpoint your position.

Some bucks are admittedly too experienced in the ways of hunters to be fooled by a mini-drive. They will cross where least expected, leave the cover at the first hint of a downwind driver, and they are difficult to pin down. One trick we've used to keep track of smart bucks is to determine where they jumped out in unexpected locations, and keep it in mind. The next time we drive that area we'll post a stander in that location, and often the buck will make the same exit and bump into the hunter. He seldom has an opportunity to fool us twice.

HILLSIDE DRIVES

This drive works very well in farmland areas where hills are abundant and butt up against small lakes. I'm mindful of one location where Kerby and I hunt, and we've taken a number of bucks there over the years.

Picture it: a sidehill laced with cedar, juniper, pine and tamarack, and less than 50 yards from a small lake. The cover is thick and slightly wider at the upwind end than the downwind end. Bucks lay up here, and each year we take a few. The reason—the deer have nowhere else to run except directly to the standers.

Only two spots offer a buck any chance of escape. One is a small gully running up the sidehill to an open field, and the other is out through a 10-yard-wide natural funnel where the curving sidehill slides up next to the lake. A driven buck must head out one of the two locations, and we always have hunters posted at each location.

The driving technique used once all standers are in place is similar to the mini-drive. The driver(s) move upwind to circle the spot before turning downwind through it.

They move downwind in stops and starts. A lone driver will zigzag back and forth through the cover with frequent pauses, and two drivers will criss-cross back and forth with frequent pauses, and

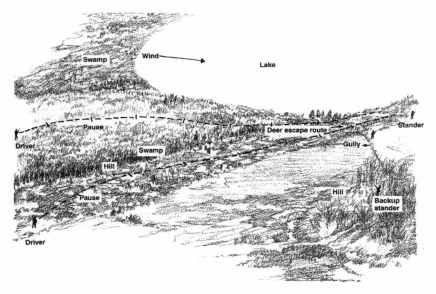

A sidehill laced with cedars, pines and tamaracks with a maximum distance of 50 yards from hill to lake. The sidehill narrows down and acts as a funnel for deer trying to escape the drivers. Standers are positioned at the narrow end, in a gully running up the sidehill and on a nearby hill.

we check out all available cover. The important thing is to thoroughly punch through every bit of cover big enough to hide a buck.

Few bucks slip behind us because we choose narrow areas where visibility is reasonably good, and the buck is forced to keep moving downwind. Sooner or later a buck finds himself moving past one of the standers who makes the shot.

Drivers must be aware of where standers are, and the reverse is true. If a stander moves at an inopportune time, the buck may spot the movement and try to crash back past one of the drivers. The driver then takes the shot.

The hard part is to find an area where a sidehill butts up against a lakeshore. The water prevents the buck from easy escape in that direction, and the sidehill acts as a funnel to move the deer where we want. The buck is caught in a box, and must travel in the direction we choose. This method puts as much venison in our freezers as any driving technique except the mini-drive. It produces bucks for our group every year.

THE DEAD-END DRIVE

This method derives its name from the fact that we force deer into a dead-end. A buck caught in this drive runs into a brick wall at the end of the alley, and has nowhere to go . . . except where we choose. It's important to realize that all drives are nothing more than a variation of the mini-drive, and differ only in the locale where they are used.

We use dead-end drives for narrow fingers of swamp. The swamp may be dry with tag alder thickets or wet and wild with standing water and thick with cedar trees. Both areas produce good bucks.

A dead-end drive necessitates locating prime cover with a road, lake or other natural barrier along one of the long sides. Everything must funnel down to a dead end, and a cover that ends at a highway

A dead-end drive has a road or lake along one of the narrow sides. Deer usually try to es-cape along a thick fencerow into a nearby woods. One stander acts as a stopgap near the lake and road.

or lake is the best scenario. Whitetails caught in this manner must filter out one side or find themselves facing oncoming traffic or deep water.

We station one man at the extreme end on the off chance a buck is willing to try crossing a lake or road, but one or two standers will be placed along the only side that offers an escape route. A gully, ravine, narrow finger of woods, fencerow or other cover along the open side will be where bucks usually try to escape. If a hunter is properly positioned he'll get a shot. The man at the dead end serves only as a stopgap measure, and seldom gets a shot.

Drivers work slowly downwind through the cover, and stop often for a brief look ahead. They zigzag, and often spot deer moving ahead as they try to find a way out of the box. It goes without saying that a noiseless approach is important, and do not hurry when making this drive.

Standers should be in position at least 30 minutes before the drive starts, and snap shooting at rapidly moving targets is the rule. Once a buck knows that he is caught in a trap he'll try to get away.

FLANKER-BACK DRIVE

We seldom use a flanker-back drive because much of the terrain we hunt, and the covers we choose, are narrow enough that a flanker covering our rear is not needed.

This drive is suited to slightly larger covers where it's conceivable that a buck could sit tight and slip back around a driver to escape through the rear. A flanker, properly positioned, will intercept the animal and get a shot.

The drive is set up like the mini-drive or dead-end drive, and although the drive is still made downwind a flanker covers the rear on two sides. The two drivers begin working downwind through the cover—one from each side—and once they are 50 yards into the cover one or two flankers slither in from the sides to cover the middle.

A deer that tries to circle behind the drivers will seldom travel along the outside edges of the cover where it could be seen. Deer generally try to circle back into the middle of the cover to stay inside the thicket.

The flankers move slowly, and stop often. They should move through all available clover, and concentrate solely on that area between them and the drivers. They must look for the flick of an ear or tail, a horizontal body line in a vertical environment, and be prepared to allow the deer to move past them before shooting to prevent an accident to one of the drivers.

Flankers must zigzag slightly but not as much as the drivers. They should stay at least 50 yards behind at all times, and move at a much slower pace.

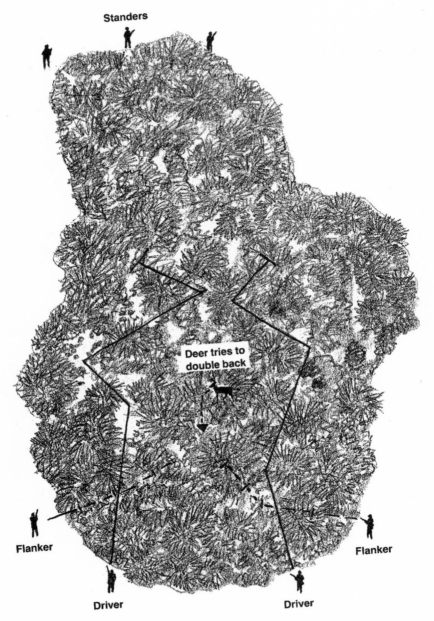

Standers

Deer tries to double back

Flanker

Flanker

Driver

Driver

This drawing illustrates how a flanker-back drive should work. The drivers move downwind into the cover first, and once they are 50 yards inside the flankers slide in from the sides to cover the middle. Flankers stay at least 50 yards behind drivers and move slower.

It surprises many hunters, but in slightly larger covers a flanker-back drive can produce good bucks. And, equally surprising, flankers often do the shooting.

This happened to me one time. We were driving a narrow but extremely thick swamp, and I was the sole flanker. The drivers were moseying back and forth through heavy cover, and I had just stopped for a quick look around. I caught a glimpse of a deer moving head-down through the swamp. It apparently had spotted the approaching drivers, laid down and once they passed got up and began moving out of the swamp. The only problem was the deer was moving my way, and although I couldn't tell whether it was a buck or doe its actions were suspiciously that of a buck.

I froze in place, and the deer kept coming. It raised its head several times to look around, but the tag alders looked like antlers to me but I still couldn't be sure. It moved slowly past me only 20 yards away, and then it reached a tiny clearing and stood upright with its head held high. It was a nice 5-point buck.

I was carrying a well-worn .30–30 carbine that day. I snuggled the front sight into the buckhorn back sight, nestled the white front sight bead behind the buck's front shoulder and touched it off. The buck lurched, bolted into the alders and seconds later I heard him crash to earth.

The buck wasn't big by anyone's standards, but he was clever enough to allow the drivers to walk past. If I hadn't been following along and bringing up the rear that would have been one buck we never would have seen. Flanker-back drives work. Use them sparingly, and make sure flankers move slowly and stay far behind the drivers.

THE STILL-HUNT DRIVE

This deer-hunting method derives its name from the fact that hunters still-hunt and drive at the same time. It is best suited for large parcels of land which cannot be successfully driven without a small army of hunters. We execute this type of drive two or three times a year, and it generally produces one or more bucks.

This technique can work in any area, although if a hunting location is too large, there are simply too many holes for a buck to slip through. The secret to this hunting method is to position as many people as possible on the upwind side of the cover, and one or two standers on the downwind side.

The standers must move into position early, and then wait for something to come their way. In reality, drivers more often score on bucks than do the standers and the reason is simple once we analyze our strategy.

The standers are positioned in a semicircle at the downwind end of the cover being driven, and then each driver slowly still-hunts downwind. Each person takes a few steps, stops and looks in all directions (including behind them) before moving again.

It's impossible to move too slowly in a still-hunt drive; it may require two or three hours to cover one third to one half a mile of prime whitetail habitat. Each hunter investigates each draw, ravine or gully in his area. The trick is to poke along while investigating blowdowns and other cover. Move very slowly, try to anticipate where a deer may bed down and attempt to position yourself in a place from which it is possible to shoot an escaping buck.

Bucks often will hear a still-hunter approach, and only when that sportsman gets too close will the animal pick up and begin moving. There's a possibility that once a buck starts to move it will blunder into another driver as he still-hunts nearby.

Even if shots are fired the still-hunt drivers should continue in the downwind direction in hopes of pushing other deer to the standers. Keep moving, keep looking and perhaps someone else will get an up close and personal shot.

The reason for lengthy pauses is to give a moving deer a chance to cross in front of another driver. One whiff of scent from

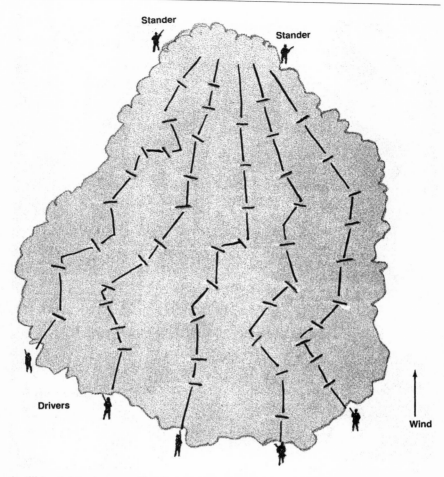

A still-hunt drive is set up like this. Two standers cover the downwind (narrow) end, and all other hunters begin still-hunting and driving from the upwind area. Each driver zigs and zags, and checks all available cover in stops and starts. This drive is best suited to larger areas which are impossible to drive with one or two men.

that hunter may spook the buck in front of still another sportsman who may take a shot.

Safety must be the priority item on a still-hunt driver's agenda. It doesn't pay to take a shot unless the sportsman knows, beyond any doubt, that the area beyond the deer does not contain another driver or stander. More people are wounded or killed in line-of-sight (where an unseen hunter is in line with the deer) accidents than for any other reason except stupidity or horseplay. There isn't a buck in the world worth wounding or killing a friend with an errant shot.

Still-hunt drives produce on occasion, and at other times fail to deliver even one buck sighting. But, if all drives were destined for success then we'd have far fewer whitetails than currently inhabit the North American continent.

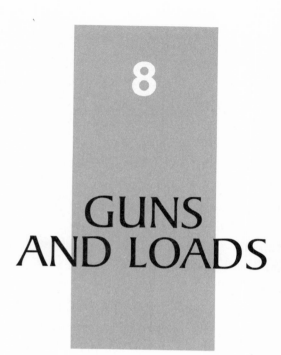

GUNS
AND LOADS

A whitetail deer isn't a terribly big animal. Even a 300-pounder from Alberta, Manitoba or Saskatchewan isn't big when compared to an elk or moose.

The average whitetail weighs somewhere between 100 and 150 pounds, and an animal this size doesn't require a lot of killing. Sure, the occasional outsized whitetail may tip the scales to 200 pounds, and some farm-country bucks or forest whitetails from the central Canadian provinces may reach 300 pounds, but the odds of a hunter encountering a heavyweight are rare.

Most firearm deer hunters pursue this fantastic animal in areas where they are of average size, and should choose their firearms accordingly. Too many people use too much fire power, are afraid of it, and can't hit the broadside of a barn with it.

A Winchester .458 Magnum for whitetail deer is the extreme in overkill in my estimation, while a .22 long rifle veers off in the opposite direction. A deer hunter doesn't need an elephant gun to drill a hole through deerskin and reach the vitals, and the sportsman shouldn't suffer with brutal concussion-producing recoil to take a buck. Big rifles just aren't needed.

My wife, Kay, uses a Thompson/Center single-shot .243, and she is deadly accurate with it. I've seen her kill a dozen deer in a year (in Michigan and other states) with one shot each. I've used her rifle many times on deer and achieved the same type of success, and one year I killed four caribou—two Quebec-Labrador and two Central Canada Barren Ground caribou—with this pint-sized rifle shooting an 85-grain hollowpoint bullet. The caliber isn't nearly as important as the bullet weight and configuration, and obviously, where the bullet hits.

My argument for the proper firearm and cartridge and bullet in this book is to use that which will competently place the bullet in the proper place, at the proper time, while doing enough damage to the nervous system and vital organs to kill the animal quickly. Some will and some won't, and that is the topic of this chapter.

The .22 rifle has probably popped as many deer across the country as the .30-30, but the .22 is not legal in any state or province I know. It is most often used by poachers who steal our game by spotlighting and shooting after dark. So, right off, we can eliminate the .22 and relegate it to rabbits and squirrels.

At the other end of the spectrum are those hunters with an Elmer Keith syndrome. I met Elmer several times many years ago and marveled at his big-bore philosophy. I didn't always agree with him and we had some interesting conversations, but his "wham, bam, slap 'em down" theory has led many beginning deer hunters astray. I respected Elmer's opinions and his right to voice them, and to use whatever cannon he favored at the time, but his choice of howitzer isn't what many deer hunters need.

This Thompson/Center .243 single-shot rifle with a set trigger is my wife's rifle and she has shot many whitetail bucks with it. One shot, and the deer is down. That means a properly sighted-in rifle and waiting for your shot before pulling the trigger. The results are a dandy buck like this.

It's like my Idaho guide on a whitetail hunt saying that many of his clients use a .338 Winchester Magnum because "Idaho mountain whitetails are so tough." That's nonsense: a whitetail is a whitetail, regardless of where it lives. It doesn't take a big-bore rifle to kill a deer, but it does require the ability to shoot straight.

Over the years there seems to have been a strong leaning toward large caliber rifles for deer. I've seen a few hunters toting bigbores into the whitetail woods that would have caused a brown bear to hightail it into the nearest alder thicket. On the other hand, I've seen hunters use a bullet too small or of the wrong configuration for deer. One is as bad as the other.

Ask 100 deer-hunting book authors the burning question, "What cartridge, firearm, bullet weight and bullet configuration is best for whitetail deer?" and you'll probably receive 100 different answers. Simply stated: There is no best all-round cartridge or firearm for deer that will work on all occasions. What works in one area, and under one specific set of circumstances, may fail miserably in another location. I feel following some of these recommendations will help establish the ideal cartridge and bullet for a situation.

Consider the big picture this way. Let's go on the assumption that you hunt whitetails in the Montana mountains, and you need a flat-shooting rifle capable of hitting a whitetail buck across a mountain canyon or valley. You're not going to hunt with iron sights and a .30-30 carbine that shoots a bullet with the trajectory of a last-second basketball shot from midcourt.

The hunter will be toting a rifle—probably a bolt action—that whips out a bullet at 2,750 to 3,000 or more feet per second. The sportsman will probably opt for a .264 Magnum, .270, .280 or 7mm Magnum. It takes the proper bullet configuration to make confident shots from any of these rifles and create severe trauma to internal body parts.

But, for the sake of trying to end the eternal firearm argument, let's assume you are hunting a Midwest cedar swamp or a Deep South

Good bolt action rifles like this Smith & Wesson Model 1500 Mountaineer are available in several commonly used calibers for deer. A bolt action almost always is a straighter shooting rifle than any other action like a lever action, pump or autoloader.

palmetto thicket. Who needs a flat-shooter? Not you or me. We want a midrange weapon that will shoot accurately at 50 yards. Of course, any of the above cartridges will do the job at that range, but rifles capable of tack-driving accuracy aren't always a requirement when shooting distances are less than the length of a football field.

Anyone who hunts where the shooting distance is measured by yards rather than as far as you can see will want something that hits on target, has the necessary knockdown power and is easy to carry. Those who hunt such thick tangles care little about being weighted down with a 10-pound-plus scoped rifle that can shoot a squirrel's eye out at 300 yards.

We want a lightweight, easy-to-carry rifle that will come to the shoulder fast, is easily sighted on the target and which, when the trigger is pulled, will dump a whitetail buck. We care little for fancy engravings, and gold triggers or inlays are mere decoration. These firearms will get battered and beat up, and some will look like we've used them to drive fence posts by the end of a season. We want reliable firearms that do the job for which they were intended, and that is to shoot deer at reasonably close range.

Conversely, a firearm shooting a bullet with a rainbow trajectory is of little use on the farmlands, prairies or mountains. Hunters who gun whitetail bucks in the open spaces want and need, something that will pop a buck at 300 yards or more. They want scoped rifles instead of iron sights, and want a flat-shooter that will shoot— and knock down—a buck at eye-straining distances.

So, this chapter is not meant to promote differences of opinion or to toss a white-glove challenge in the face of hunters who feel differently. These are my opinions based on hunting and shooting bucks at spitting distances and out to 300 or more yards. It is meant to stress the obvious: Use a firearm that will do the job at the range for which it was intended, and do it in the most expedient manner possible.

It also means that hunters must choose the firearm that is right for them, and correct for the country or terrain being hunted. It also indicates that some hunters should be converted to using the ideal bullet weight and configuration for the distance and terrain being hunted. Nothing more, and nothing less, is intended in this chapter.

I'm a firm believer in the proper firearm and load for the area. My arsenal, as noted earlier, is considerable but well chosen to meet a variety of terrain needs. So which of these many firearms do I use most of the time?

The answer is easy—none of them. It's my practice to hunt deer almost every day of the Michigan season, and in several other states and Canadian provinces as well. The five or six firearms are my basic first choices, and I pick and choose as often as four times a day depending on the terrain being hunted.

No one firearm does yeoman service for me; instead, I try to match the firearm to my immediate needs. There isn't any one firearm totally suited to deer hunting across North America; there are too many variables to limit a hunter to just one choice.

The Ruger M-77RL Ultra Light rifle also is available in several calibers. The Ruger action is popular with many deer hunters.

In many off-season deer hunting seminars I tell people to hunt with whatever is right for the terrain, and choose a firearm noted for reliability. The choice is yours, but whatever you do, choose one that will shoot where you want and be extremely familiar with it before you enter the deer woods.

I firmly believe the bullet you push out the barrel of a deer rifle must be up to the job. It must enter the vitals of a whitetail, expand rapidly and produce tremendous shocking power while doing considerable damage to internal organs and surrounding tissue. Properly placed, the correct bullet will kill a deer in a heartbeat.

A full-jacketed bullet has little place in a deer rifle unless the hunter is skilled enough to make brain or spine shots. Body shots with a full-jacketed bullet often result in a wounded deer getting away.

All too many sportsmen choose bullets for deer that are better designed for use on animals with big, heavy bones and thick skin, and that are capable of taking more than one shot to be put down. Deer have thin skin, and a bullet must expand quickly, deliver a powerful blow to the internal organs and nervous system, and reach full expansion while inside the chest cavity.

Many hunters use Core-Lokt or Silvertip bullets on whitetails. Many of these bullets, especially in larger calibers, are too powerful and pass through a deer before they expand properly. The result is often a deer with a hole through it, but unless the bullet passes through the heart, liver, lungs or spinal column, the deer may go down but the shot may not kill it immediately. It can run for long distances, mix with other deer tracks, and not be recoverable simply because the hunter chose the wrong bullet.

Pointed soft-point or hollow-point bullets work very well on deer-sized animals. My wife's single-shot .243 shoots 85-grain jacketed hollow points very well. I often use my .264 Winchester Magnum for longer shots, and the 140-grain Nosler Partition is deadly.

As this book is being written in late 2000, my wife has made 13 one-shot kills with her firearm and load and I have made seven. Of these 20 deer between us, none needed a second shot and all but two dropped where they stood when shot. The two that did run off left a blood trail a blind man could follow, and none went over 50 yards. Most cartridge manufacturers print a guide for specific bullets for specific game, and my advice is to choose recommended deer loads.

Without overplaying my point, use fast expanding and reliable bullets for deer. Save the heavy bullets designed for big bears, elk and moose for those critters.

Round-nose bullets have had many admirers over the years due to their supposed "brush-busting" abilities. Those in favor of heavy, round-nose bullets claim they will bust through brush and retain their direction of travel.

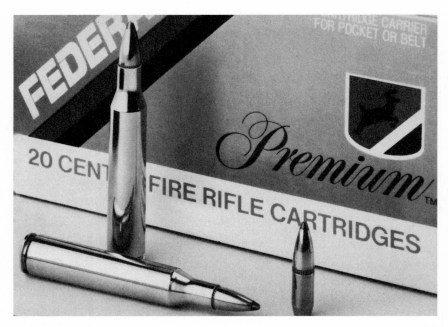

I've shot all types of factory ammunition, but Federal Premium cartridges are some of the best for those people who do not reload.

That theory is simply not true. Any bullet, regardless of configuration or design, will ricochet away from the target on encountering a twig, sapling, or low-growing bushy cover. If a bullet hits a sapling dead-center, it generally disintegrates.

The round-nosed bullet was designed originally for lever action firearms where bullets are stored, one after another, in a straight tube magazine. The fear once was that a pointed bullet could hit the primer on the next cartridge during recoil. Another problem with round-nosed, and to a lesser extent pointed soft-point bullets, is a tendency for the exposed lead tip to become deformed while putting it in and taking it out of the magazine or chamber. Defaced lead-nose bullets seldom fly to the correct point of impact.

So, what bullet styles do I prefer? I use nothing but hollow point or pointed soft points for whitetail deer. Let's take a look at the loads I favor for my deer arsenal.

I'm a firm believer in the 240-grain hollow point in my Ruger .44 Magnum, and I stuff my .264 Magnum full of custom reloaded 140-grain Nosler Partition pointed soft-point bullets. My .270 shucks out 100-grain hollow points with precision accuracy.

Whenever my wife allows me to use her single-shot .243, I use what she shoots—an 85-grain Federal Premium hollow-point bullet. It is deadly accurate, a joy to shoot and she has made numerous kills to 250 yards with it.

If I'm going to shoot a whitetail buck, I don't want to chase them over ridges and through swamps because of poor bullet performance. I want, and expect, instant results when I squeeze the trigger.

The above loads perform well for me wherever I hunt. They open up immediately on punching through deer skin, and they do their job inside the animal instead of expending their energy and mushrooming qualities after having passed through a whitetail.

I reloaded for many years, and have nothing against the practice. In fact, I still use custom-reloaded bullets for my .264 Winchester Magnum and my 7mm Magnum for bears, elk and moose, but I'm in favor of most people using factory ammunition. It's easier, and error-free.

My custom reloader, on the other hand, is so meticulous that his reloads are perfect . . . every time. He's really the exception to the rule.

Let's use my .264 Winchester Magnum for example. My reloader always uses new factory brass, and measures the empty cartridge so every one is perfect. Those less than perfect are rejected. The same goes for the bullets. Only perfect 140-grain bullets are used, and he'd never use a 138- or 142-grain bullet. Each one is perfect and weighs exactly 140 grains.

Powder loads are measured to the exact speck of powder. The depth of the chamber is measured so each cartridge and bullet fits properly into the chamber and throat to achieve the utmost in accuracy. My .264, when I first bought it in 1961 and began developing loads, was capable of shooting to the same point of impact with everything from a 77-grain Norma bullet to a 160-grain Hornaday, and that included the original 100-grain and 140-grain factory loads. Factory loads now available for the .264 Magnum only are made with 140-grain bullets.

That rifle, although now 40 years old, is still capable of placing bullets more precisely than I can shoot them. Glaucoma over the past 15 years has robbed me of most of the vision in my left eye and a portion of vision in my right eye, but I can still shoot well with my right eye if proper optics are used. My Swarovski 2 × 10-power scope enabled me to drop two deer this year at 250 yards, and I made one muzzleloader kill at 188 yards.

There are any number of excellent deer rifles and cartridges on today's market. Top-of-the-line Federal Premium cartridges are a

Craig Pollington admires a fine buck with heavy antlers that he shot with factory loads in his bolt-action rifle.

superb value, and Winchester or Remington's premier cartridges are excellent as well. Weatherby also makes great shells.

Factory loads are good only when the hunter knows how to shoot and is capable of putting a bullet where it counts. This means an intimate familiarity with the firearm, the load and the scope. It also means plenty of shooting practice.

It means a firearm must be sighted in properly. One common problem among many deer hunters is they seldom touch their rifle until the day before deer season opens, and then they twist off two or three rounds and call it good enough.

Well, it's not good enough. A whitetail deer is an amazing animal, and as such should be afforded better treatment than to be gut-shot by some dude who cranked off three rounds at a pine stump and managed to hit it once. The proper deer rifle should be able to hit dead-on at the ranges you expect to be shooting, and the hunter should be capable of placing a bullet where he wants to—every time.

Many years ago I worked in a sporting-goods store that sold a multitude of deer rifles in every imaginable caliber. My job, for the six weeks preceding Michigan's November 15 to 30 firearms deer season, was to sight in hundreds of rifles for customers. Many would buy a scope for their centerfire banger, bring it to me and ask me to sight it in for them. I did the job because that was my job.

I always spoke with each hunter, and suggested they sight the rifle in. I would offer to work with them, and informed them that everyone looks through a scope differently than I may, and this could cause their shot to go high, low, left or right of the target. Such shots would either miss or wound the animal, and I knew most of them were not competent to blood-trail a wounded deer very far.

My arguments never seemed to get through. Perhaps only one person in 100 would take my advice. Most were too lazy to do it themselves, and then would gripe after the season when they missed a buck. The only thing I guaranteed was that their rifle would be sighted in when they picked it up, but it would be sighted in according to how I held the rifle and looked through the glass. I would furnish them with a target showing three holes within a one-inch circle, and for most of them, it was good enough.

Down through the years since I sighted in rifles for a living, I have developed a method which would accurately sight in most rifles with nine shots . . . maximum. I heartily advise any hunter to sight in his own rifle, and to use this system. Learn your firearm, and know what it will do. Some rifles consistently shoot high or low, or off to one side or the other, after one or two shots and this is something each hunter should learn before hunting season starts.

Here's how I sighted in up to 200 rifles each fall. It worked then, and it will work now for any hunter willing to spend some time with his firearm.

SIGHT IN A RIFLE WITH NINE SHOTS

You say you missed a standing broadside shot at a big buck last year? And at 25 yards, no less?

If this happened and you wish to correct the problem before next season, don't despair. Thirty minutes on the range, and nine cartridges for the rifle, is usually enough to change things. You'll need to shoot the rifle yourself but it will be good practice.

Years ago, before bore sighters were invented, I would remove the rifle bolt and position the firearm on sandbags. I would line the rifle bore up with the bull's-eye at 25 yards and then adjust the scope until the crosshairs or post and crosshairs were properly aligned with the bull's-eye. I now use a Bushnell Bore Sighter, and do exactly the same thing.

It's important to remember that no two people hold and shoot a rifle exactly the same, and no two people look through a scope in the same manner. Head and cheek positioning on the stock vary

Teresa Herman sights in her deer rifle using the 9-shot system outlined in this chapter.

from one hunter to another, and the only way in which a firearm can be accurately sighted in is if you shoot it yourself. Dodge this most important issue, or get someone else to sight in the rifle, and you're missing the boat and will probably miss the deer.

Most hunters think a scoped rifle will always hit the target at 100 yards. This is true when a rifle is properly sighted in, and not true if it isn't. If you're missing at that range, it's because the rifle and scope are not working together. They are not sighted in; here's how to do it.

The best way to sight in a rifle is to begin at a 25-yard range. Use a bore sighter first to align the bore and scope before shooting the first cartridge.

Once the firearm is bore sighted at 25 yards, put on some shooting muffs, get a firm rest on a shooting bench, place a soft sandbag under the fore-end and under the bottom of the buttstock, and aim directly at the bull's-eye.

The next step is very important. Take a deep breath, let it all the way out, and squeeze the trigger. Don't jerk it, and do your best not to flinch (involuntary reaction to the firearm's noise and recoil). Concentrate on keeping your face against the stock, force yourself not to look up as you squeeze the trigger, and center the crosshairs on the bull's-eye.

Fire three shots with at least five minutes between each shot to allow for barrel cooling. Three rapidly fired shots heat up the barrel, and cause shots to stray across the target. Remember, when deer hunting, the first shot is almost always the best shot you'll have and it will be from a cold barrel. It's important to have a cold barrel when sighting in a rifle.

If you've carefully taken aim, didn't flinch and slowly squeezed off each of the three shots with ample time between each to cool the barrel, all shots should be within one or two inches at the 25-yard range.

Sam Johnson put two out of three shots from his .375 H&H Magnum into the bull's-eye at 100 yards. Accuracy with a heavy caliber rifle is necessary because hunters often are using it on dangerous game. It reduces recoil and muzzle jump.

Make the necessary adjustments, up or down, left or right, and consult the directions that come with the scope. Many scopes adjust at a quarter, half or minute-of-angle (one inch at 100 yards) per click, but some scope makers use a different increment for each click of the elevation or windage settings. Compute your changes to correspond to a 100-yard range, and place a target at that distance.

We'll pretend the rifle produced a sample grouping at 25 yards by being three inches low and two inches to the right. At 25 yards we'd have to multiply by four to get the proper sighting at 100 yards to make the correct adjustments.

If the scope has ¼ minute-of-angle clicks the sportsman will have to move the elevation dial 12 clicks up (four times three inches) and to the left eight clicks (four times two inches). This should bring the point of impact very close to the bull's-eye at 100 yards with a good rest.

Take another firm rest and fire three evenly spaced shots at the bull's-eye at 100 yards with a lengthy pause between shots to allow for barrel cooling. Take a pen and ruler, and walk to the target and measure from the center of the grouping to the bull's-eye. All three shots should again be in a circle of two or three inches or less.

It's time to make final adjustments for elevation and windage. If the scope is calibrated to ¼-inch clicks, four clicks will move the point of impact one inch at 100 yards. If calibrated in ½-inch clicks two clicks will move it one inch at 100 yards.

Don't guess at the clicks, but count each one as the dial is turned in the proper direction. A dime or screwdriver will work, and many dials have tiny knurled wheels which can be turned with finger pressure. Make the final adjustments with care, and don't hurry the process.

Fire three more carefully aimed shots from the shooting bench. If everything has been done properly you should be right on the money. Just be certain which direction is up, down, left or right when making scope changes.

The line of sight through a scope is slightly higher than the bore, and this causes the bullet to cross the line of sight twice from muzzle to target. A rifle sighted in at 100 yards to hit at point of aim will also hit at about the same point of aim at 25 yards.

Many sportsmen will sight in scoped rifles to hit three inches high at 100 yards. A flat-shooting rifle sighted in three inches high at 100 yards will hit at point of aim at 25 yards and again somewhere between 200 and 250 yards, depending on bullet weight and configuration. It will shoot about one inch high at 50 yards, three inches high at 100 yards, one and one-half inches high at 175 yards and dead on at 200 to 250 yards.

Some hunters, if they know a shot will be taken inside of 60 yards, will sight in their scoped rifle to hit dead-on at that range. Any deer between muzzle and 60 yards can be hit by holding the scope's reticle directly on the target.

This method of sighting in a scoped rifle is easy. There is nothing mysterious about sighting in a rifle, and the job is best done by the person who will be shooting it. Become familiar with the rifle, and practice shooting it several times before deer season opens.

Thirty minutes or less of your time spent sighting in your favorite rifle can spell the difference between eating venison steaks this winter or grilled hamburgers. How well you shoot, and whether you score, will depend on how well the rifle is sighted in and how much you practice with it at various distances before the season opener.

GUNS AND LOADS

It's often been said that any caliber rifle bullet will kill a deer, and exponents of that theory will get little argument from me. But, just because a given caliber and bullet will dump a nice buck for one person doesn't mean it is capable of standing up to continued use from most of the hunting fraternity.

The following, from the smallest deer hunting rifle caliber to the largest, are my recommendations for what to use for whitetail deer.

Cartridge	Bullet Weight	Bullet Type	Muzzle Velocity
.222 Remington Magnum	55 grains	PSP	3240
.222 Remington Magnum	55 grains	HPPL	3240
.223 Remington	55 grains	PSP	3240
.22/250 Remington	55 grains	PSP	3730
.243 Winchester	85 grains	BTHP	3320
.243 Winchester	100 grains	SP	2960
6mm Remington	80 grains	PSP	3470
6mm Remington	100 grains	PPSP	3130
.25-06 Remington	87 grains	HPPL	3440
.25-06 Remington	117 grains	SP	3060
6.5mm Remington Magnum	120 grains	PSPCL	3210
.264 Winchester Magnum	140 grains	PPSP	3030
.270 Winchester	100 grains	PSP	3480
.270 Winchester	130 grains	PPSP	3110
7mm Remington Magnum	125 grains	PPSP	3310
7mm Remington Magnum	150 grains	PPSP	3110
7mm Remington Magnum	175 grains	PPSP	2860
.30-30 Winchester	125 grains	HP	2570
.30-30 Winchester	150 grains	OPE	2390
.30-30 Winchester	170 grains	HPCL	2200
.300 Savage	150 grains	PPSP	2630
.308 Winchester	110 grains	PSP	3180
.308 Winchester	125 grains	PSP	3050
.308 Winchester	150 grains	PPSP	2820
.30-06 Springfield	110 grains	PSP	3380
.30-06 Springfield	125 grains	PSP	3140
.30-06 Springfield	150 grains	PPSP	2920
.300 Winchester Magnum	150 grains	PPSP	3290
.303 British	180 grains	PPSP	2460
.35 Remington	150 grains	PSPCL	2300
.44 Winchester Magnum	240 grains	SP or SJHP	1760
.444 Marlin	240 grains	SP	2350

Abbreviations for the various bullet configurations listed above include: HP—Hollow Point; SP—Soft Point; PEP—Pointed Expanding Point; JHP—Jacketed Hollow Point; PP—Power Point; SJHP—Semi-Jacketed Hollow Point; BTHP—Boat Tail Hollow Point; HPPL—Hollow Point Power-Lokt; PPSP—Power Point Soft Point; OPE—Open Point Expanding; HPCL—Hollow Point Core Lokt; and PSPCL—Pointed Soft Point Core Lokt.

Note that hundreds of different bullets in various calibers and configurations are available from manufacturers or reloading supply houses. All offer fine bullets in weights unavailable from ammunition manufacturers.

HANDGUN LOADS FOR DEER

Shooting a whitetail deer with a handgun represents a big challenge for some folks. The handgun (preferably scoped) needed to down a buck at ranges from 30 to 100 or more yards is indeed a handful. Such handguns bellow and bark, but in the hands of an expert they offer deadly accuracy, sufficient knockdown power and reasonably mild recoil if Mag-na-Ported.

Granted, a whitetail handgun isn't for everyone. Outfit one with a scope and the rig takes on enough weight as to be uncomfortable to carry and fire with one hand. Larry Kelly of Mag-na-Port Arms in Mt. Clemens, Michigan, is an advocate of handguns for deer. He often uses a sling attached to the butt and barrel of his handgun, and with one of several hand-held cannons of various calibers has managed to drop elephants, lions, other assorted and sundry African beasts and more than a few Michigan deer.

"Laws vary from state to state but U.S. residents may not take handguns into Canada for any purpose," Kelly said. "I do not recommend using a .25, .32, or .38 Special handgun for deer hunting. Even the .357 Magnum is marginal, in my opinion.

"A handgun can be extremely accurate, but the use of one for deer hunting means constant practice. A hunter should be able to consistently place six shots in a pie plate at ranges from 25 to 100 yards, and if he can't . . . well, he should either practice more or consider using a centerfire rifle."

Kelly believes the sportsman must determine the exact distance at which he can accurately shoot, and then practice at that range. He believes a scoped pistol or revolver will increase any handgunner's ability to place an accurate shot on a buck, and a rest to steady the aim is a good hedge against misses.

"My choice for a hunting handgun is a .41 or .44 Magnum, and the latter is my favorite," Kelly said. "I recommend a full metal-jacketed bullet in either caliber, but a jacketed soft-point bullet will work. Don't scrimp on barrel length; a 5-inch or longer barrel is preferred, and I attach a sling for easy carrying."

Kelly's firm specializes in Mag-na-Porting pistol, revolver and rifle barrels to reduce muzzle jump and to enable hunters to get on target faster if a second shot is needed. This process reduces recoil by about 30 percent, eliminates most of the muzzle jump and it enables hunters to recover much faster for another shot.

He deer hunts from a blind or on stand, and tries to position himself so if a buck crosses his line of fire he will have a broadside shot at the animal. He feels hunters should aim for the center of mass (the heart-lung area), and avoid neck shots except at very close range. He believes neck shots increase the risk of a handgunner wounding and eventually losing the deer.

Single-shot pistol, single or double-action wheelgun (revolver) or semiautomatic—the choice is up to the hunter. I once dumped a small buck with a Smith & Wesson Model 469 in 9mm with hardball ammo, but most serious handgun aficionados lean toward larger handguns. The single-shot Thompson/Center Contender is a solid choice for many, and heavy revolvers like Colt, Smith & Wesson or Ruger offer a wide choice of single- or double-action revolvers in various barrel lengths. Few serious handgunners use semiautomatics unless they are in law enforcement and wish to hunt with their regular duty sidearm.

Michigan's rock 'n' roll Motor City Madman—Ted Nugent—has taken numerous deer and other wild game with a .44 Magnum revolver. I've watched him shoot on several occasions, and the man is deadly accurate at ranges to 100 yards. He has good vision, and the last I knew he was still shooting with iron sights.

"I stress safety at all times," Nugent told me. "I wear shooting glasses and muffs over my ears to protect my hearing. Anyone who wants to deer hunt with a handgun must practice religiously. It takes time, lots of practice and experience to shoot a revolver like I do, and to hit where you are aiming. It's not overly difficult to learn but it isn't easy either. It requires far more practice than most hunters are willing to put into it."

The following cartridges and bullet styles will work for handgun deer hunters:

HANDGUN LOADS

Cartridge	Bullet Weight	Bullet Style	Muzzle Velocity
.256 Winchester Magnum	60 grains	HP	2350
.357 Magnum	150 grains	FMJ	1600
.357 Magnum	158 grains	JHP	1450
9mm	125 grains	MC	1120
.243 Winchester	85 grains	BTHP	3320
.243 Winchester	100 grains	PPSP	2960
.270 Winchester	100 grains	PSP	3480
.30-30 Winchester	125 grains	HP	2570
.30-30 Winchester	150 grains	OPE	2390
.41 Remington Magnum	210 grains	Lead	1050
.41 Remington Magnum	210 grains	SP	1500
.44 Remington Magnum	180 grains	JHP	1610
.44 Remington Magnum	200 grains	JHP	1650
.44 Remington Magnum	240 grains	JSP	1625
.44 Remington Magnum	240 grains	SJHP	1180
.45 Winchester Magnum	230 grains	FMC	1400

Abbreviations: FMC—Full Metal Case; SJHP—Semi-Jacketed Hollow Point; JSP—Jacketed Soft Point; SP—Soft Point; OPE—Open Point Expanding; HP—Hollow Point; JHP—Jacketed Hollow Point; BTHP—Boat Tail Hollow Point; MC—Metal Case; and PPSP—Power Point Soft Point.

Note that handgunners have other specialized "wildcat" cartridges available which offer good possibilities. It's important to know that the muzzle velocities for the .243 Winchester, .270 Winchester and .30-30 loads listed above will be considerably less when fired from a shorter-barreled handgun. The muzzle velocities for the so-called rifle cartridges were fired from rifles with a 20- to 24-inch barrel rather than the five- to 10-inch barrels on most hunting handguns.

SHOTGUNS AND LOADS

The always popular shotgun makes a fine sporting arm for deer hunters, and in many portions of the country (particularly in the heavily populated eastern and midwestern states), a shotgun and/or muzzleloader is the only legal firearm during firearm deer season. Some states allow the use of buckshot, and others do not, but whenever they are legal, buckshot and slugs offer sportsmen a fine alternative to a rifle.

Single-shots, double barrel side-by-sides, over-unders, pumps and semiautomatics—all are adequate for deer hunting. The same shotgun used to chase ruffed grouse or bunnies, ducks or geese, pheasants or woodcock, will serve admirably in the deer woods.

However, with the advent of slugs-only seasons in many states some firearms manufacturers such as Mossberg, Remington, Smith & Wesson and Winchester have begun making shotguns designed specifically to shoot rifled slugs. These slug barrels are generally 18 to 20 inches long and are made with iron sights.

A scope can be mounted atop the receiver, and any scope will increase a slug gun's range and effectiveness if properly sighted in. A scoped shotgun in the hands of a practiced shot can deliver consistent kills out to 70 to 80 yards.

Winchester-Western, Remington, BRI, Lightfield Hybred Sabot Slugs and Federal make rifled slugs, as does Brenneke, a German firm. Slugs are available for shotguns from 10-gauge down to the puny .410,

Paul Kerby uses a short-barreled 18½-inch barreled 12-gauge 3-inch magnum shotgun when deer hunting in heavy cover when he knows the shots will be close. He chooses 3-inch magnum No. 4 buckshot.

but the .410 is not recommended for deer although a precise shot in the vitals will drop the animal. Most slug guns used for deer fall in the 12- and 20-gauge class; a few big men who can handle the heavy recoil will use a 10-gauge. Few hunters these days choose a 16-gauge.

I've known a few brave souls who have tried to reload shotgun shells with buckshot or slugs. Me, I prefer store-boughts and consider reloads with slugs to be a dangerous situation. I'd rather spend the extra money for factory-made shotgun slug shells than try to crank out my own.

If arguments I've listened to concerning buckshot deer loads were worth a buck apiece I wouldn't have to work for two or three weeks. The argument always hinges on the effectiveness of single-ought (0), double-ought (00) or triple-ought (000) buckshot for 12-gauge shotguns. There are many who will disagree and argue about my thoughts on the topic, but I could care less. I never use any of the big buckshot loads.

I've patterned 2¾-inch and 3-inch 12-gauge loads in all available sizes through my Remington pump, and the three different ought (0, 00 and 000) sizes of buckshot, and can't get any of them to shoot accurately enough to suit me.

If I'm going to use a cornshucker for deer, and anticipate close (within 25 to 40 yards) shots, I stuff mine full of 3-inch magnum 12-gauge shells loaded with No. 4 buckshot. Each of the 41 shot in that round are about the same size as a .22 caliber bullet, and they seem to hold together at 30 yards in a tighter pattern, regardless of choke, than do the larger buckshot. The knockdown power of this load at close range is unbelievable. It's deadly on farmland whitetails.

Of course, in other shotgun gauges, No. 4 buckshot is not available. I wouldn't suggest using this load past 40 yards, and only then in a 3-inch magnum. The 2¾-inch magnum pushes out only 27 pellets, and although it offers a wider spread of pellets than 0, 00 or 000 buckshot, the others may have the edge in the smaller magnum shells.

My advice to shotgun users is to use the maximum number of buckshot pellets in a load commercially available from manufacturers. Do not attempt to handload buckshot or rifled slugs, and whenever possible stick with the heavy magnum loads.

BUCKSHOT

Gauge	Shell Length	Powder Dram Equiv.	Shot Size, Number
10	3½ inches	Super Magnum	4 Buckshot — 54
12	3-inch Magnum	4½	00 Buckshot — 15
12	3-inch Magnum	4½	4 Buckshot — 41
12	2¾-inch Magnum	4	1 Buckshot — 20
12	2¾-inch Magnum	4	00 Buckshot — 12
12	2¾-inch	Maximum	00 Buckshot — 9
12	2¾-inch	3¾	0 Buckshot — 12
12	2¾-inch	Maximum	1 Buckshot — 16
12	2¾-inch	Maximum	4 Buckshot — 27
12	2¾-inch Magnum	Maximum	000 Buckshot — 8
12	3-inch Magnum	Maximum	000 Buckshot — 10
16	2¾-inch	3	1 Buckshot — 12
20	2¾-inch	Maximum	3 Buckshot — 20

SLUGS

10	3½-inch	Magnum	1¾ ounce
12	3½-inch	Maximum	1½ ounce
12	3-inch	Maximum	1½ ounce
12	2¾-inch	Maximum	1¼ ounce
12	2¾-inch	Maximum	1 ounce
16	2¾-inch	Maximum	⅘ ounce
20	2¾-inch	Maximum	⅝ ounce
20	2¾-inch	Maximum	¾ ounce
.410	2½-inch	Maximum	⅕ ounce

MUZZLELOADERS

Muzzleloading rifles have undergone tremendous changes from the old Kentucky or Pennsylvania long rifles used by Davy Crockett and Dan'l Boone. The transformation may still not be complete as we enter the 21st Century.

The old smokepoles used black powder, round balls and used a flintlock system to ignite the powder charge. Some were very accurate with extremely long barrels and others were woefully ineffective. Moisture was always a problem with frontloaders, and many a fur trapper or scout met an early demise when a "flash in the pan" failed to touch off the powder charge.

The original long rifles slowly evolved into a similar rifle but the powder was ignited by a percussion cap. These rifles were much more reliable, but in 1985, muzzleloading underwent a dramatic new change.

William "Tony" Knight produced his first MK-85 in-line muzzleloader that year, and muzzleloading changed for the better. The first MK-85, and numerous other models that followed over the next 15 years, looked more like a centerfire rifle than a blackpowder rifle. They feature the sleek lines of a modern centerfire rifle, have a positive double safety, and although the early models relied on a percussion cap, the newer models feature a newer and more positive DISC ignition system

Knight Rifles, made by Modern Muzzleloading of Centerville, Iowa, helped lead sportsmen from the still reliable Hawken and other replica muzzleloaders into a brand-new world of blackpowder accuracy. Gone are the nipples and replacing them are new muzzleloaders with larger flash chambers for more positive powder ignition.

Tony Knight is the founder of Knight Rifles. He is shown with a trophy Iowa whitetail buck taken with a .50 caliber rifle.

The next important change in muzzleloading was the synthetic Pyrodex that replaced the original FFg black powder. Pyrodex isn't as corrosive to muzzleloader barrels as black powder, and produces enough velocity for any modern muzzleloader.

The next major change to occur, and Knight led the way with his popular new in-line rifles, was the use of sabots and pistol bullets. The original sabots allowed sportsmen to use a .44 or .45 caliber bullet, and the sabots helped increase accuracy. The sabot industry has now evolved to where a hunter using a .50 caliber muzzleloader can accurately shoot a bullet weighing 325 grains.

"The new Knight in-line rifles have taken the country by storm over the last 15 years," Knight said. "They are easy to load, easy to disassemble and clean, and are extremely accurate. A good shot with a scoped .50 caliber can easily kill game at distances of 200 yards. The accuracy is unparalleled, and the shocking power of a heavy

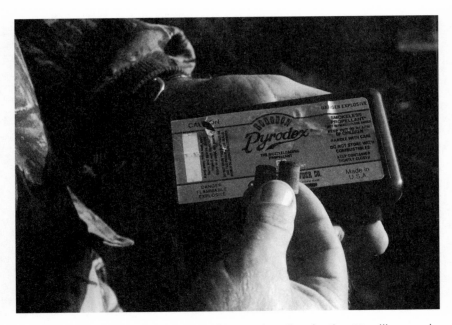

Pyrodex or Pyrodex Select powder comes in 50-grain pellets for the .50 caliber muzzle-loading rifle. They have a thin line of finer, faster igniting powder at the bottom to provide guaranteed ignition.

This is the common load for most .50 caliber in-line muzzleloading rifle shoots: two 50-grain Pyrodex Select pellets, a saboted Barnes Red Hot bullet and a DISC (with shotgun prime) for positive ignition.

saboted bullet will drop anything that walks on the North American continent."

New in 2000 was Knight's .45 caliber rifle. It's lighter, is drilled and tapped for a scope, and is very accurate. Mike Murphy of Knight Rifles, Gary Baynton of Buckley, Michigan, and I became the first modern hunters to use this new muzzleloader. We traveled to Quebec for the famed Quebec-Labrador caribou in September, 2000, and we each made one-shot kills with the rifle.

One might ask: "Why stray from the old-fashioned blackpowder rifles that are so much a part of our hunting heritage?"

It's a good question, and Knight has the answer.

"If mankind didn't progress, and radical changes weren't made, everyone would still be reading by candlelight and driving a Ford Model A," he said. "Many of the old muzzleloading rifles were difficult to shoot and some were inaccurate. The new rifles are based on a very old principle dating back to the seventeenth century that pointed out the best ignition occurred if the spark that ignites the black powder was in line with the powder charge. I developed the first in-line blackpowder rifle to meet the needs of sportsmen tired of trying to shoot with flintlock or percussion cap rifles.

"Accuracy is the primary key to this new rifle. In today's world, sportsmen must become known for making clean killing shots. Many of the old and even some replica rifles simply weren't able to provide precision accuracy. Each rifle we sell is shot and tested thoroughly before it goes out the door. We want hunters to be responsible, shoot straight and make killing shots when they pull the trigger on an animal."

Sighting in a Knight muzzleloading .50 caliber rifle is easy. Adjust the scope for proper eye relief, and fire the first two shots at 25 yards to develop a pattern. Always shoot with a cold barrel.

Knight makes the new Master Hunter, American Knight, DISC, Bighorn, T-Bolt, MK-85, Wolverine II, TK2000, and every muzzleloading accessory needed for a great hunt except for black-powder or Pyrodex. Knight's in-line rifles are made in .45, .50 and .54 caliber, and they also make an awesome blackpowder muzzle-loading shotgun with an extra-full turkey choke.

"Muzzleloading is supposed to be fun," Knight said. "For it to be fun for the average hunter, he must be able to hit what he shoots at. Muzzleloading is the fastest growing aspect of hunting and the shooting sports, and we are responsible for making it fun and pro-ductive for North American deer hunters."

There is a wide range of sabots and bullets available. They weigh from 180 to 325 grains, and proper sabot fit is critical for each bullet. (Other bullet weights include 220, 240, 250, 260, 265, 300 and 318 grains.) The best load for my rifle is a 250-grain Knight Red Hot bullet with two 50-grain Pyrodex Select pellets. It gives me

The Barnes Red Hot Bullets with sabots is my choice for whitetail deer. I killed a nice whitetail during the 2000 season at 188 yards with 100 grains (two 50-grain pellets) of Pyrodex Select. This load is very accurate, and for hunters who desire a little more power and a slightly flatter trajectory, all Knight .50 caliber rifles can be loaded with 150 grains of Pyrodex Select.

superb accuracy and one-shot kills—including one deer in December, 2000 at a distance of 188 yards.

All of Knight's muzzleloading rifles have a Green Mountain 1:28-inch twist that delivers the accuracy needed for clean kills. The barrels are strong enough to shoot 150 grains of Pyrodex Select for greater speed but I'm a little guy; the recoil is 50 percent more than my 100 grains, and is too much for me. I can shoot it but after several rounds I go back to my 100-grain loads.

Muzzle velocity varies somewhat between the different bullet weights, and according to the powder charge. For years I used only 90 grains of Pyrodex Select powder, but when they began making Pyrodex powder in pellet form (50 grain pellets) I switched to 100 grains of powder because I occasionally will have a shot at distances in excess of 150 yards.

"One of the nice things about this muzzleloader is it can handle various powder charges, bullet weights and recoil," Knight said. "I'm so accustomed to shooting 150 grains of powder that it doesn't bother me but beginning muzzleloaders may wish to start at 90 or 100 grains and move up if they choose. Hunters, within reason, can tailor their rifle to their specific needs."

Actions and barrels are available in stainless steel or blued, and thumbhole stocks are available on some models. Stocks can be had in Realtree Hardwoods camo, Walnut, Mossy Oak Break-Up, black composite, and Shadow Black.

Other muzzleloader companies have jumped on the in-line bandwagon, and some companies include Connecticut Valley Arms, Markesbery, Remington, Thompson/Center and White.

Chances are if you are reading this book you already own a muzzleloader, pistol, revolver, rifle or shotgun. You may possibly own one of each or just a hand-me-down rifle passed from grandfather to father and now to you.

But no matter what you own, what's important is that you use the correct loads, and that you shoot them accurately.

9

BOWHUNTING TACTICS

I've killed whitetail bucks with a bow, muzzleloading rifle, center-fire rifle, 12-gauge shotgun and a handgun. Each animal has provided me with good sport and a wholesome day in the deer woods and some great eating, but the bucks that have stayed with me and really stoked a fire in my belly and mind are those I've taken with a compound bow.

The late Robert Traver (John Voelker), the widely acclaimed trout-fishing writer and a longtime personal friend, once said: "Trout fishing with a fly is the most fun you can have with your clothes on." He may have had a point, but it's my contention that bowhunting for whitetails falls into the same category.

Bowhunting offers a distinct challenge that is often missing when using a firearm. A bowhunter must be able to approach a high-strung quarry and get within striking distance without being detected, and must become proficient enough with bow and arrow to consistently hit the animal and make a clean kill.

It's easier said than done. Many bowhunters lack the skill to shoot straight and true while feeling the heart-pounding thrill of a buck at close range. For many, practice on a regular basis is required to change them from a person with a camo suit, bow license and bow into a complete and competent bowhunter.

Simply stated, taking a buck with a bow isn't the easiest thing to do. Anyone who thinks a whitetail buck is spastic, around the bend with nervous energy and always ready to run because of its inborn phobias about sight, smell and sound, should consider the bowhunter's plight as he tries for a shot.

I've shot well over 200 whitetails over 45 years of hunting the animals, and have taken deer in countless places across North America, but I've yet to shed the heart-thumping thrill of seeing a nice buck at distances of five to 20 yards. So far I've not been able to tame my wildly beating heart, the shortness of breath, and the adrenaline rush that sweeps over me when I know a bow shot is imminent.

Somehow, taking a buck with a muzzleloader, centerfire rifle or shotgun just isn't the same for me. A bow puts the hunter in close and personal with a buck, and if that buck is traveling with a doe, taking him can be more difficult than one thinks.

Then again, it can be easier than many beginning bowhunters believe.

I'm convinced of one basic fact: bowhunters are better and more skilled hunters simply because of the limited range of their bow. It takes nerves of steel to sit out the gaze of a buck who knows something is out of place, and it takes internal reserves to resist the temptation to loft an arrow at a nice buck at 40 yards when with patience a 15- or 20-yard shot may be possible.

Claude Pollington with a huge whitetail taken on Oct. 1, 2000 on his Buck Pole Deer Ranch near Marion, Michigan. This animal scored about 180 points with twin double brow points and an outside spread of over 30 inches.

Bowhunters often must sit motionless, operate around erratic breezes which can carry scent to deer, allow numerous does and fawns (and yes, perhaps even small bucks) to pass before coming to full draw on a nice buck.

Add to that mix the time of year when bowhunting takes place. In many states, bowhunters are afield long before firearm hunters.

Seasons start in September or October, and I know of no better time to be afield than during autumn's color changes. Factor in mild weather, early-season whitetail patterns, and the simple joy of being in a ground blind or treestand and watching a buck move your way. There is nothing finer.

The popularity of bowhunting for whitetail deer has skyrocketed in the past 20 years. Bowhunter numbers are high, and are expected to continue rising. One reason for the increase is the time of year. Bow seasons open during the autumn, a glorious time of year to be afield. The weather is warm and autumn foliage is at its peak.

The single most important factor in the dramatic build-up in bowhunting interest over the past 20 years, however, is the advent of the compound bow. In some cases, the switch from firearm to bow is the result of the compound being much easier to draw, hold, aim and shoot than the recurve or long bow.

The long bow and recurve bow industry took a hit when compounds were first invented, but the past 10 years has seen many confirmed bowhunters return to their roots. Compounds, up to a point, have made shooting a bow easier. Those hunters who wish a greater challenge have forsaken the easy-to-draw compound and switched back to the more primitive recurve or long bow.

WHICH BOW FOR YOU?

Choosing a hunting bow boils down to a number of options: cost; paying your money and taking your chances; heft, feel, and comfort of one brand over another; for compound bow users, the option of choosing a 30, 40, 50, 65, 70, or 85 percent let-off—all can have an effect on which bow a hunter chooses to buy.

However, there are a number of rules to follow that can make bow buying easier.

Many first-time bow buyers walk into a local sporting goods store or archery shop, examine the gleaming products as if they were judging the fine lines of a new car. They "ooh" and "ahh" over the finish, the marvelous grain of the wood handle, and seldom realize the wood handle will be covered with camo spray paint or enclosed in a camo bow sock to hide the shiny finish.

Hunting bows fall into one of three categories—compound, long or recurve. Most hunting bows sold today are compounds with cables, cams, eccentric wheels and other features that offer a certain

Kay Richey, the author's wife, poses in the autumn woods with a young buck taken with her Oneida bow.

degree of let-off (a degree of reduced poundage being held when the bow is pulled to full draw). A 70-pound draw weight bow with a 50 percent let-off means the hunter is only holding 35 pounds when the bow is at full draw. This allows hunters to pull, hold at full draw and shoot a bow easier than when a long or recurve bow is of similar draw weight. There is no let-off when a long or recurve bow is pulled back to full draw.

Obviously, for smaller guys like me, a 50 percent let-off allows me to use a slightly heavier draw-weight than is possible with a re-curve. Those people who are amply endowed with bulging biceps and strong back and shoulder muscles will be able to handle a 30- or 40-percent let-off on their compound bow. I shoot a 50-percent let-off Oneida bow, and customarily hunt with a 60-pound draw weight.

There are countless manufacturers who make compound bows, and numerous small companies that make long or recurve bows. If a hunter wishes to go the more traditional route, then a long or re-curve bow is the best bet. For those who want more speed, and some let-off, a compound is the best choice.

Down through the years I've shot Bear, Browning, Darton, High Country, Hoyt, Mathews, Martin, McPherson, Oneida, Stemmler and several other compounds. All have features I like and features that are meaningless to me.

I used a Browning four-wheel compound for several years. It was short, light, and relatively easy to shoot but this was back in the days when few good bow releases were available. I shot the Brown-ing with my fingers, and the finger pinch involved in drawing and releasing an arrow made it unacceptable.

My first Oneida Screaming Eagle was the fastest and easiest drawing compound I ever shot, but once an arrow was released, it made all kinds of racket. That problem was soon corrected, but the point is that few compound bows fall into the "perfect" category, which also is true with long and recurve bows.

George Gardner, an archery manufacturer's rep, tunes an old Stemmler bow. Each bow must be tuned for the person shooting it to obtain maximum arrow speed and the finest accuracy.

Much was made 10 years ago, and even today, of arrow speed. Every compound bow maker wanted their bow to shoot the fastest arrow speed possible. Twenty years ago many manufacturers felt it would be impossible to get a bow to shoot 200 feet-per-second (fps) but that plateau was reached and surpassed by almost every compound bow made. The bar for arrow speed continued to be raised, and year by year, arrow speed became ever higher until now it's not uncommon for a compound bow user to achieve arrow speed of 300 fps.

Compounds began to undergo even more changes. Cams and wheels evolved to achieve faster arrow speed, and limbs and risers changed to provide a more comfortable feel in the hands of the shooter. Bows, following the trends in outdoor clothing and other gear, began being manufactured with various camouflage finishes.

The bow-sight industry went from pins to lighted sight pins and evolved into Red Dog sights that effectively make the shooter more proficient at hitting the target.

Shoot-through arrow rests replaced the old plastic arrow rest and the Burger Button arrow stabilizing unit. Arrows evolved from wood to aluminum to graphite and aluminum-graphite that are much straighter, more accurate and much faster than ever before.

The entire archery industry has seen dramatic changes over the past 20 years, and more changes are coming in the future. What does this mean to the bowhunter?

It means that in today's market there is a great choice of options for the compound bow shooter. With the advice of a good archery technician, it's possible to tailor-make a basic compound bow into a unit that is the best hunting outfit available.

Claude Pollington of Buck Pole Archery in Marion, Michigan, is the new owner of C.P. Oneida Eagle bows, and is the nation's largest Oneida dealer. He obviously feels strongly about the bows he sells, but feels the choice of which bow to buy is a personal decision that can only be made by the person who shoots the bow. He does offer some advice to would-be bow buyers.

"One mistake people make is they rely on a friend's advice about which model of bow to buy," Pollington said. "That can be a major mistake. What suits one person's needs may not be applicable to someone else.

"What archery shops sell—besides bows, arrows and archery accessories—is service. The best advice I can give is to buy a quality product, and one that feels good in your hands and is easy to shoot."

He said a bowhunter who buys a cheap bow at one of the major chain stores is buying trouble. A mall store may sell bows but that's all they do. If a person has a problem with the bow there is no one available to solve the problem. They get stuck with a cheap bow they can't shoot accurately, and easily become discouraged.

An archery shop is in business to make money, but even more importantly, they are in business to service what they sell. If a lower limb hits a tree branch and the bow is knocked out of tune, an archery shop can fix the problem. If the arrows don't fly straight, paper tuning can point out the problem and the shop can determine which arrow size is most appropriate for that bow's draw length, draw weight and the shooter.

Theoretically, a new bow fresh out of the box should be tuned properly. Some are but many are not. An archery shop can tune the bow to the hunter's needs, provide the service of properly positioning the arrow rest and placing the arrow nock in the correct location, and then begin the final tuning. The end result is a bow that works as it was designed to work, and shoots well for the individual shooter. A straight-shooting bow encourages bowhunter confidence, and in the end, enables the hunter to accurately place an arrow in a deer so it dies quickly.

"Buy a bow that feels good," Pollington said. "Never buy a bow that doesn't feel comfortable in your hand, is difficult to draw or is overly heavy. Each bow must be chosen after consultation with the archery shop technician, and when coupled with a proper arrow rest, sight and correct arrows, the hunter will be able to shoot well."

The cost of a bow, arrows and accessories should not be the reason why a person buys a particular bow. As is true with many things, quality costs more than whatever else comes in second best. A quality bow, properly cared for, will last many years and provide many seasons of reliable service.

Claude Pollington, the man Outdoor Life *magazine called "The Whitetail Wizard," is shown tuning an Oneida bow. Pollington is the owner of Oneida bows.*

It's important to determine what comes with a bow. One over-looked item is the choice of a wood or metal handle. Aluminum or other metal handles will freeze your fingers off in cold weather. A wood handle is warmer to hold for long periods of time while waiting for a buck to turn and offer a shot.

The bow must be a functional unit, one that complements the hunter. An analogy is the comparison of a car used to take fishermen along two-track trails to a secluded beaverpond for brook trout. A bow is meant to be used, and not hung on a rack to admire like a piece of artwork.

With bows, what you see is what you get. All the glitter, fancy words on advertisements or cheap gimmicky items will not help a hunter shoot a buck with a bow. Again, quality is most important. Choose a good bow—one you can shoot—and you'll score on a whitetail providing you are as good a woodsman and hunter as you are a bowshot. Choose a fancy bow, and neglect your hunting skills, and you're an also-ran in the deer woods.

One last bow tip: The best bow won't kill a whitetail unless you know how to hunt. Too many hunters practice constantly on paper targets but fail on deer. The reason is that paper doesn't breathe, hear, see or smell like a live buck.

Given my druthers, I'd rather hunt with a guy who practices just enough to know where his arrow is going rather than one who can hit the bull's-eye every time but doesn't have a clue where to shoot a deer.

ARROWS

Arguing arrows and arrow length or fletchings versus plastic vanes is like espousing personal views on politics or religion. There are no winners.

Archery shop salesmen may be able to keep these things in their minds, but I can't remember which aluminum shaft or graphite shaft is best suited for draw length or draw weight. All the numbers become confusing.

The best thing to do is consult a chart published by Easton Aluminum or Game Tracker, aluminum or graphite respectively. If I know my draw length and the pound-pull of my bow, it's easy to make a wise arrow purchasing decision.

Arrow shafts are available in aluminum, fiberglass (mostly for bow fishing), graphite and wood. Wood arrows are almost a thing of the past except for long bow and recurve hunters. A few people still use *good* wood arrows for use with their compound bow, and for years I shot the best cedar shafts out of my compound. They produced countless deer, a few black bears, two or three caribou, and they worked fine although I wouldn't suggest anyone drawing more than 60 pounds to use wood shafts because of the danger of them blowing apart.

My personal choice in recent years has been Carbon Express arrows made by Game Tracker. They fly straight, hit hard and provide maximum penetration.

I like carbon or graphite arrows. They are smaller in diameter, tough as nails, often provide complete penetration through a deer, and one year I shot a black bear, caribou and whitetail buck with the same carbon arrow. Try that with most aluminum arrows and it would be impossible because the shaft usually gets bent or broken on the first animal.

Arrow speed has been the name of the game for many years, and shows little sign of reaching its peak. There are a number of ways to gain more arrow speed: lighter shafts, a short or long overdraw, using graphite (rather than aluminum) inserts, using graphite rather than aluminum arrows, reducing size and weight of broadhead or increasing the draw weight.

The Easton Aluminum Arrow Chart, available from most archery shops, explains how to choose an arrow. The two major things to know are draw length (length of arrow from nock to broadhead insert) and draw weight (how many pounds it requires to come to full draw). Know these two things, and choosing an arrow is easy.

For instance I once shot a 29-inch aluminum arrow from a bow set at 58 pounds. A quick glance at the chart indicates the proper choices include: 2213 (473 grains), 2217 (535 grains) or 2018 (542

A hunter comes to full draw on a buck walking below his stand, about 15 yards away. Quality arrows can make the difference between success and failure.

grains). If my shooting style and preference was for a lighter, slightly faster arrow I'd pick the 2213. However, if I wanted an arrow with slightly more weight (which I do) to deliver better penetration, I would choose the 2018 shaft.

I've seen many bowhunters purchase the most expensive bow available, spend hard-earned bucks on rests and sights, and dump money unwisely on other bowhunting accessories, and then skimp on arrow quality.

That is one of the strangest things a bowhunter can do. Anglers have long known that fishing line is the main connection between rod and fisherman and the fish, and they know that trying to save money on cheap line is unwise. Too many bowhunters fail to heed this lesson, and spend 10 bucks on a few cheap arrows and wonder why they miss a standing buck.

Buying quality arrows makes sense just as buying the best bow a hunter can afford is wise. Quality is quality, and cheap is cheap, and one wonders why anyone would invest good money on a fine bow only to buy the cheapest arrows possible.

Good arrows, depending on locale, will run $60–80 per dozen, and that is money well spent. Easton Gamegetters are good arrows but are not the top-of-the-line. Easton XX75 are better, and Easton XX78 are superb arrows. Add camo finish to the arrows, and the price jumps slightly. I favor camouflaged arrows with a flame orange or pink nock to help me follow the arrow in flight. Others choose to have a white nock feather for the same reason. A bright nock, feather or vane also aids in recovering the arrow if it flies into the woods or ground or is buried under forest duff.

Earlier I mentioned arguments between feathers or plastic vanes. It's well-known that certain features help correct human error when a shot is taken, and feathers are great except they can't take much punishment. Rain and/or snow will dampen or wet feathers and make them slightly nock-heavy which can affect accuracy. Conversely, plastic vanes are not as forgiving of human shooting error but the elements have no affect on the arrow's flight.

I prefer shooting vanes rather than feathers. My eyesight is poor, and I seldom shoot past 20 yards. At that distance the vanes work very well and the arrow flies straight if the bow is properly tuned for that particular arrow. Hunters who shoot at longer distances may prefer feathers for a long and more stable arrow flight.

How many arrows to buy? The best deal (price) on arrows is to buy a dozen at a time, and that has been my practice for many years. My procedure is to buy 12 arrows with the proper spine for my draw length and draw-weight, and I save the best six arrows for hunting and use the other six for practice.

Being a maverick is somewhat comforting to me. The tried and true belief of many hunters is to outfit six arrow with broadheads and six with target points. I'm one who often goes against the grain of tradition, and there is a perfectly good reason for doing so. I target practice with the same weight and style of broadhead that is used for hunting.

Target points seldom weigh the same as the chosen broadhead, and one or two grains difference can raise havoc with accuracy. I weigh my broadheads, and usually use 125-grain broadheads for hunting. My six target arrows are fitted with 125-grain broadheads, and this ensures that my arrow goes where I want it to hit.

Target points are not as aerodynamically designed as a good broadhead. I want my bow to shoot to the same point of impact with target arrows as with those used for hunting. Broadheads, because of the wider blades, can plane or curve slightly to one side or the other on a shot. It's important to know what they will do when hunting.

The results of a clean killing shot. The arrow punctured the lungs, hit the heart and the animal traveled only 60 yards before falling.

BROADHEADS

Three basic types of broadheads are available—fixed-blade, replaceable blade and open-on-impact or mechanical heads. Which is best is a matter of opinion.

I've used all three of the basic broadhead types, and have had varying degrees of success with each one. My personal preference is a two-blade, fixed-blade broadhead that weighs 125 grains.

I shoot the Patriot broadhead now but have used Bear, Zwicki and several other fixed-blade heads. I like the sharp pointed two-blade because it starts cutting on impact, slices easily between or through rib bones, and almost always give me complete penetration which leads to a better blood trail. I've shot three bucks with a two-blade head, had the arrow completely penetrate their chest cavity, and they have stood in place and died without moving.

Mind you, it requires an at-ease whitetail buck for this to happen. All too often the buck is alert, senses aware, all nerves ajangle, and these bucks will run when hit with any broadhead. I've found, when properly tuned, my bow, arrow and broadhead will fly perfectly straight without planing with a two-blade, fixed-blade broadhead.

This type of broadhead can be resharpened easily, and I commonly remove dirt from my target broadheads, sharpen them with file and hone, and use them for hunting. Try that with a replaceable-blade or open-on-impact broadhead.

I have used replaceable-blade three- and four-blade broadheads on many occasions. They work well under most circumstances, and some always work.

It's my choice and decision to use a Game Tracker string tracking device when hunting whitetails, and I normally tie a slip knot, remove the broadhead, slip the loop over the broadhead's insert, and screw it into the arrow shaft. I pull the knot tight, and snip off excess string.

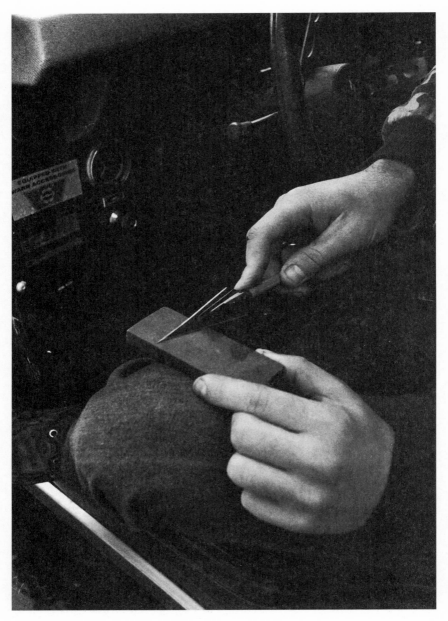

Sharp broadheads are needed for bowhunting. An arrow and broadhead kills by cutting arteries, capillaries and veins, and destroying vital organs. Broadheads must be razor sharp, and this photo shows the sharpening of a fixed-blade broadhead.

My major problem with replaceable-blade broadheads is the blades often fall out when I try to tie on my Game Tracker string. Who wants to climb 10–15 feet up a tree, and then drop one blade from a broadhead? No one wants to climb down until dark, so they pull out another arrow and try it again after replacing the first arrow in a bow quiver.

If a sportsman hunts in country like I do it's nearly impossible to find the fallen broadhead blade. If this happens three or four times a season the hunter will have lost one complete broadhead's component of blades.

Another thing I dislike about some (not all) replaceable-blade broadheads is the blades are touted as being razor sharp. Some are but many are not.

I've had wonderful success with Barrie, Game Tracker First Cut, Kolpin, Rocky Mountain, Satellite and Viper replaceable-blade broadheads.

Open-on-impact broadheads are wonderful . . . when they work, which is often. Some of the earlier models of seven or eight years ago might or might not open. If they didn't, the result was a wounded deer and a blown ground blind or treestand location.

I hunted in Kentucky with Kevin Kreh a few years ago, and he was using a Gold Tip Gladiator open-on-impact broadhead. He opened my eyes with one shot.

The 140-class buck he shot was hit behind the front shoulder, and it left a massive blood trail before dropping 75 yards away. The entrance hole was small but the exit hole and damage was massive, and it was a perfect example of how well an open-on-impact or expandable broadhead like the Gladiator or Game Tracker's Silver Tip will work.

It should be stated that anyone using an open-on-impact broadhead should be drawing at least 50 pounds to achieve maximum cutting advantage. A lighter draw-weight bow may not enable the blades to fully extend for maximum cutting action.

One important thing to remember: broadheads kill deer by causing massive hemorrhage as they slice through arteries, capillaries and veins. There is little or no shock to a broadhead hit (which is why my two-blade broadhead caused deer to stand motionless after being hit until they bled to death). A broadhead kills through blood loss but the cutting edges must be as sharp as a barber's razor. To prevent rust, I coat my sharpened broadheads with a thin layer of Vaseline petroleum jelly, 3-in-1 oil or WD40. Rusty broadheads are dull and will not cut as well as clean blades.

Broadheads, like the bow being used, is a matter of personal choice. Choose one that works well for you, is sharp or can be sharpened to a keen edge, and practice with it until the head flies straight and true.

PROPER SHOOTING FORM

Shooting a whitetail buck is much different than shooting at a paper target. Paper doesn't look around, sniff the air or listen with extended swiveling ears. Paper targets do not generate the adrenaline rush that a buck will do.

My youngest son was given a bow, arrows, target points and broadheads when he was 12 years old and had completed his Hunter Education training, passed the test and received his certificate that would allow him to buy his first archery hunting license. He was ready to bowhunt deer!

Guy practiced day in and day out, and shot many dozens of arrows each day to hone his form and shooting skills. He could put five arrows side-by-side in the bull's-eye at 20 yards, and could do it every time he shot from ground level or from a treestand. The kid was good, and being 12, somewhat cocky.

"Shooting a deer this fall will be easy," he said. "I'll nail the first one that comes past me within shooting range."

Constant practice is required to shoot a bow accurately. This means daily practice during off-season months to get prepared for when the season opens.

I informed him that shooting deer was different than shooting a paper target. I told him about adrenaline rushes, heavy breathing (he seemed to know something about that but in a different context), and how he had to study deer before shooting.

"Nothing to it," he boasted.

I took him out hunting on opening day, and put him in a stand where he would see 12 to 20 deer during a late afternoon-early evening hunt. I told him to stay put until I came to get him.

"Bring your knife to field dress my deer," he said, as I turned to leave. The kid was still cocky, and would soon be singing a sadder tune.

I sat in a treestand 200 yards away with my bow across my lap and binoculars to my eyes. I wanted to watch the kid in action without him knowing it.

Time passed slowly as I watched. He sat still, didn't move, and scanned the nearby brush for deer. An hour before sundown I watched him ease slowly to a standing position, come to full draw, aim and shoot.

He sat back down dejectedly. His shot missed the deer.

Ten minutes later along came a doe with two fawns. He eased upright in a slow motion move, drew again, aimed and released. Again he sat back down after another obvious miss.

Guy repeated this scenario four more times until his bow quiver was empty, and I watched him climb down, looking over his shoulder in all directions, climb back up with his arrows in his quiver and proceed to clean each one of dirt.

After six misses, the deer decided to move elsewhere. I climbed down 30 minutes after sundown, walked to the car and drove over to pick him up.

"Hey, partner, get a deer?" I asked with a hopeful lilt in my voice.

"No," he said.

"Any shots?"

He gazed at me with a strange look, trying to determine if I had seen him picking up his six arrows, thought about it for a moment, and said he had shot.

"Did you hit one?"

He shook his head that he had not.

"How many times did you shoot," I asked as we stood in the darkness.

Another lengthy pause, and he answered "six times."

"I thought you said shooting a deer would be easy," I said. "You told me it would be a done deal with only one shot. I've got my knife ready. What happened?"

"You were right," he said. "It's much tougher hitting a deer with a bow than hitting a paper target. Those deer stood with each one facing in different directions and looked around, sniffed the air and their ears were moving constantly."

This was Guy's introduction to bowhunting. The next time he was told to study the animals, look for the proper moment to draw and shoot, and never take a low-percentage shot. I moved McKenzie targets around my backyard for him, and asked him to tell me when it was a high- or low-percentage shot, and he gradually learned that arrowing a whitetail required much more than the ability to shoot straight.

It must be something about my mental make-up, but I can't shoot targets well but I haven't missed a deer with my bow in many years. The difference, I guess, is that I don't concentrate on paper targets but every sense is tuned into drawing, aiming and releasing on a deer. That I can do right.

Proper form is a big part of the secret to shooting deer. It means using proper form every time a shot is taken, and this form will differ slightly from one person to another. Such things as body build, facial features, length of arms and many other factors enter into the success or failure of a shot.

George Gardner, an archery tackle representative, has spent hours with my wife and me in order to develop good shooting habits. He advised us to be consistent, and to use the same anchor point time and again.

"The most common anchor point for bowhunters," Gardner said, "is the corner of the mouth. But, the hunter must hold his bow the same way on each shot and touch the corner of the mouth each time while making the same release time after time. It's not easy."

Claude Pollington shoots from a treestand in a cedar tree. His anchor point is the corner of his mouth.

He suggests grasping the bow like you were reaching out to shake hands. This automatically turns the inside of the elbow to a more vertical position, and this will remove the possibility of an "idiot mark." An idiot mark results from the bow string slapping against the inside of the upper arm, elbow or lower arm and wrist. String slaps are painful, can cause flinching and can be avoided by holding the bow properly or by using an arm guard.

"The first step after determining where the nocking point should be (this can be done at any archery shop)," Gardner says, "is to come up with a firm, never-changing anchor point. Depending on shooting style, I recommend the release aid touch the right corner of the mouth for a right-handed shooter and the left corner for a southpaw."

Claude Pollington teaches a somewhat different shooting form. Both instructors urge beginning bowhunters to turn their body so the left side is facing the target (for a right-handed shooter) or have the right side of the body facing the target for a left-handed shooter. Both feet should be spaced even with the shoulders for steady balance when drawing a bow.

"Don't try to choke the bow handle to death," Pollington said. "Grasp the bow lightly so it is balanced between thumb and index finger. The bow should just float there."

Stand erect with head up, and look at the target where you wish to hit. Begin drawing the bow as it comes up, and when the hunter reaches his anchor point, the sight pin, Red Dot sight or lighted pin will be perfectly aligned with the eye.

"The big thing is not to shift the head to one side or another," Pollington said. "Keep the head up, achieve your anchor point, and if the bow is properly fitted to the hunter, the eye, sight and arrow will be pointed at the target. It's the best and easiest way to achieve proper form and it is the best method for perfect shooting."

Once a person masters the mechanics of proper stance, shooting form and bow balance, shooting standing up is easy.

Much of the time when we hunt from the ground we will be sitting, and I always sit in a treestand because standing requires too much movement and isn't as safe as shooting from a sitting position. I believe sitting in a treestand reduces my silhouette, reduces body movement and is far more stable and much safer than standing to shoot.

Once perfect form is achieved, and it becomes second nature to obtain the same anchor point each time, hunters can then experiment with different body positions including shooting from a sitting position. It's not as easy is it appears, and it is more difficult to draw the same poundage while sitting than when standing.

I often set my bow at 58 to 60 pounds of draw weight during the early fall. However, when late fall arrives with colder temperatures and wind and/or snow, I crank my bow down to 55 pounds to compensate for added clothing and stiff muscles.

I remember one November when the rut was in full swing. It was damn cold, and my treestand overlooked a trail used by rutting bucks. I'd seen a nice 8-pointer working the trail daily for a week. He always came just before legal shooting time ended, and seemed to mosey along in an indifferent manner until he came to his scrape line 50 yards away.

I sat and waited, and an hour and then two dragged by as the wind chill seemed to turn my bone marrow to ice. It was 15 minutes before shooting time ended when I saw the buck swagger down the trail. When his head went behind a nearby tree I raised my bow, and started my draw.

The bow string wouldn't budge. I was too cold, and my muscles too cramped to pull my bow. I slowly lowered the bow, flexed my muscles slightly and tried again.

I still couldn't break the 58-pound compound. I couldn't get the string far enough back to roll it over the hump, and I had to let it

When to shoot is always a matter of importance for bowhunters. The doe on the right is offering a high-percentage quartering-away shot, while the buck at left is a low-percentage, quarter-toward shots. In cold weather, back your bow off a few pounds for easier shooting.

down again. By this time the buck knew something was wrong, and was staring intently at my treestand.

I didn't move, and minutes later he started past my stand. I allowed him to pass and tried to come to full draw again. I struggled, gritted my teeth, and the arrow fell off the rest and onto my finger and made a slight tinkling noise as I replaced it on the rest.

The buck whirled around just as I muscled the bow back, finally to full draw, but my arms were quivering from the cold and strain. My anchor point was less than perfect. The buck was nearly broadside but quartering away slightly, and my release was a total disaster.

I missed that buck clean, and never saw him again. Chalk up an educated buck to a bow that couldn't be easily drawn because of the cold.

Is there a lesson to be learned here? You bet; my first lesson was to practice drawing more from a sitting position. Different muscles are used, and it's awkward the first few times but constant practice from a sitting position will be advantageous during the archery season.

The second lesson learned that day was to crank my bow down a few pounds during cold weather. Practice with the new setting, and know where the arrow will hit. Heavy clothing and a hefty draw-weight will do strange things to the human body once the weather turns cold.

INSTINCTIVE SHOOTING OR BOW SIGHTS

My first 10 years of bowhunting were spent shooting instinctively. I looked down the arrow, over the broadhead and at my target. When everything lined up and felt right, I turned the arrow loose. Several bucks were downed; a dozen caribou fell to my arrows; two black bears and a wild boar were shot instinctively.

Then it all fell apart. My eyes changed with approaching middle age, and with that change came bifocals. I couldn't hit a bull in the backside at 10 yards while shooting instinctively. My arrows hit the top, bottom, right and left edges of the paper target—when they hit the target at all. I sprayed arrows like water from a garden hose.

It meant giving up bowhunting or start using sight pins. I chose the latter, and am happy I did. It gave me renewed confidence to hunt big game again.

Things cruised along smoothly until I reached my late-40s, and glaucoma set it. Five surgeries on my left eye and three on my right eye made it impossible to use sight pins as I had in the past.

It was back to the beginning again. Finally I decided that wallowing on my personal pity pot didn't solve a thing. My eyes, after the surgeries, were as good as they would ever get and feeling sorry for Poor Me was like self-flagellation; it served no useful purpose and solved nothing.

I decided to try a Red Dot sight, and practiced with it, and eventually it helped me to bowhunt again. The internal red dot does not shine any visible light on the deer, is fully adjustable as the sun goes down, and the internal red dot is easy to see through the 1× scope against a deer's body.

I learned it was important to shoot with both eyes open even though my left-eye vision is "fingers-only" movement at six inches. Keeping my left eye open, even though I can't see a deer, helps keep the bow level and the dot on the target.

The Pollington Pro-Point red dot sight has kept me bowhunting when I once felt my archery days had ended. This doesn't mean a red dot sight is for everyone although anyone can learn to shoot with one, but it does mean that people with poor vision can still learn to shoot accurately.

A beginning bowhunter of 35 years of age or less will almost always start out shooting instinctively or with pins. As we pass over the bumpy hill into middle age, the maturing process can do strange things to our vision, and sight pins become somewhat easier to use.

Sight pins come in varying sizes for use at different distances, and some have fluorescent pink or red rings, others have crosshairs like a rifle scope, and others are lighted. I tried them all years ago before my vision began heading south, and I favored yellow, green or red lighted pins, and the smaller the lighted area the better. I often placed a tiny dot of fingernail polish on the lighted end to reduce its size, and it worked for me. If the lighted area on a pin or red dot sight is too large at dusk it will blot out the deer, and make it nearly impossible to make a truly accurate shot.

Over the years I've used Altier, Bear, Bowscope, Browning, Chek-It, Cobra, Fine-Line, Fisher, Logan, Martin, Pollington Pro-Point, PSE, Range-O-Matic, Tru-Shot and Zero Peep lighted pins or sights, and all have worked for me.

Instinctive or sights for bowhunters is a personal choice. Try them, and decide for yourself which offers the best accuracy.

BOWHUNTER CLOTHING

It's said that clothing makes the man, and that also holds true for bowhunters. Good clothing is important, and since bowhunters do their thing in camouflage it pays to purchase quality clothing which will hold up to the countless treks through briers, brambles and shinnying up and down trees.

I've worn wool for many years. It's warm during cold or wet weather, and it is quiet. Is wool still the answer for bowhunters?

It can be but there are countless synthetic fabrics that are quiet, warmer, capable of wicking away perspiration and hold up well during a bowhunt.

Down is warm when dry but heavy and cold when wet. I haven't worn a down garment to hunt in for nearly 20 years because the nylon or synthetic shell on them is also too noisy for me. I can't sit quietly in a ground blind or treestand without rustling.

King Of The Mountain Sports' wool garments are quiet and warm, and scarcely a whisper is heard when my bow comes to full draw or my rifle is raised for a shot. I wear mine often, but one draw-back is the weight.

Other registered or trademarked synthetic brand names of in-sulated or uninsulated quiet cloth or clothing liners include Gore-Tex, Polar Fleece, PolarGuard, polyester, polypropylene, the various saddle cloth garments, Thinsulate, and other insulating materials are now available. Whatever insulating material is used must be coupled with a soft and quiet outer layer. Sadly, some makers of hunting clothing do a good job of insulating the body but a poor job of producing a quiet fabric.

I use a simple test before purchasing any clothing. I rub my hand in 12-inch strokes against the outer fabric. If the noise it creates is anything other than a soft whisper, that garment gets a thumbs-down from me.

Several companies make wool or wool-acrylic blended garments. These serve the purpose well if worn as outer garments. Check all gar-ments for noise before purchase.

The whole secret of quiet movement once a buck approaches within bow range is to wear clothing that will not scratch or make noise as the bow arm is extended and the hunter comes to full draw. Nylon, cotton and many hard-fiber synthetic materials fail this test.

CAMOUFLAGE CLOTHING

Name the pattern, and some camouflage company will make the design. Years ago, hunters used basic U.S. Army camouflage, and it was more green than any other color but it seemed to work in many areas.

Now, dozens of companies have camo patterns to permit sports-men to hunt in any type of terrain. Hunters can blend in against bare earth, cornstalks, desert country, maples, oaks and a variety of other colors. Snow camo clothing is available for hunting in some Canadian provinces or on snow-covered terrain.

Choose your camo clothing so it blends in with your surroundings.

Companies like ASAT, Gunflint Select, Nature's Edge, Predator, Realtree, Realtree Advantage, Realtree All-Purpose, Mirage, Mossy Oak, 10-X Shikari Cloth, Timberghost, Trailcover, Trebark, Wall's Whisper-Soft, Wolf Mountain Hunting Wear and countless others make camo clothes that allow hunters to match their camo pattern with the environment.

Bowhunters can stick out like a sore thumb if they wear the wrong camo pattern at the wrong time of year. For instance: green Army camo clothing in a bare birch, maple or oak tree will look out of place. The same is true if a very light-colored camo is used while hunting in a cedar swamp.

My normal mild-weather bowhunting uniform consists of: blue jeans, one pair cotton and one pair wool socks, a brown or camo chamois cloth shirt, green or brown wool stag pants and a camo wool sweater. My footwear is a pair of knee-high LaCrosse rubber boots, and I tuck my jeans and wool pants into my boots to avoid leaving human scent while walking into the hunting area. I often wear suspenders because leather belts can squeak when moving or turning in a stand. Brown jersey gloves cover my hands and wrists, a camo face mask covers my face, and I wear a camo hat.

Cold-weather bowhunting clothes are another story. I wear one or two pairs of long underwear, insulated underwear top and bottom, one pair of cotton and two pair of wool socks, wool stag pants, and my King Of The Mountain bibs on the bottom portion of my body. On top, I wear long underwear, thermal underwear, a down vest under a heavy chamois cloth or wool shirt, a wool camo sweater and a green-black wool jacket. A wool scarf is wrapped about my face and neck to prevent heat loss, and a wool stocking cap is pulled low over my forehead and ears to prevent valuable heat loss. Brown jersey gloves go over my hands, and they are followed by wool gloves with or without a flap for hand and finger movement. If a winter deer shows up, I often remove the heavy gloves while retaining the cotton jersey gloves. I keep my hands in my pockets until it is time to shoot.

If the weather is really cold I wear IceMan boots with a heavy felt liner to keep my feet and toes warm. Cold weather always affects my fingers and toes first, and this is a result of getting frostbitten fingers on several occasions.

BOWHUNTING ACCESSORIES

Bowhunters are as gadget crazy as trout fishermen. We spot something new, and must have it. It's not that these items aren't needed or do not have practical applications, it's just that many of us complicate our hunting with too many gadgets.

There are certain items that fall into the "must-have" category. One of mine is a backpack. In it I carry a rope to drag out my deer, plastic bags for heart and liver, sharp hunting knife, binoculars, small limb saw, compass, first-aid kit, extra gloves, scents, camo face mask, extra broadheads, lighter, rainwear, fire cubes, Space Blanket, haul rope for pulling my bow up into a tree or lowering it, safety harness, scent eliminating spray, extra release and other items that may come and go as the need develops.

I use a release aid when bowhunting. On more than one occasion I've dropped one, and either had to climb down to retrieve it or sit tight to avoid spooking a buck. I carry an extra one in the event I drop one.

At one time it was my practice to carry what I needed into the tree and leave my backpack on the ground. That changed when I first dropped my release. Now the backpack goes into my stand, and I use a small screw-in L-shaped hook to hold the bag within easy reach but out of my way when drawing, aiming and shooting.

My bow has Cat Whiskers (string silencers) on both ends of my bow string and dark-colored Muffs on my cables to silence my bow when drawing it. I cover the sight window and above and below the arrow rest with stick-on brown carpet to silence it.

I favor a Bo-Doodle shoot-through arrow rest. Once properly installed and set, it provides an excellent way to shoot arrows silently. I do add shrink-wrap rubber tubing to the fingers of the rest to allow an even more silent draw.

A Roll-Aid archery release means a smooth release every time.

I use a Scott rubber grip handle with one of Pollington's Gator Jaw releases. The Gator Jaw system allows me to attach the twin release jaws on the bow string above and below the arrow nock, and it provides an instant and trouble-free release.

There are any number of bow quivers on the market. My favorite always has been the Quikee Quiver, and rubber inserts can be purchased to hold the larger diameter aluminum arrows or the smaller diameter carbon arrows. I remove the quiver from my bow while hunting, and never shoot with it on. It's just one more piece of equipment that could make a noise at a critical time.

A few bowhunters still rely on the Indian-type back quiver. They work fine when walking but I wouldn't wear one in a treestand. There is just too much chance an errant clink of arrows bumping together could spook an incoming buck.

Binoculars serve a useful function for farmland deer hunters. They allow the hunter to glass an animal long before it approaches bow range, and it helps hunters determine antler size. My Bausch & Lomb binoculars work well when deer are outside of 50 yards, but a small pair of compact permanent-focus binoculars come in handy once a deer gets close enough for a shot. Hunters must use caution because lifting binoculars up or lowering them, or stowing them away before a shot, can cause enough movement to spook a deer.

One of the most useful items a bowhunter can attach to his bow is a Game Tracker. This string tracking device attaches 17-pound red or white center wound line just behind the broadhead, and when the arrow hits a deer the line peels off and gives the sportsman an easy means of following the animal. If the arrow goes through the deer a hunter will be able to follow a double line. It has saved deer for me that may otherwise might not have been recoverable.

Paul Jalon inserts a fresh roll of Game Tracker string into the string tracking device. This center-wound line is attached to the arrow behind the broadhead, and when the arrow hits a deer and the animal runs off, the string peels out of the canister and the hunter often can walk right to the dead deer.

Paul Jalon is shown attaching the Game Tracker line to the arrow.

WHEN TO SHOOT, WHERE TO AIM

There isn't a deer hunter worthy of the name who doesn't dream of seeing a buck in the standard calendar pose. You know the scene: a buck standing broadside to the camera with nostrils quivering and every sense alert. The bowman just knows he could thump that animal and track down the prize of a lifetime.

I've killed countless whitetails with a bow, and so have many of my close hunting buddies. We agree that the calendar pose is one of the toughest shots to make, especially on a mature buck. Standing deer, especially those with their head up, are tough to shoot.

Disagree? Well, what do you think will happen when you come to full draw and the arrow whispers off the rest when you make a release? Do you really think the buck will stand rooted in one spot and wait for destiny to overtake him? I doubt it.

Hunters have heard of deer "jumping the string," i.e., moving when they hear the string go forward as it releases the arrow. Well, it's true; whitetails do jump the string after a fashion. Most often, they go down rather than up but it makes no difference to the hunter unless he is holding low. Their reflexes are so sharp that only bad hits are the result, and more often than not, it means a complete miss.

Now is a good time to point out an important fact that few bowhunters realize. If a deer is within 20 yards of the hunter, and the arrow is traveling in excess of 180 fps, the broadhead will hit the deer before it has time to react to bow twang. Of course, this applies to relaxed deer . . . not alert animals.

It's somewhat difficult to counsel others on when to shoot or where to aim. A friend of mine, with hundreds of deer on his spread and countless bucks to his credit, detests a standing target. His reasoning is simple.

A buck makes some noise as it walks, feeds and whenever it moves. A walking deer is much easier to hit than a standing animal.

He advises bowhunters to wait for their shot. Never go for the shot being offered by a buck; instead, wait for the animal to turn to provide the ideal high-percentage shot needed to regularly kill deer. My buddy likes to take his shot after the buck passes his stand and is moving slightly away. A quartering-away shot allows the arrow to slide up through the soft belly behind the ribs and into the heart-lung area.

A quartering-away shot is deadly. The next best shot is a broadside shot as the buck moves across in front of the hunter. The worst shot is a head-on or tail-on shot.

The best advice anyone can offer is to wait for high-percentage killing shots, and pass up low-percentage opportunities. Picking the shot means watching deer, and knowing what they will do at any given moment.

Such judgment only comes from experience. It means watching the deer's head, and being able to time their movements so it's possible to guess when the head will come up to study nearby terrain. It also means watching other deer; one wrong movement when other animals are within range, and the object of your attention may disappear over the nearest ridge because other deer spooked your target.

My favorite time to make my draw is when a buck has his head down feeding or scent-trailing an in-season doe. Keep body movements very slow, and do not be afraid to stop in middraw. I've sat for long minutes with bow arm extended when a deer caught my minor movement, and then completed the draw and shot the animal after it decided there was no danger. I always wait for the buck's head to go down before coming to full draw, aiming and shooting.

Be alert to a common whitetail trait. They often put head fakes on anything they may be suspicious of, and like a basketball player trying to juke an opponent, they lower their head and

There's no shot available yet. This bowhunter must wait for this buck to sneak past the brush and work into the open for a shot. Too many bowhunters rush into taking a poor shot at this point, and either miss or wound the animal. Wait for the proper time to shoot, and take only high-percentage shots.

abruptly raise it again in hopes of spotting some movement. Let deer do this two or three times without moving, and they will soon tire of trying to spot movement and give the hunter time to draw.

Many years ago an old bowhunter offered some advice. I've followed it every time a deer is within bow range, and it has paid off with many bucks.

"Draw down on every deer that passes within bow range," he told me. "Pretend you plan to shoot every buck, doe or fawn within range. You'll soon learn when to draw on the animal and where to hold off. It gives the hunter the power of life and death, and within a season a sportsman could shoot every deer within bow range if they wanted to, and this experience will be invaluable when it comes time to turn loose an arrow."

I've followed this philosophy for over 40 years. Each year I draw on at least two dozen bucks within bow range. During 2000, from October 1 to October 27, I had drawn on and passed up 28 bucks. That, my friends, averages slightly over one buck daily. Not one of the bucks I drew down on knew I was there, and all were within 20 yards and a few were inside of 10 yards of my treestand.

It's my decision to not shoot early in the bow season, and two reasons dictate my actions. The first is I want to see what bucks are in the area, and the second is it would put an end to my bow season far earlier than I wish.

There isn't a single deer that passes my ground blind or treestand that I don't draw on, and amazingly enough, my draw and aim hasn't been spotted in many years. I always have bucks dead to rights, and choose to pass up the shot. One day I passed up 27 does and fawns, and shot the 28th deer—a nice buck. It's great practice.

It helps hunters get past the jitters when a buck finally does offer a shot. The hunter is more relaxed, more confident, and seldom makes a mistake.

Where to shoot a deer is a matter of preference for a killing shot, and it depends on the degree of archery skill possessed by each bowman. I personally abhor head-on, tail-on and inside the back leg (femoral artery) shots because they are too chancy.

The best advice is to wait for the high-percentage shot. Settle for the heart-lung areas from a broadside or quartering-away angle, and pass on everything else. Learn to wait for your shot; don't get antsy and shoot at the deer but pick a precise target.

Come to full draw, aim confidently and make a smooth release when the deer is in the proper position. Make a mental note of

Television show host Tim Hooey poses with a heavy, wide-racked buck taken by hunting from a carefully located stand site. He used a portable blind to hunt from, and it paid off.

where the arrow hit, and give the deer at least 15 minutes before following the blood trail. Listen immediately after the shot, and often you'll hear the deer fall. If all your senses are attuned to the hunt it should be possible to walk right up to a bow-killed buck.

It's then you will have achieved the ultimate in deer hunting; the taking of a nice buck with a bow in an ethical and legal manner.

10

SCENTS: SENSE OR NONSENSE?

There are several ways to get your nose bent into a different shape. Arguing politics, religion, or insulting another hunter's dog are three that quickly come to mind.

A fourth topic is deer scent, and whether it works or not.

I have firsthand knowledge of how deer scent discussions can turn ugly in a hurry. I stopped into a local sporting goods store once, and was minding my own business before buying a bottle of a popular deer sex scent. The whitetail rut was underway, and my supply of buck lure had run out.

"I'd like a bottle of that deer scent," I said to the clerk in a friendly way, pointing to the scent display on the counter behind him.

A nearby gent's eyebrows knotted while a frown creased his face. He acted like he smelled something bad.

"Only a dummy would use bottled deer pee to shoot a buck," he snarled. "Why don't you be a man and hunt deer like a real hunter? Scents take advantage of bucks."

"I didn't think my manhood was in question," I said, recognizing him as a local poacher. "After fathering four kids it hardly seems likely that hunting with or without a sex scent has anything to do with my virility or manhood. Besides, how do men like you hunt . . . with a spotlight after dark?"

It was a dumb choice of words. He was in my face in a heartbeat, had me by the front of my shirt and my booted toes were doing a tippy-tap on the floor as he berated me for being a loudmouth (so true), a know-it-all (also true), and less than a man (not true) for using deer scents. He was getting ready to let me have it when the store manager stepped in and broke things up. Mr. Personality stomped out, a far better alternative than stomping on my face, and I made my purchase without further incident. Two days later I arrowed an 8-pointer while sitting in a treestand downwind from a mock scrape spiced up with deer scent.

The buck walked out, stood nearby for several motionless minutes while checking the area for an estrus doe. The buck, his nose in the air and lip curling, began following a drag line of deer scent and was soon within 20 yards of my treestand. His movement led to a quick one-shot kill.

The problem with deer lures and scents is there is no middle ground. Hunters either like to use these scents or consider the gels or liquids to be a manufacturer's greedy method of separating innocent sportsmen from their hard earned money.

The anti-deer-scent side considers scent use as hocus-pocus; a mythical or supposedly secret scent that might work, might not or is designed solely to make hunters hit the hip to pay an exorbitant fee for a two- to six-ounce bottle of stuff that smells worse than unwashed two-week-old sweat socks moldering in a damp closet.

This treestand hunter has placed his stand properly for an easy shot at a buck coming in to a deer lure placed nearby.

Of course, the pro-scent faction feels the various scents have a place in the deer woods and use one brand or another. Some shoot deer over their scent placement, and some do not. The same holds true for people who do not use scents.

The burning question for many bow and firearm deer hunters is: Do scents work and make sense or is it just a bunch of nonsense?

My answer after two years of experimentation whenever I hunted may lack a strong scientific sampling methodology but it did prove three things. Some scents often work, some never do and others may occasionally help a hunter get his buck.

FACTORS AFFECTING SCENT EFFECTIVENESS

Weather conditions and wind velocity or direction play an important role in how effective a deer scent can be. Heavy rain, a steady drizzle, and wet falling snow can and will decrease the effectiveness of most scents. Increased moisture in the air causes deer scent to settle onto the ground and a deer must be very close to smell it.

Swirling winds of medium to high velocity can have an adverse effect on scent use. Deer seldom move well in strong wind, and there is always a chance that a deer will smell a waiting hunter before smelling a deer scent on the ground or vegetation.

Several rules apply to hunter use of deer scents during the pre-rut, rut and post-rut periods.

1) A hunter must totally believe in the scent he buys; if he doesn't, he may or may not be successful. This falls into the same category as a favorite pike lure for Canadian fishing trips.

Some anglers favor spinnerbaits while others prefer red-white spoons for jumbo northern pike. The reason is they have caught big fish using their favorite lure, and that lure accompanies them on every trip. The fact that they believe in the lure makes them concentrate more on how they fish it. The result is better catches.

This analogy applies to scent-using deer hunters as well. If they believe in the product being used it will make them a better and more successful hunter.

2) Proper preparation is a key to success. The hunter must be odor free, and this means bathing before going into the woods and wearing rubber gloves and boots when placing deer scent on the ground. Hunting clothes must be odor free as well, and I highly recommend three products that I've found to work. Clothing should be washed in Atsko Sport-Wash, and when it is dry hunters can spray it with Scent Shield or Vanishing Hunter to prevent human odor from destroying any chance for a shot.

   It also pays to have two or three travel routes to a ground blind or treestand. Try to avoid brushing bare skin or clothing against vegetation. The use of high rubber boots is important. Leather boots retain odor from whatever they come in contact with, and deer are paranoid about foreign odors.

3) Deer scents can make hunters more effective. One reason is that sportsmen who use scents hunt harder and are more intuitive about stand and scent placement, wind direction, and where deer feed, bed and travel. They become thinking hunters.

   The best scent made won't help if the hunter lacks knowledge of deer bedding and feeding areas, travel routes and countless other factors. A sportsman with horrible body odor who hunts upwind of a known travel route will spook every deer within smelling range. Such individuals smell like a locker room after a basketball game.

4) Proper knowledge of how, when and where to use deer scents is very important. A strong estrus scent may have little impact on hunter success if used before the rut begins or after it ends. On the other hand, a strong estrus scent can work well when bucks are chasing does prior to breeding them.

5) Much has been incorrectly written in outdoor magazines about bucks charging wild-eyed to a scrape reeking of an estrus scent. Some writers would have hunters believe that a buck in rut is as dumb as a fence post.

A nice buck eases into a fresh scrape to investigate the odor.

A buck, caught up in the fall rut, may lose some caution during this period but a sense of survival is a strong trait in an adult buck's makeup. Trophy bucks often will wind-check a scrape from 20 to 40 yards downwind. They ease in, sticking to heavy cover and the hunter must be properly positioned to intercept the animal.

6) Deer scents always seem to work best in areas with a high number of does than in locations where whitetail numbers are low. It stands to reason that the more bucks that live in an area, the better the chance of one finding a scent location.

7) Be picky about your choice of deer scents. Buy proven products from manufacturers with strong national reputations. Twenty years ago about 24 companies sold deer scents. At my last count there were about 150 scent companies. Do your homework,

The author has had good success using Pete Rickard's Indian Buck Lure and Super Doe Buck Lure.

and determine which company has the best reputation for quality products.

8) I use cover-up sprays to remove human odor, and use them every time I hunt. I never use food scents like acorn, apple, or corn, and never use masking scents like cedar, coyote,

earth, fox, pine, raccoon or skunk although they do work at times.

I've hunted areas where coyotes are a deadly winter and spring predator, and every time a coyote masking scent is used, the deer vanish like ghosts in the night.

SEX SCENTS

A sex scent is designed to represent an estrus whitetail doe. The primary reason for using these scents is to capitalize on a buck's willingness to breed any doe that will hold still. When a buck encounters a sex scent he will move slowly forward, and depend on his eyes, nose and ears to tell him that a doe is waiting patiently nearby in quivering anticipation of his amorous advances. A good scent, properly placed where deer normally travel, reinforces the buck's desire to breed.

If a searching or trailing buck smells any human odor in the vicinity, he'll turn around and flee so fast that you might not even know he was there. It only makes sense to be as clean and odor-free as possible when using any sex scent. One tip to remember: Never place a sex scent on your body or clothing. I've never seen an estrus doe in a tree.

HOW DEER COMMUNICATE WITH SCENTS AND SCRAPES

A whitetail sex scent is only produced when a doe is in estrus. This estrus cycle lasts about 24 hours, and if she is not bred, the doe will recycle approximately 24 to 28 days later. A buck, once his antlers are hard and barring any accident or illness, can breed until reduced levels of testosterone cause the antlers to fall off.

An estrus doe will urinate frequently, and the urine will dribble down her hind legs and over the tarsal glands. Urine, during this 24-hour period, is highly charged with hormonal secretions and

Many hunters add attractants to foot pads or boots before they walk to a stand.

pheromones that trigger a dramatic change in any antlered buck in the vicinity. Just don't be fooled by a company that advertises products containing natural pheromones.

These sex-oriented pheromones exist in deer, and are powerful attractants to bucks, but they have not been created in any laboratory.

They are short lived in the wild, and I feel bottling urine from ranch-raised deer makes it impossible to capture and maintain the life of pheromones.

This points out the need to buy the freshest bottled doe urine as possible. If taken from an estrus doe, it is much "hotter" than urine taken at any other time. However, deer sex scents may or may not be taken from estrus deer.

In recent years I've personally strayed from the traditional sex scents offered for sale. Instead, a Michigan manufacturer—Hawgs, Ltd. Buck Fever Synthetics of Manton—makes a man-made pre-rut and rut formula that really works. Another of their products called Deer Stop also appeals to deer, and his Vanishing Hunter spray makes human odor disappear.

A doe will generally deposit urine and occasionally fecal matter in or near a scrape being tended regularly by a buck. This is a signal that she is ready to be bred.

Bucks urinate down their legs and over the tarsal glands while standing in an active scrape. This gives a similar signal to the doe, and in the case of dominant bucks, it serves as a warning to smaller bucks to stay away from his action.

Last year I watched a young buck get pounded by the dominant buck in the area. The action began after shooting time had ended with two does and a 4-pointer hanging around the area. They had me pinned down until they chose to move off.

As light faded the little guy made his move. He walked over to the active scrape 30 yards upwind of my treestand. He stood in the scrape, sniffed the overhanging licking branch, and tried to act like he knew what he was doing. He was trying to impress the does that were a year or two older than he was.

The dominant buck stepped out of heavy tag alders only 10 yards from me, and the little buck paid no attention to him. The much larger buck's neck hairs raised as he charged the smaller buck

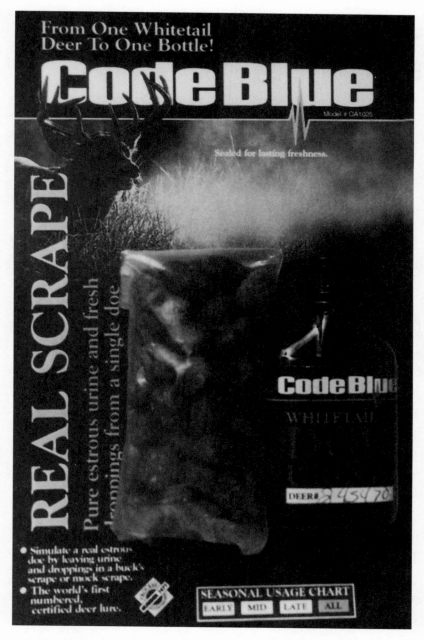

Code Blue Whitetail Deer Urine and fresh droppings from a doe. Place these deer scents in an active scrape and hunt nearby.

There often is a direct tie-in between rutting scrapes and rubbed trees. This buck was photographed rubbing a leaning tree within 20 feet of his scrape.

with his head down. He tined the juvenile in the rump with his antlers hard enough to lift him off his feet, and pushed him to the ground before slowly backing up. The youngster, after having learned a hard and painful lesson, leaped to his feet and ran off. I saw the little guy once more during the season and he was walking with a noticeable limp and seemed to have no interest in any doe.

Scrapes and tree rubs also play an important role in deer behavior during the rut, and should be of interest to hunters who plan to use scents.

A favorite time of year for me is during the rut but it's important to know when the rut occurs and where to look for scrapes and possible hunting sites. My preference is to create a mock scrape. Here is my method of creating a scrape that bucks will come to before, during and after the rut.

MAKING A MOCK SCRAPE

I choose a mock scrape site near a tree that will be downwind of the scrape because I know bucks often wind-check scrapes from downwind. Unlike many treestand hunters I dislike aspen, birch, maple, oak or other trees that drop their leaves during the autumn. My choice is a cedar or pine because the green needles offer a natural scent, provide good cover for a hunter and are often found in locations where bucks make annual rutting scrapes.

The tree must be downwind of a thicket, alder tangle or heavy brush-choked river bottom that bucks commonly travel from bedding to feeding areas. My tree must be within 30 to 40 yards of smooth barked trees with a small but pronounced natural opening where deer travel. In my area, popple trees are commonly used for rubbing the velvet off antlers and they often have low growing branches that provide the necessary licking branch three to four feet off the ground.

I carry a clean, freshly washed sheet of plastic to my mock scrape site, and prepare it in early September. The plastic is laid on the ground, and I always wear rubber gloves and boots. My clothing is freshly laundered and free of any cooking, gas or human odors.

The next step is to choose a location directly below an overhanging limb that is three to four feet off the ground. Use a gardening trowel or sharp toothed rake to remove all grass, weeds, twigs and other forest debris from the site. Scratch out a depression two or three inches deep into the soil and use pruning shears to remove small tree roots. The idea is to have nothing but bare earth below the licking branch.

Use a sharp knife to fray the ends of two or three twigs at the end of the licking branch. Hold the limb with one rubber gloved hand while fraying the ends, and then scrape some bark off the trunk of the tree two to three feet above ground level.

My choice for the last three years has been Hawgs Pre-Rut formula. Squirt a quarter of a bottle directly into the newly created scrape and place several drops on the roughened tree trunk bark. Gather up all debris removed from the scrape and dispose of it at least 100 yards away.

I try to return to every mock scrape at least twice weekly during September to freshen the scrape and rub with scent. Another trick is to squirt Deer Stop for 20 yards in each direction of the scrape to simulate other deer moving through the area.

A hunter should begin to see activity in the scrape, rubbing on the tree and nibbling on the licking branch within two weeks. Continue to freshen the scrape and rub as often as necessary during the pre-rut period of the hunting season. Switch to Hawgs Rut formula when bucks are seen chasing does.

In 2000, I reworked a mock scrape near a favorite treestand, and within a month the scrape had expanded from a two-foot circumference to four feet.

Our rut was late in 2000, about two weeks later than normal. By the time the rut actually began, the mock scrape was five feet in diameter and six inches deep, and the overhanging limb was nearly destroyed. Bucks had made two satellite scrapes within 10 yards of the primary scrape, and by mid-November, 15 inches of snow covered the ground but the mock scrape was still being kept open by deer.

The Michigan bow season kicks off on October 1, and I was in an auto accident on October 27, suffering three broken ribs which put an end to my pursuit of a 150-point 10-pointer I had seen twice but had been unable to shoot. Twenty-six days of hunting near mock

Theron Luft uses a synthetic lure from Hawgs Lures and sprinkles about a quarter of a bottle of the Rut lure into a mock scrape.

Tink's #69 Doe-In-Rut Buck Lure.

scrapes had produced 28 antlered bucks within 20 yards. Alas, the big 10-pointer was always screened by heavy brush whenever I saw him.

Scents, and in my case, man-made scents and mock scrapes were responsible for putting 28 bucks within bow range. Had I not been picky it would have been easy to fill my two buck tags.

Bear in mind that bucks often return to a mock scrape if they used it the year before. My mock scrapes have produced 20 to 30 buck sightings within 20 yards for each of the last four years, and I suspect 2001 will be another good year.

SCENT TRAILS & HOW TO MAKE THEM

Land topography can be used to the advantage of hunters who use deer scents and make scent trails. Doing so is easy but I'm always surprised that more people do not understand or fail to use scent trails while deer hunting. Scent trails can be made while walking into the stand, and thus the freshest scent is always closest to the stand.

I use a clean dark towel and wrap a flat stone in it and sew it shut with 20-pound monofilament. Tie a five-foot piece of clean unscented rope to the opposite end, and saturate the towel or a Knight & Hale Deluxe Scent Drag with scent. Drag the scented and weighted towel or drag to a ground blind or treestand. Leave the scented towel or scent drag 15 yards upwind of the stand but remove it before leaving the woods.

A hunting buddy uses a drag rag to lay scent trails that lead from heavy cover to his nearby stand. He often will lay three or four scent trails every time he hunts.

"I make my trails from every direction except directly downwind of my stand," he said. "My reasoning is that a cruising buck may encounter one of the drag trails 75 to 100 yards from my stand and then follow it to where the other drag trails meet in front of the stand. This gives me greater scent coverage in my hunting area and it frequently leads to far more buck sightings and better chances at mature bucks."

He carries three or four Zip-Loc bags for storage of his drag rags. When his hunt ends, he collects each rag or towel and stows it in a separate plastic bag and zips it closed. He freshens each drag rag with more scent before they are used again.

This young deer hunter is laying a scent trail. He tied a rock inside a towel, sewed it shut, tied a rope to the towel, placed deer scent on the towel and dragged it along the ground. He begins the first drag at about 45 degrees on each side of directly downwind of his stand. Each drag begins about 100 yards away and meets within 20 yards of his stand. Any buck that cuts the scent trail may follow it toward the tree for an easy shot from the stand.

Knight & Hale Deluxe Scent Drag. Pour scent on it and make drag trails to lure deer within bow or firearm range.

SCENT BOMBS

The idea of a scent bomb isn't new. They are easy to make and carry, and can be used time and again. Empty 35mm film containers are most commonly used. They are thoroughly cleaned inside and out, and kept in a sealed Zip-Loc bag after use.

Fill each scent bomb with clean cotton balls but never use bare fingers to handle the container or cotton. Saturate the cotton and place at strategic areas along nearby runways.

Use a small pointed stick to lift up some cotton from the canister after removing the cap. Likely locations for scent bombs are along deer trails, near rubs or scrapes, or wherever a buck may be found as he moves through heavy cover toward a bedding or feeding area. Place scent bombs upwind and crosswind of your location. They can be used along with scented drag rags.

I'm so mindful of the first time a scent bomb was used. My stand was in a cedar tree 12 yards from an active deer trail. I climbed into my stand, checked for the ideal location to shoot, climbed back down and placed an opened scent bomb on the ground at the hotspot.

Thirty minutes later a deer was heard walking through dry autumn leaves behind me. It was moving slowly down the trail and I watched as it walked to within 10 feet of the scented cotton. The deer stopped, stuck its neck out, sniffed, rolled its upper lip back in the Flehman (lip curl) response that allows a deer to taste the scented air. Satisfied, it walked forward and placed its nose to the film canister.

That deer was in a state of bliss. I eased back to full draw, aimed at the quartering-away animal and made a smooth release. The 7-pointer still had his nose to the film canister when the arrow bored through his ribs and heart. He wheeled and ran 50 yards before falling.

To make a scent bomb stuff unscented cotton into a 35mm film canister, add scent to the cotton and place the canister(s) within 20 yards of the treestand and properly positioned for a good shot.

SOME SCENT REMINDERS

Hunt with scent on days when the wind ruffles the leaves. Calm or very windy days are never as good. Deer like soft breezes best for checking ahead for danger.

Dry days are better for using scent than during rainy or snowy weather. The peak of my scent use takes place from about 10 days before the second full moon after the autumnal equinox until about 10 days after the second full moon. This normally hits the peak of the rut in northern tier states such as Michigan. The rut occurs much later in southern states like Alabama, Georgia and Texas.

The major reasons why hunters fail when using deer scents is human odor and movement. The use of scents isn't a panacea for a person's hunting ills; it can work and work well only if a hunter follows the rules. Hunt downwind of where deer are expected to appear and don't fidget or wiggle around. Be silent and still to succeed.

Soft, noiseless camouflage clothing is very important for bow-hunters. A silent bow is needed to avoid any telltale squeak that can spook approaching deer. Firearm deer hunters, even those wearing Blaze Orange clothing, should choose garments that are soft and quiet.

Deer scents work but the hunter must pay attention to wind direction. I've often moved from one stand to another in the middle of a hunt just to avoid being winded by approaching deer.

Deer scents are not miracle workers. They can produce when properly used, and will probably fail if improperly used. It's as simple as that.

It's vitally important to do your homework with deer scents before the season opens. Read the manufacturer's directions, follow them, and always stay downwind of where deer should appear. Sit still, let the deer come close, and then shoot straight.

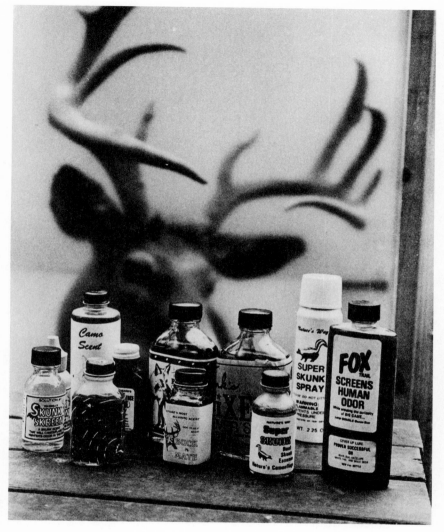

Several different types of cover-up scent used to mask human odor.

Dozens of manufacturers sell deer scents. Among those I have successfully used are Buck Stop, Hawgs, Pete Rickard, Safariland and several others. What works one day in one area may fail to produce in a different location the next day.

A final thought: Never brag about your scent hunting success in a sporting goods store or a tavern. Keeping your mouth shut can help avoid having your nose forcibly rearranged or mandating an immediate visit to the nearest dentist.

Hunting with deer scents is a controversial topic. It makes little sense to act as a lightning rod for someone else to focus their displeasure on. Keep quiet about your hunting techniques, and enjoy the extra enjoyment that scent hunting can bring.

11

CALLING AND RATTLING

The buck was a 2½-year-old, and the poor guy didn't have the first clue what was happening to him. It was during the rut, and I'd spotted him leaving a palmetto thicket in Alabama and he was crossing through an open area between two tiny creeks swollen with rainwater.

He had walked past my treestand once, and when he was a football field length away, I grunted softly. He stopped, his backside to me, and looked around. I gave another short series of grunts, and here he came on the run. Nose up, ears spread wide and nostrils flaring; he was looking for some sweet lovin'.

I raised my rifle to my shoulder, centered him in the scope, and waited to see what he would do. He milled about, seemingly puzzled, and slowly turned to walk off toward one of the creeks. I let him get out about 50 yards and started to call again.

The buck wheeled and came back to within 15 yards of my tree and stood motionless as he looked around. He was trying to locate a receptive doe that seemed to be calling his name, but she kept playing hide-and-seek.

He turned for the third time and walked off. I let him go about 50 yards, lifted the Knight & Hale EZ-Grunt-ER Plus to my mouth, and blew both calls—the inhale and exhale grunts. He almost turned inside his skin and came running back, apparently figuring he had the ol' girl pegged. He stopped 30 yards away to look, and I called again.

The flatulent sound drifted on the breeze, and he swiveled his hips and began walking stiff-legged toward the call. We had been playing this game for 20 minutes, and darkness was only 45 minutes away. I wanted him to leave in hopes a bigger buck may show as dusk began settling across the swamp.

I was tired of the game, but he acted like he would play all day. This time when the buck turned to leave I stuffed the call back into my pocket and let him go. He would be a very nice trophy in another year, and I didn't want to shoot him. I'd already taken a nice buck and was now looking for a real trophy.

Calling deer is nothing new. Indians used some of the same techniques years ago, and now deer hunters are picking up the challenge as they lure bucks in for close shots. I felt like the Pied Piper with that buck, and hunters can achieve a tremendous feeling of holding life and death of a buck in their hands once they become accustomed to trying different calls.

Duck, elk, goose, predator and turkey hunters have used calls for years to lure these critters within range of their bow or firearm. However, deer hunters are now learning how much a whitetail deer will vocalize with other deer. Scientific studies have proven that it is possible to call a nice buck within easy range.

Calling in a nice buck like this can be easy if conditions are right. Make sure you're well hidden, and pay particular attention to the area downwind of your position.

They also are learning that calling deer is not difficult. In fact, it's so easy that many hunters successfully use calling techniques and score the first time out.

There are several things to learn, but the hardest one of all is to develop confidence in the call. It really is a mind-over-matter situation.

THE MENTAL ATTITUDE

The important thing to overcome is a feeling of foolishness. Many hunters feel silly blowing on a call that makes a sound like a rude dinner guest after a hefty meal of beans.

"No way am I going to sit in my treestand and make stupid sounds," one hunter told me after a deer hunting seminar. "Every deer within earshot will hit the road the moment I start blowing on a grunt call."

I cajoled the guy for five minutes, gave him a demonstration, wiped off the mouthpiece and offered it to him.

"Give it a try," I said. "There isn't anyone around except you and me."

He gave me that steely-eye look often reserved for people he probably didn't care much for, but I knew he would try it. He just had a role to play before giving in.

"OK, I'll try it," he said. "Don't laugh at me."

I assured him I wouldn't giggle. After looking around to see if anyone was watching, he exhaled and inhaled through the call.

"That wasn't hard, was it?" I asked.

"At least you're not laughing at me," he muttered. "What kind of sound cadence should I use?"

Aha, another convert. He had learned how easy it was within two minutes, and once he gained some self confidence, he was grunting like a champ. I spent the next 15 minutes with the guy, and he was off in search of a grunt call to buy.

David Hale using a grunt call. This technique works on the ground or from an elevated stand. Too much calling can spook deer, however.

The big trick is to rid yourself of feeling like an idiot. Blowing a grunt call can be as easy as standing up against a barn and breathing in sunshine. Some tapes are available from various manufacturers, and listening to someone call can make a hunter's calling even better.

And the calls are easy to use. It's not like mastering a diaphragm call for elk or turkeys, and it's far easier than learning to blow a duck or goose call. Many models are breath-through calls, some are breath-in calls and a few can be used by breathing in and breathing out.

CALL MANUFACTURERS

Over the years I've interviewed many of the leading deer call manufacturers, picked their brains and have come up with a solid game plan that will work most of the time. Nothing works all the time.

Some of the calls I've used were made by A-Way of Beaverton, Michigan; Kelly Cooper of Picture Rocks, Pennsylvania; Knight & Hale Game Calls of Cadiz, Kentucky; Quaker Boy of Orchard Park, New York; Trophy Hunter Products of Rock Falls, Illinois; and Woods-Wise Products of Franklin, Tennessee.

Each company has a number of calls that work for deer. The secret to good calling is to have an assortment to cover almost any situation.

TYPES OF CALLS

Adult buck grunt, doe bleat, doe grunt, fawn bleat, snort, social calls, tending buck grunt, grunt-snort-wheeze (I still haven't mastered this combination call) and others are commonly heard. Some deer researchers feel a deer can make 25 to 30 different sounds.

The adult buck grunt and tending buck grunt are common. A doe bleat or grunt is common, and fawn bleats are commonly heard when the youngster has lost track of its mother.

Some calls are more aggressive. For instance, the tending buck grunt or the grunt-snort-wheeze call are aggressive. One hunter told me once that "if you call, and hear a buck do a grunt-snort-wheeze, drop the call, and grab your bow or rifle because that animal is looking for a fight."

Deer vocalization is just now being studied by numerous deer researchers. Most of their work is done with penned animals, but a

buck is a buck, and the sounds penned bucks or does make are replicated in the wild.

A tending buck grunt is very common. It sounds like a rutting pig.

Once it's been heard, a tending buck grunt is easily recognizable in the deer woods unless you happen to be hunting near a pig
farm. It is a deep, abrupt, nasal and often raspy grunt. It's difficult to
confuse it with any other sound in nature.

FRED ABBAS INTERVIEW

Fred Abbas of Houghton Lake, Michigan, and his son Greg
of Beaverton, Michigan, make the A-Way Bowgrunter Plus call. It
can be attached to a bow or firearm, and the mouthpiece at the end
of the rubber tubing activates the call.

"This is the world's only patented social deer call," Fred said.
"Deer are very social by nature, and they verbally communicate
with one another throughout their lives. A deer's vocal communica-
tion is so soft and subtle, and we have duplicated this sound."

He said the sound of deer vocalizing is very soft, and in many
cases, a hunter can't hear it. The exceptions are when a deer snorts
at danger or when a tending buck grunts as he trails an estrus doe.

The Bowgrunter Plus can be a soft and subtle call that can only
be heard five yards away to a raspy rutting grunt that can be heard
for 100 yards.

"We urge hunters to attach the calling end to the bow or
firearm—or even to the clothing—and then pin the tube near their
mouth," Abbas said. "The reed is adjustable for a dominant buck
grunt, young buck grunt, doe grunt or for a fawn call. It's easy to use;
just inhale on the tube after setting the reed for the desired call.
Give three short grunts every 15 to 20 minutes. This call frees up
your hands to shoot."

KELLY COOPER INTERVIEW

His Locater Call (deer bleat) is not a mouth call, and it's so simple to use that my grandchildren have fun playing with it during the off season. This call operates by turning it upside down.

That's it, and the deer bleat can be heard for 50 yards or more. It's a good call to use during the rut because the bleat can attract a buck or doe. If a doe comes to the bleat, and is in estrus, a buck may be right behind her.

"It's a call that many experienced hunters use," Cooper said. "Simply turn it upside down, and it delivers an unsurpassed quality of sound. It really works."

KNIGHT & HALE INTERVIEW

Harold Knight and David Hale produce the EZ-Grunt-ER Plus, the call that I described using at the beginning of this chapter.

"We feel deer calls work best before and during the rut, and once the rut ends only does seem to be attracted to this call," Knight said. "We've had bucks run 200 yards to a call just before the rut gets into full swing. They are eager to investigate the call, and are as hot to trot as a barnyard rooster in a henhouse."

Hale said he first tested the call in several states and shot several big bucks. He feels if a dominant buck is present, and if the animal is visible, the buck will often respond to a properly used grunt call.

"Many hunters have heard a buck grunt as he follows an estrus doe," Hale said. "But, in many cases, they didn't know what it was. The best description of a tending buck grunt is it sounds similar to a grunting barnyard pig. It is low and gutteral, and often can be heard for 100 yards."

Knight said does also make a grunting sound, but the tending grunt call is most often heard as an amorous buck follows a doe in

David Hale shows how to muffle the sound of a grunt call by squeezing the plastic tube together. The flexible tubing can be bent one way or another to simulate the sound of a buck or doe moving around.

heat. The sound is a series of six or seven evenly spaced low grunts with as much as a second pause between grunts.

"The buck's head is usually lowered until he sees the doe," Knight said. "His neck is swollen from the rut and the animal trails the doe at a rapid pace."

Hale said the call can be used by breathing in or out even when deer are not visible, but when a buck is seen, the tending grunt call is much more deadly. A dominant buck grunt is longer, sharper and may be used in an area where the deer hunter suspects a trophy may be found.

They feel the dominant grunt may attract the larger bucks in an area simply because one may feel another animal is trying to horn in on his territory. The call should be longer, more drawn out, and can be muffled against the chest to deaden the sound as a buck approaches.

DICK KIRBY INTERVIEW

Kirby is the top honcho at Quaker Boy Calls, and his Phantom Buck call is a tube call with two different sized plastic tubings. He feels one reason grunt calls are so popular is that a deer's voice has some of the same characteristics of a human voice.

"No two bucks will sound the same," he said. "Variation in pitch, rhythm, volume and intensity give deer vocalizations recognizable differences."

He said the Phantom with its optional ability to vary voice quality offers hunters the versatility of reproducing the many grunt calls made by bucks.

"It is designed to be used primarily during the rut when bucks are most vocal and responsive to other deer calls," Kirby said. "However, it can be used successfully throughout the deer season.

"During the mating period when does become receptive to servicing, they will be attended by amorous bucks. This Attending (or tending) Grunt has been given to calls made by bucks at this time. It

Marty Pollington used a grunt call to bring this dandy 8-point buck within bow range.

will vary in intensity, volume, pitch and frequency according to the excitement level or sexual drive and age of the buck."

He said the grunt is easy to reproduce and is the one call most used with the highest success rate. A buck may react to a grunt call out of curiosity, jealousy, or their natural sex drive, and will respond by coming in on a dead run or by sneaking in.

"The two interchangeable sound tubes offer hunters the ability to reproduce a variety of deer grunts from young and older bucks," Kirby said. "The deep guttural grunts of older bucks are made with the thinner tube while the nasal, blatty calls of younger bucks are reproduced with the larger tube."

He said there is no perfect sequence when calling. It is better to call softer and less frequently than to call loudly and too often. A good series may consist of from one to four grunts over a minute or two with long pauses before the next series.

TED LAWSON INTERVIEW

Lawson owns Trophy Hunter Products, and has been calling deer for years. He produces the Trophy Model call that emulates a young buck sound, a Pro Model with an intermediate sound, and a Magnum Model for the dominant buck grunt.

"It's fun to call deer and it is a very effective hunting technique during the rut which often coincides with the late bow season and the firearms deer season in many states," Lawson said. "But one problem that many beginning grunt call users make is they call too often."

He said he likes to call and rattle, and his normal sequence is to rattle for a minute or more and then call several times. He then waits 10 to 15 minutes, and runs through the calling and/or rattling sequence again.

His calls differ from most call makers. Some of his must be inhaled through while others produce the proper sound by exhaling through them. He feels each type of call has its own advantages.

JERRY PETERSON INTERVIEW

Peterson's Woods-Wise Products is the maker of several deer calls. His Buc-N-Doe call makes buck and doe grunts, bleats, contact calls and distress bawls. He also produces a Fawn Meow call, Doe Contact Bleater, Boss Buck Grunter and a Bucksnorter call, and all are mouth-blown calls.

"Many mouth calls used for deer calling are made to be blown into," Peterson said. "Most of my calls are used by inhaling through the call to produce the desired sounds. Inhaling through a call rather

A rifle, bow and grunt call can spell big trouble for a buck that comes to investigate a calling sequence.

than exhaling through it prevents moisture condensation on the reed, and eliminates any possibility of it freezing up or going out of tune in cold weather. Anyone who has had a grunt call fail or make an unnatural sound will understand why an inhale call works best."

He says there are three basic deer sounds for hunters to remember: bleats, grunts and snorts.

Bleats are fawn related sounds that express distress or frustration. Grunts are the social noises made by whitetails and snorts are danger or warning calls.

"There are three types of grunts," he said. "The attention grunt is one or two half-second gentle volume calls that can be made anytime during hunting season to call bucks, does or fawns within range or to calm down 'spooky' deer by reassuring them that all is well. This call must be made very softly at less than half the maximum volume.

"A tending grunt call is a series of five to 20 low-pitched 'hollow' guttural grunts given two seconds apart and fairly loud and aggressive in tone. This call says a buck has found an estrus doe, and is pursuing her while warning other bucks in the area that she belongs to him. It is only made by a buck tending a doe in heat.

"Aggressive grunts are higher pitched and sharper in tone," Peterson said. "They are louder in volume, but are only a quarter-second in length and are given only once or twice. This is a good call to use while rattling."

HOW AND WHEN TO USE CALLS

It really makes little difference which type of call is used. The secret to any deer call is knowing how and when to use it.

I'm so mindful of a Georgia hunt several years ago. I sat in a treestand in a dense thicket overlooking a well-used runway along a stream that was being traveled at least once a day by a big buck. A big thicket of honeysuckle lay across the stream and upwind of me.

My first calling attempt began late in the afternoon before deer started to move out to feed. I was convinced the buck was bedded down in the honeysuckle about 100 yards away, and felt he might move in to several low tending grunts because the rut was in full swing.

"*Uhhhh, uhhhh, uhhhh,*" I grunted. Several minutes passed, and I gave three more short guttural grunts followed by a longer and more drawn out grunt that slowly tapered off in intensity and volume, "*Uhhhh, uhhhh, uhhhh, uhhhhhhhhhhhh.*"

Two minutes later a deer could be heard crossing the creek upwind and crosswind from my stand. The splashing noise came up the stream bank, and stopped behind a wall of brush almost within spitting distance of me.

I could hear the buck raking his antlers against the brush and small saplings. Twice his massive antlers came into view less than six yards away, but the animal wouldn't move two more steps into the open to offer an easy shot.

The buck was waiting for the doe to come to him. I was playing the part of the doe, and it was obvious I couldn't go to him. He was now so close that I didn't dare risk calling one more time. Deer can literally place a call, and even if they can't see a hunter, it isn't smart to make any sound when deer get too close.

Darkness fell that evening over a Mexican standoff. The buck wouldn't move any closer, and I couldn't shoot through the heavy cover screening his body.

The next day I slid quietly back into the same area but silently climbed a different tree on the opposite side of the brush. The same scenario played itself out again; I called, and the buck came to the call.

This time he stopped where he had stood the evening before, and was looking for a doe or a feisty scrap with another buck. Boy, was he fooled when I gave him a broadhead through the ribs from

10 yards away. Another buck had fallen to a deer call and a bit of hunter ingenuity.

Deer calling will work regardless of whether a hunter can see the deer or not. However, I feel it works best if the buck can be seen because it allows the hunter to gauge the deer's actions but it can be equally effective on unseen bucks.

Harold Knight said calling can be overdone. If a buck is seen, and is heading toward the hunter, let him come without any additional calling. If he stops, and appears uncertain, give one or two very low grunts to help establish the direction.

David Hale feels a trick he uses may be beneficial to hunters. He imagines a buck within 100 yards of the caller at all times. This necessitates working into a ground stand or treestand as quietly as possible, and it means paying close attention to the wind direction. One whiff of human scent can ruin a hunt before the hunter gets a chance to warm up his deer call.

Get into the stand, and remain motionless and quiet for several minutes to allow the woods to settle down from your passage. Ready all equipment and begin with a short series of low and soft grunts. A buck may be within 50 yards, and a call that blasts out at high volume can spook a deer standing nearby.

Call several times, and wait five to 10 minutes before calling again. Watch in all directions for approaching deer, but pay particular attention to the downwind area as subordinate bucks often try to circle the call to wind-check for estrus does or the dominant buck.

A deer call will not spook nearby does if the hunter doesn't move or isn't winded. Short, medium volume grunts are common vocalizations among whitetails, and does pay little attention to the call but are quick to spot hunter movement.

Once a buck moves within range, shift the call behind your back or tuck it inside your jacket or shirt. The last thing a bowhunter wants or needs is to take a shot and have the bow string catch on the call.

Once you get into your stand, settle down and remain motionless and quiet for several long minutes before starting to call.

A word of caution: Be alert at all times. Bucks usually can determine precisely where the call comes from, and can approach with all the stealth of a cat burglar. One minute there will be nothing there, and the next, a buck can be directly under your treestand.

Experience is the best teacher, so experiment as I did at the beginning of this chapter. Nothing short of movement, being winded, or making a danger snort will spook deer, and trying different sound combinations can lead to interesting results.

Deer calling may not be new, but the technique has been revised over the past two decades. Whitetail bucks will come to a deer call, and the close-up encounters will create an adrenaline surge the hunter will remember all winter.

RATTLING

The art of rattling bucks with natural or imitation antlers is another old hunting method that more and more hunters are trying. It got its start in Texas' back country where ground cactus, rattlesnakes, mesquite and whitetail deer are found.

The basic trick is to imitate two fighting bucks in hopes that it will lure in a trophy whitetail buck. Sometimes it does and sometimes it doesn't, but over the last 20 years the method has strayed from Texas to wherever whitetails are found.

Is it a successful technique? The answer is a qualified "yes." Does it always work? The answer is "no" although some hunters would have other sportsmen believe differently.

Rattling works best in the pre-rut and during the rut. I've seen little evidence of much success once the rut has ended. Again, there are some who claim otherwise.

I've tried it many times in Michigan and other states, including during my Texas deer hunts, and have met with varied success. I've rattled in bucks wherever it's been tried, but frankly I've had my best success when rattling from ground level.

Let's face an obvious fact: How many fighting bucks have you seen in a tree?

Your answer is probably the same as mine. None. Can it work for two hunters? Again, the answer is yes. In fact, in my experience, it works best with two hunters.

The ideal situation would be to have the hunter in a treestand where he can see the rattler concealed in a ground blind. Nonverbal communications are required between both people, and an easy set of hand signals can be determined in advance.

The treestand hunter must be limited in movement. If he sees a buck coming, he can hold up one finger while using his leg as cover and point in the proper direction. I normally wear brown jersey gloves, and cut the fingertips out of two glove fingers so the visible skin is easily seen by the ground rattler. A palm held upright would mean to stop rattling, and a downward movement of the open hand (like pushing air down) could mean reduce the volume. All fingers pointing upward would indicate a big buck.

I remember rattling one time in southwest Texas just a few miles from the Mexico border. I was sitting in a natural rocky outcropping that provided good cover except from above. My rattling antlers lay on a nearby rock, and all rocks were of uniform height and just right for an easy rifle shot in every direction.

I completed one rattling sequence, and sat quietly for 10 minutes. It was in December and the rut was underway, and I was reaching for the rattling antlers again when I saw a nice 10-point desert whitetail 100 yards away. I clicked the antlers together softly, laid them aside and watched as the buck moved through a mesquite strip and closed to within 60 yards before stopping again.

The buck was partially screened by rocks along the hillside but I could see his antlers glinting in the late afternoon sun. Two more soft clicks of the antler tips made him step out for a closer look. One shot put him down.

As a big buck searches for the source of clashing antlers (made by a second hunter), this treestand hunter gets ready for a shot.

Although I met with success on that occasion and during a few other individual efforts, I've learned that two hunters can do a much better job. It's difficult to rattle from a treestand, and although it can be done, I much prefer rattling from ground level because any movement made by the rattler may be sensed by a buck to be that of the two fighting animals he hears.

ANTLERS FOR RATTLING

A heavy set of mature 8- or 10-point antlers is ideal. The best antlers have thick bases, long heavy tines and are prepared for use by cutting or filing off the brow tines and any small bumps at the antler base. Drill a hole through the bottom inch or two of each antler, slide a leather thong through one hole, and tie two or three overhand knots to hold it in place. Do the same with the other antler, and then the antlers can be draped over one shoulder or the neck for easy carrying.

It's important that all but the main beams and main points be removed. The first time I tried rattling with antlers that still had brow points and small burrs on the bottom of the antler was a disaster. I banged my hands and fingers so often that I could hardly wait to get home and remove the little bumps and brow points. The base of the antlers is what the hunter must grip, and all protruding knobs must be removed.

Numerous synthetic rattling antlers are on the market, and although they work, I don't believe they have the same resonance or sound of natural antlers. I've seen synthetics in brown, green or white colors, and of the three I use green antlers. They don't flash in sunlight (a safety precaution in heavily hunted areas), and all colors are impervious to moisture, weather or damage.

MY RATTLING TECHNIQUE

I learned about rattling from noted deer hunter Bob McGuire over 10 years ago when he was passing through Michigan. I took time to interview him, shoot photos of his methods, and have adopted some of his techniques to my personal style of hunting.

People who rattle often develop their own way to hold the antlers. Some prefer to hold them as if the rack was still growing off a buck's head. They hold them so each side faces the other, and this method works although it is much easier to smash your fingers by holding them with the points facing each other.

My preference is to hold the left antler the way it would grow out of a deer's head but the right antler is turned so it almost lays inside the other when they are brought together. This eliminates many pinched or bruised fingers.

There are two ways to start a rattling sequence, and both work at different times. The first way is to softly click the antler tips together several times. If you watch two bucks go at it, they often begin by gently touching and clicking their antlers together before pulling away and then going at it.

Click them several times softly, pause for several seconds and then crash them together. The more force used in the initial clash, the more noise it makes. It sometimes pays to do a soft clash first, twist the antlers back and forth to make a clackety-clack sound, and then follow up with a harder clash.

After the one loud clash, taper the sound down by twisting the antlers back and forth and separate them with a loud noise.

The second variation, and McGuire favors this method, is to start with a loud clash of rattling antlers and he feels the louder the better. He then tones down the volume by raking the antlers against each other, twisting them together and tickling the tips. He feels some antler sound is better than dead silence.

There are other tricks to rattling that work. The hunter can rake brush or small trees with the antlers like a buck doing mock battle with a tree, and smashing one antler into a leafy bush or tree will work.

When deer fight, the sounds of battle often are accompanied by the thudding of hooves on the ground. This sound can be replicated by pounding the earth with the outside edges of the antlers.

My scenario begins with the tickling sounds of antlers faintly clicking together, a loud clash as they are brought forcibly against

Bob McGuire likes to start with a loud crash, then tone down the volume.

Vocalization is a big part of any rattling sequence. Bob McGuire lays his rattling antlers in his lap, and makes grunts without calls. Hunters lacking this skill can use any one of a number of grunt calls, doe bleats, tending buck grunts and other calls to add realism to the rattling of antlers.

each other, the thudding of antlers hitting the ground three or four times, the raking of brush, the sounds of antlers scratching forcibly against a rough tree, a softer clash, the wrenching sounds of the rattling antlers twisting together, more earth pounding and bush raking, another clash, and then a tickling of antlers.

The occasional heavy raspy grunt of a tending buck can be used to break the silence, pause for a minute with more brush raking, and another guttural grunt to key nearby deer to the activity, and then a short pause. Begin the sequence again.

BE SCENT-FREE

Bucks have a tendency to circle fighting bucks. The doe often stands nearby, casually feeding, while real bucks fight for her. It's very common for a normally subordinate buck to try slipping in to scoop up the doe while the big bucks try to establish which one is the dominant animal.

Bucks that circle will eventually come in downwind from the rattling area. Any whiff of human odor will send an investigating buck hightailing it for the next county. I spray everything from my hat and face mask down to my boots and gloves with a scent eliminating spray before a rattling sequence begins.

It helps to have an open lane, deer trail, forest opening or other area downwind of the hunter but it should be surrounded on three sides by heavy cover. Fighting bucks take up a lot of room as they push and shove each other around, and if the hunter has ever seen a true buck fight, it is a noisy affair.

There is some grunting as they try to gain dominance, and plenty of noise created by pounding hooves trying to get a firm footing on the ground to push back. Try to recreate all of these sounds.

Once a buck has been spotted, and is responding to the rattling and calling sequence, it pays to tone down the volume of the calls and rattles. A bag of rattling sticks can be gently shaken to duplicate the soft sounds of a buck tickling the antlers of the other deer. Softly shaken, the sound can be heard for 50 yards. It's important to watch the buck to see how he responds to the sounds.

Some bucks will be thoroughly spooked if the sounds are too loud, and may become suspicious if there is no sound at all. Bucks may fight hard for 20 seconds or two or three minutes, but fighting is exhausting work. Deer often will take a breather between bouts, especially if they are evenly matched, but a normal buck fight won't last very long and it can stop as abruptly as it started.

Watch the deer. If it appears tentative, some soft coaxing or rattling may cause it to keep coming. It also may run a smaller buck off. Each scenario can be different.

One thing is certain: If you capture the attention of a trophy buck, and he comes busting in, the hunter must be ready for a quick shot because if he doesn't see either one of the bucks around, he may cut out as fast as he arrived.

Rattling, or ratting and calling at the same time, is a technique that works. It seems to work best just as the pre-rut ends and the rut begins. I've tried it late in the season once the rut has ended, and it has never paid off although I've talked with a few hunters who claim to have called in bucks after the rut.

This is a technique that requires personal experimentation. It's important to be in an area where bucks are found, and being scent-free makes sense. It does little good to perform a good rattling sequence, and have a buck fooled, only to lose him because he smells human odor.

DECOYING DEER

I've played with using deer decoys for two or three years and have had mixed results. Like calling or rattling, it works part of the time and fails at other times.

There are a number of deer decoys on the market. Some are full-bodied decoys and others are silhouettes, and of the two, a full-bodied decoy works best because it looks like a deer from any angle. If a moving buck approaches a silhouette decoy too closely, or gets in front or directly behind it, the decoy will seem to disappear.

I tried a full-bodied Flambeau decoy twice during the 2000 bow season, and had success luring in a buck both times. I didn't shoot either time although the second episode brought in a 135-class 8-point but it arrived just after legal shooting time ended.

Rules are rules, and I obey them. I set my watch daily, and in Michigan, we can hunt until 30 minutes after sundown. Our Department of Natural Resources prints up their rule book, and in it is daily morning and evening shooting times. I follow it to the letter each and every day, and put away my bow or firearm when closing time arrives.

The first day I used the decoy was just as the rut started. I positioned my doe decoy so it's hind end was placed so a buck had to walk past my stand to sniff the doe's rump. I had attached a light brown cloth to the rear of the plastic decoy, sprinkled some doe-in-estrus urine on the cloth, and sat back in my treestand to wait.

Two or three does filtered down the trail and walked past the fake doe with only a sideways glance at her. The last deer out was a young 4-pointer, and I watched him approach the area. He stopped once downwind at 30 yards, stood motionless and stared at the decoy. He took several steps closer, caught the scent on the soft breeze and homed in on her like a sailor heading for the closest bar in port.

He ambled past my treestand at a slow pace and was only 15 yards away. I drew down on him, aimed and let up. I had no intention of shooting but wanted to practice my draw. He approached the doe from the rear, walked to within six feet of her, stretched out his neck and sniffed with obvious satisfaction.

He eased closer, put his nose to the scented rag tail, and seemed to inhale deeply. This young lad was obviously in love. He didn't try to mount the decoy, but kept prancing back and forth behind her.

When she didn't move he wandered over to a nearby scrape, urinated in it and nibbled the licking branch, and returned to his post directly behind her. He repeated that same posturing by sniffing her, going to the scrape and returning two more times. I drew on that little buck again before he finally wandered off.

The next time was a bit more exciting. I positioned the decoy in another location, and was sitting in a bushy pine tree. Fifteen minutes before shooting time was to end a young spikehorn walked in, sniffed the decoy from afar before moving closer, and eventually was standing perfectly broadside to me. Again I drew and aimed before letting the bow string back down. I wanted a spike even less than the 4-pointer.

Shooting time ended and I took my arrow off my bow string, cut my Game Tracker string, put my release in my pocket and the arrow in my quiver, and sat back to watch. I don't leave a treestand when deer are nearby.

Suddenly, the spike's head came up and he stared to my left. I eased my eyes in that direction, and 15 yards away stood a big 9-pointer that was staring at the spike.

The spikehorn decided to take a hike before the big buck whipped his butt. I watched the 9-point, and even if shooting time had not gone by, there was no way for a shot unless the buck moved. It was partially screened by heavy pine boughs.

The buck stood there for five minutes, circled my tree and approached the decoy from the rear. He cozied up next to the decoy, and I went through the motions of drawing and shooting the buck even though I didn't have my bow in hand at the time. It would have been a slam-dunk to shoot that buck.

Several things I've learned from using deer decoys on occasion is that bucks will approach a doe decoy from the rear and will approach a buck decoy from the front. This is important to know so the decoy is properly positioned in relationship to the hunter.

My decoy is a doe so I always face it into the wind and slightly to the left of me when I'm in a treestand. I want the buck to walk to it from the rear which would give me a perfect broadside or quartering-away shot.

Another trick I learned, although I haven't tried it yet, is to use white toilet paper for a tail. A friend tied two-pound monofilament to the end of the toilet paper and the other end goes through a screw eye in a tree limb above the decoy, and the line goes through another screw eye in the tree near the hunter. Occasionally the hunter will tug lightly on the line, and that causes the tail to move up and down like a live animal. He has shot two bucks including a very nice 8-pointer using this trick.

Whenever I hunt with a decoy near a scrape I do not put the doe in the scrape but about 10 feet away. I want the double-barreled attraction of a decoy and an active scrape working for me. A buck often will wind-check the scrape from downwind, smell it and the doe decoy, and once he sees the decoy will often come marching right in.

Calling, decoying and rattling deer are three techniques that can produce bucks from farmlands, swamps and thickets. The important thing to remember is when, where and how to use each method.

They can be used separately or in conjunction with each other, and that can lead to more venison steaks this winter.

12

RECOVERING WOUNDED DEER

Recovering a wounded deer can be a major problem for some hunters. Experience in blood trailing is an acquired talent, one best suited to sportsmen with good vision and careful attention to detail.

The problem is that some sportsmen take a lazy approach to looking for their wounded animal, and if it runs into a nasty tangle and the blood trail becomes faint or cannot be found, it's easy to say "the hell with it. I must have missed or just grazed it."

The truth is that if a deer is hit by an arrow, rifle bullet, or shotgun slug it is wounded and in most cases is recoverable. It may require a long and exhaustive search, but most deer can be found under proper conditions.

Spend as long as it takes to find a wounded deer. This hunter made a good shot, and didn't have a long tracking job.

Dry ground or dry leaves or snow represent little problem for an experienced tracker. Rainy weather can wash blood away and make it difficult to find blood or the animal.

Hunters owe it to a wounded animal to spend as much time as necessary to recover it or conclusively prove the deer wasn't severely injured. Years ago I learned by watching a master tracker and his assistant recover two different whitetails that other hunters had shot but had given up all hope of finding.

The late Art LaHa of Winchester, Wisconsin, had been a bowhunter for more than 50 years when I interviewed him in the late 1970s, and had killed hundreds of deer and other big game all over the world. He owned the famous Bear Ski Lodge, catered to hunters, and of all the game he killed with a bow he never lost an arrow-hit whitetail.

"Achieving this kind of success was no accident," LaHa said. "The methods I use to retrieve wounded deer should enable any bowhunter to recover the deer in almost every case providing he made a good hit. It may take a full day, a day and a night or even two full days, but venison will hang eventually if my trailing techniques and observations are closely followed."

The key to making a killing shot and recovering a deer is knowledge of a whitetail's anatomy. LaHa said a hunter should know the exact location of major internal organs and blood vessels from every conceivable angle.

He recalled an incident that took place in 1958 when he shot a whitetail buck, froze the carcass solid, and then cut it in half length-wise through the spinal column. Each organ was fully exposed in its normal position.

That homespun anatomy lesson taught him the exact location of arteries, organs and veins, and it taught him where to shoot a deer for easy recovery. An anatomy lesson should be given to every hunter, and Hunter Education classes should provide these fundamental lessons to every young sportsman.

Learning to recognize deer hair is an essential part of deer recovery. LaHa feels if a bowhunter or firearm hunter learns to recognize deer hair from various parts of the animal's body, that recovery would become much simpler.

"After a deer is shot, a bowhunter or firearm hunter will find deer hair laying on the ground under or near where the animal was shot," he said. "In many cases, studying those hairs will tell precisely where the animal was hit, how soon it will die, how far the animal will run before dropping, and how long the hunter should wait before taking the trail."

One easy solution to this problem is to save the hide from the last deer taken. Study the various colors and types of hair on the hide until you know the length, color and texture of hair on all parts of a whitetail's body. Whenever you have the chance, refresh your knowledge by examining freshly killed animals.

To get the most from this chapter it will be important to study the pictures and drawings. The text blocks tell how deer react to various hits. The study of deer hair is not an exact science because deer from various parts of the country may have slightly different colored hair on various parts of their body. The photos represent deer taken from Michigan, Wisconsin and Minnesota, plus other northern-tier states.

A COMMON ERROR

Many hunters strive for a perfect shot at a buck standing broadside well within accurate shooting range. They want to sink a broadhead or bullet into the chest cavity behind the front shoulder. The objective is to take out the lungs, heart or both organs.

"However, this doesn't always work," LaHa said. "I've seen deer shot behind the front shoulder that ran off only to be shot days or weeks later by another hunter."

Most deer hunters wonder how this can happen. It rarely happens with a bullet because of the hydrostatic shock of a bullet striking flesh, but it can occur with a broadhead.

LaHa said if a deer is standing broadside, and the arrow strikes directly in the center of the sixth rib from the front and exits between the sixth and seventh ribs on the opposite side, the arrow (especially a two-blade broadhead) can slide between both inflated lobes of the lungs, and the result is a lost animal with a nonfatal hole in it. The deer seldom dies and is seldom recovered.

"A friend who hunts with me frequently has seen this happen on two occasions," he said. "Once a hunter made a perfect hit but the deer bounded away, and didn't appear hurt. A week later the same man was in the same stand and a deer came down the trail.

"The hunter dropped the animal with one shot, and close examination showed it had a half-healed arrow wound between the sixth and seventh ribs. It was healthy and moving in a normal manner when shot. We did an autopsy on that buck, and it revealed the path of the first arrow that had hit it a week before. It showed no sign of being sick or weakened from the earlier wound."

One of the most basic tenets of hunting is to always strive for a one-shot kill. This is normally the case with bowhunters because they seldom have time to nock, aim and shoot a second arrow.

It does occur often with firearm hunters. We've all heard five to 10 rapidly fired shots on opening day, and in most cases, if the first shot missed all other shots will be at a running animal. It is difficult if not impossible for most rifle hunters to make a killing shot after having fired several times in rapid succession.

Take your time. Concentrate on the first shot, and squeeze the trigger. A good first shot will kill the animal, and preclude the need for firing additional rounds.

It is critically important to note where a deer was standing when shot, and if the deer runs off, to mark the spot where the animal was last seen. The bowhunter should try to locate the arrow (if a pass-through shot was made) and examine any blood, hair, fat or stomach and intestinal matter on the ground, the arrow shaft or fletching. LaHa says it pays to check for this sign within 20 to 30 yards of where the deer was hit.

A broadside shot from above. Bowhunters should wait for the buck to take one more step forward, moving his right leg to expose the heart-lung region.

TRAILING TIPS

LaHa believes the raven, common in northern states and throughout Canada, is a hunter's ally when a blood trail is lost. He said if they lose a blood trail at night, they return to the area at dawn, and wait for circling ravens to reveal the deer's location.

Ravens soar high over the woods and will usually locate a wounded or dead deer by 10 or 11 a.m. Ravens, like crows, announce their find by the excited tone of their calls, and other meat-eating birds will often join the feast.

Marge Engel, a guide who worked for LaHa, used ravens to track down over 250 arrow-killed deer for LaHa's clients. She said that over 150 of these deer were recovered the next day, and each one was still alive. Without the ravens, LaHa feels the deer never would have been found.

"Night trailing is legal in every state I know of providing the hunter is not carrying a bow or loaded firearm," LaHa said. "If night falls before a wounded deer is found, two hunters can take the track after giving the animal the required time to lie down to stiffen up or die. The hunters must move slowly to avoid spooking a wounded deer.

"Slow trailing is needed to follow a track or blood trail at night. One person carries a large flashlight or Coleman lantern, while the other hunter sorts out the scuff marks, disturbed leaves and the intricacies of a blood trail.

"If a hunter believes from visible sign that the deer is down but still alive, they should flash the light ahead often as they follow the track. If wounded and bedded down, the deer will look at the light from almost ground level, and hunters can see the bright eye reflections. This gives them advance notice of the bedded deer's location before they spook it and complicate further tracking."

Never hold the light on the deer's eyes for more than one or two seconds. A deer may bolt if you overdo the use of direct light.

He cautions hunters that if a deer is still alive, one hunter should sit down nearby and downwind of the animal, and wait while the other hunter returns to camp. When legal shooting time arrives, the second hunter can carry the other man's bow in to him. A second arrow is used to make the legal kill.

Blood trailing isn't easy unless the arrow or bullet causes tremendous hemorrhaging and organ destruction. It's often a step by step process, and with faint blood trails where only a single drop is found every 20 or 30 yards, the search may have to be conducted on hands and knees.

One major problem in trailing wounded deer is having too many people in the party. It's best done by one or two people to keep others from scuffing up leaves or walking over a faint blood spot on snow. Too many people get in each other's way, are impatient, and rush about destroying any chance of finding blood.

At times it requires a keen eye to spot the tiniest spot of blood. I was in on two trailing jobs in 2000 when the animal suffered a high lung hit. The blood trail was very faint for the first 60 yards with just a tiny spot here and there in widely separated spots.

If the person who shot the deer had not been paying attention, and did not know exactly where the arrow entered the deer, it could have resulted in giving up and losing a recoverable animal. We knew that high lung hits often bleed little until the lungs fill with blood so we kept going, an inch at a time. It took nearly two hours to cover 60 yards, and then we saw more frequent spots of blood.

Eventually blood was easily seen in splashes and sprays on vegetation about three feet off the ground. Nearby vegetation was drenched in blood. We followed the strong trail for 20 yards, and the deer suddenly veered off to the left.

"That buck is right up ahead," Gary Baynton whispered. "He's probably long dead by now, and I bet we find him within 20 yards."

He was right. The buck folded up his tent 15 yards away and crashed into wind toppled tree roots. The lesson here is obvious: take things slow, look carefully, check all deer trails for 30 yards in each direction, and if necessary, get down on your hands and knees to look for spoor.

The other thing about blood trailing is to put the person with the best vision on point. One person can stand at the last blood sign, and if both people can see blood well at night, mark the last blood with blaze orange or white surveyor's tape. Restrain the urge to charge after a deer. Instead, take it slow and easy and don't overlook the possibility of a deer suddenly changing direction.

Knowing deer habits and the habitat being hunted can be key factors in recovering a wounded deer. It's commonly believed that wounded deer always head downhill or toward water when hurt, and in many cases this is true. But it isn't always a sure bet; wounded deer have a strong sense of survival and go where they wish.

Deer often head for the thickest cover around. I blood-trailed a buck for a young hunter one time. He didn't know where it was hit but he thought it was hit in the heart or lungs. That buck, when recovered, was just nicked high in the lungs and it bled very little and the trail was impossible to follow at night.

We returned the next morning, and from previous experience with wounded deer in that specific location, knew the animals usually headed for an alder thicket that bordered a small stream. The boy and his father tried to sort out the track where the deer entered heavy cover while I cut through it to where previous trailing jobs had taken me, and after covering 200 yards I began looking.

I found blood immediately in the thick tag alders, and followed the trail to the creek. The last blood on the alders was at the edge of the creek. I checked 50 yards in each direction along the opposite bank and found no blood.

The next step was to walk up and down the creek. I knew that deer often moved freely in the shin-deep water. I walked downstream 100 yards and around a bend, and there in the shallow water lay the boy's first buck.

I hollered for them: "I've got blood down here."

They began moving my way and hollered when they were 100 yards away. "Still got blood, Dave?"

I yelled back and said I did. They kept coming until they were only 10 yards away but they were still in the thick alders and couldn't see me.

I stood motionless, one foot on either side of the buck, and waited.

"Still got the blood trail," they yelled.

"Yep, I've still got blood," I answered. "Just keep coming toward my voice."

The boy burst through the alders on a dead run, looked at me, and asked if I still had the blood trail. Then he looked down, saw his buck between my feet, and fell to the ground praising the Lord for granting him this animal.

There was no magic in my recovering that deer. It was based on previous trailing experiences, and I knew where that buck would go. It was a much simpler job finding the deer in daylight when tiny specks of blood could be found. Those little blood droplets eventually turned into a gusher, and even though the animal ran 100 yards down the river, the blood could be seen on overhanging alders.

Know deer habits, know the habitat being hunted, and commit every trailing job to memory. Hunters will find that other deer often use the same trails once used by other wounded bucks.

LaHa says that coyotes are a common problem in many states. Several of his clients' arrow-hit deer had been taken by night-running coyotes, and it underscores the reason why hunters should stay near wounded deer at night.

I've hunted in several areas where it can be a footrace between the hunter and coyotes to recover an animal. If coyotes are heard yapping at dark, hunters should proceed on the blood trail and try to recover the deer before the brush wolves find it. If coyotes find the deer first, and have a chance to feed on it, there won't be enough usable meat left to make a big hamburger.

If a coyote cuts the blood trail of a wounded deer, it will follow the track. A deer, even if wounded, can bluff one coyote. However, they often will howl or yap, and coyotes a mile away can hear the racket. Within minutes, three or four coyotes will close in on the wounded animal. The predators will sit and wait until the deer goes into shock and its head begins to rise and loll from side to side. Once this happens, the coyotes will kill the whitetail and render it unfit for humans to eat.

LaHa says a hunter that is close to the animal can chase coyotes away and save his venison and trophy. In many cases, if I'm hunting alone and have a deer down, I hang my coat and hat near the animal while I go for help. If the deer is dead, and the hunter needs help getting it out, cover the dead animal with a coat. Human scent on a coat will keep coyotes at bay for a short time.

One last thing: a Coleman lantern with a reflector is much better for spotting blood than a flashlight. The soft glow of a lantern is less harsh to nighttime vision, and a handle on the lantern makes it much easier to carry. Always start out with a full tank of fuel in the lantern, and carry two extra mantles in your pocket. A stumble and fall can destroy the mantles. A small flashlight can be helpful for backup if the lantern goes out.

DIFFICULT TRAILING CONDITIONS

I've blood trailed wounded deer in every imaginable type of terrain. In some areas trailing is easy but in others, it can be a lesson in frustration.

One of the worst places I've trailed wounded deer is near my wife's bow stand. A big pine plantation is just behind her, and most of the deer run through the pines to reach the safety of an alder swale and swamp with a small creek running through it.

Blood is difficult to see on pine needles unless there is a steady flow. A high lung hit can be very difficult because the deer doesn't bleed much until the lungs fill. It's one reason why she always uses a Game Tracker string tracking device. It's much easier following a white string than looking for blood, but strings occasionally break and it becomes necessary to go back to the old blood trailing methods.

I've hunted deer several times in southwest Texas, and as is usually the case, the ground is very dry with a layer of fine dust everywhere. I shot a big 10-point desert whitetail there several years ago, knew where I hit the animal, but couldn't find a single drop of blood. As soon as blood hit the talcum powder-like dirt it was soaked up and never left a trace of the deer's passing.

The deer was finally found but it had covered 75 yards and holed up in a arroyo filled with mesquite. The deer made it that far, and I walked past it twice before it was located. There were so many deer in that area that tracks were everywhere, and without blood to go by, it was trial and error.

I stood where the deer had entered the arroyo and then any trace of it disappeared. The blood we found was under the animal. If I hadn't been paying attention, and knew where that animal went, we never would have found it.

Some rocky or mountainous terrain can prove difficult in following a blood trail. Tall marsh grass also can present a difficult trailing job unless the animal is bleeding heavily. In marsh grass it's important to follow known deer trails but wounded bucks won't always follow a major trail.

They may light out and run where their head leads them, and with a high lung hit, blood can be difficult to find. I found a buck once after three hours of searching because I twisted one stem of marsh grass around and spotted a tiny pearl of blood on the stem. It took another hour to find the next droplet, and I looked back at my last marker, lined up the two locations, and continued on along that sight line. Ten yards farther I found another drop, and then the blood really began flowing. Recovery of that animal took nearly five hours, but finishing the job is a major part of the hunting experience.

That leads us into the next portion of this chapter on recovering wounded deer. There are good hits on deer, and several low per-

A southern deer hunter approaches his deer. A lung-hit deer like this will usually go less than 100 yards before collapsing.

centage shots that make recovery very difficult. It's the hunter's role to always strive to take the best possible shot, and be alert enough to know where the arrow or bullet hit the animal.

HITS THAT COUNT

LUNG HIT

This is a deadly hit, but death is somewhat slower than with a heart shot. A deer hit low in the lungs will die faster than one hit high. A high-lung hit takes time for the deer's lungs to fill with blood, and that means it will run farther before it succumbs to the wound.

A lung-hit deer often runs hard and straight for 40 to 50 yards before slowing down. They often meander a short distance, wobble in place and then stand for a moment or two before falling. Others will run until their heart gives out and then die in a skidding slide.

Retrieval of lung-hit deer should be 100 percent providing a hunter waits for an hour (unless coyotes are plentiful or you are on open state land where a deer thief may steal the animal before you can get to it) before trailing begins. Blood flow increases with a pass-through arrow or bullet wound because the blood will flow out the entrance and exit holes. This a high percentage shot.

HEART HIT

A deer hit in the heart usually leaps wildly, humps up briefly and kicks his back feet to the rear and runs hard. Look for blood on arrow fletching or vanes, and heavy bleeding occurs within 20 yards although the animal won't fall to the ground until it runs 70 to 80 yards. A deer hit squarely in the heart with a bullet will often die on the spot. Heavy blood flow provides a good blood trail if the animal runs, and this high percentage shot seldom requires a lengthy tracking job.

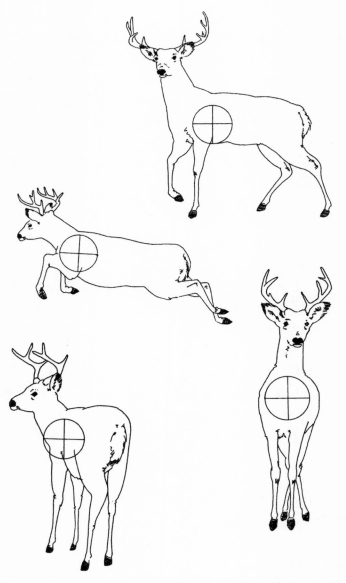

Your target should always be the heart-lung area. For a broadside shot, aim behind the front shoulder, halfway between the top and bottom of the body. From head-on, aim at the base of the neck in the center of the chest. If the deer is angling away, aim just behind the ribs. If it is running straight away from you, aim above the back at the base of the neck.

LIVER HIT

A whitetail hit in the liver will leave a steady blood trail, and may run up to 100 yards before slowing to a tail-down walk. Blood spray is common for 80 yards, and droplets are thumbnail-sized. A deer may live for up to four hours with a liver hit from a broadhead, and hunters should wait 30 minutes before trailing. Recovery of liver-hit animals should be 100 percent. The only problem with this shot is if the arrow or bullet hits behind the liver, a gut-shot deer can cause tracking problems.

KIDNEY HIT

A deer hit in the kidney will jump forward, slow down and then walk away. Bleeding is heavy, and provides an easy trail to follow. The deer will often drop and die within 80 yards. The problem with this shot is the kidney is a small target, and if a shot goes high it can result in a clean miss.

TENDERLOIN HIT

Any hit between the kidneys and spine will sever the aortic artery in the tenderloin, and bleeding is heavy and immediate. The result is a heavy blood trail, and recovery normally takes place within 100 yards.

SPINE HIT

A solid spine hit will drop a deer immediately. Effective targets may be from the base of the skull to within six inches of the root of the tail. A bullet hit here will kill the animal quickly and prevent it from running off. However, a glancing hit off the spine with an arrow may temporarily immobilize the animal, and hunters must be prepared for a quick second shot if the deer regains its feet.

A buddy of mine once shot a nice buck in the spine. The deer flip-flopped on the ground while I urged him to shoot again. He didn't, and the animal flopped around for 10 seconds before the arrow popped out, and the deer regained its feet and ran off.

There was no blood trail to follow, and other than partially paralyzing the deer for a few seconds, the broadhead did no other damage.

LOW-PERCENTAGE HITS

BELLY HIT

A deer hit in the belly may walk away after a few short jumps. They often walk or run with legs splayed and the back is humped up. A deer will soon lie down after being hit, but do not trail it for at least four hours in cold weather and up to 10 hours in warm weather. There is little blood sign, and what there is will often be dark due to intestinal or stomach contents.

Check the arrow for blood and stomach matter. Such deer will remain alert, and often will watch their backtrail. Hurry the tracking job on a belly-hit buck, and chances are good the animal will get up and run again and again. If a stomach hit is obvious, give the animal plenty of time to lay down and die of blood loss or shock.

HIND LEG HIT (FROM SIDE)

The femoral artery lies on the inside of the hind leg. Deer bleed out quickly when this major artery is severed. Press a whitetail slowly to keep it moving, but do not press it too hard. If the femoral artery is cut there will be an instant and heavy blood trail. If the hit misses this artery and bleeding is minor, take the trail slow and easy but realize that the blood may start to fizzle out and become difficult or impossible to follow. It's difficult to hit the femoral artery from the outside of the leg, and I would never recommend this shot, even for a skilled rifle shooter.

HIND LEG HIT (FROM REAR)

This angle gives easier access to the femoral artery but it can be a rather difficult hit to make with an arrow, and the other problem is it destroys some of the finest eating steaks on a whitetail. However, heavy bleeding occurs, and offers a strong blood trail to follow. The animal seldom covers over 100 yards, and recovery is 100 percent.

NECK HIT

This is a deadly hit with a rifle but an iffy hit with an arrow. Neck shots often result in a good hit or a complete miss.

A hit below the spine will sever the carotid artery and/or the windpipe. The deer is normally recovered within 80 yards. A hit above the spine results in light to heavy bleeding, but is seldom fatal and the deer normally lives. A direct spine hit results in immediate paralysis, and the animal goes down. An arrow hit here will immediately kill the animal if the spine is severed but be prepared for a quick second shot if the spine is not destroyed.

BRISKET HIT

This is a low-percentage shot for bowhunters because everything depends on direct penetration. Obviously, a rifle bullet will do the job but an arrow may not. If the arrow enters the brisket, punches through the sternum or cartilage and ribs, or if a side penetration hits several inches back from the front of the brisket, either shot can kill the animal. A glancing wound without full penetration is seldom lethal. The amount of bleeding will determine the outcome.

DEER HAIR AND WHAT IT MEANS

Deer hair cut from the hide of an arrowed animal or one shot with a rifle bullet or shotgun slug has different characteristics. The various colors, lengths and texture can provide positive clues to where the animal was hit.

Study these photos, and practice on deer that you kill. Learn where and what type of hair is located on the animal, and commit it to memory. The study of deer hair can tell a hunter where the animal was hit, whether it was a fatal or nonfatal wound, how long to wait to take up the blood trail or whether to take the trail immediately.

1. HIGH BELLY HAIR

Hair from this area is coarse, hollow and a brownish-gray, and the tips are not as dark as from the spinal area.

2. HIGH BACK, KIDNEY OR TENDERLOIN HAIR

Deer hair from the high back is very dark in color along the spine from the base of the skull to the root of the tail. It is shorter in length than other deer hairs.

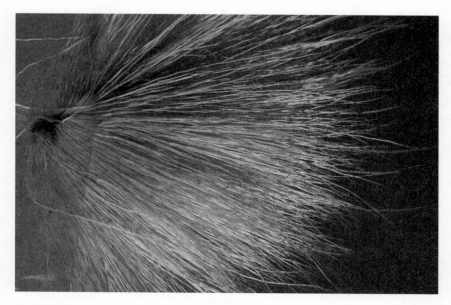

High belly hair.

High back hair.

3. HIGH NECK HAIR

This is dark brown hair with light brown tips. It is slightly longer than high back hair.

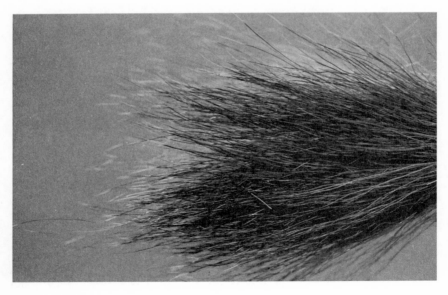

High neck hair.

4. LOW NECK HAIR

Hair from the lower neck is a grayish-white color and is easily recognized. It appears slightly darker near the roots.

5. HAIR BETWEEN REAR LEGS

This hair is white, silky and fine. It shows a tendency to curl at the tips, and is not hollow.

6. TAIL HAIR

It is black or a grayish-brown on the top surface to pure white underneath. It is long, coarse and wavy.

7. LOW BELLY AND NAVEL HAIR

Low belly and navel hair is coarse, whitish and hollow, and tends to be curly or the tufts may spiral away from the belly.

Low neck hair.

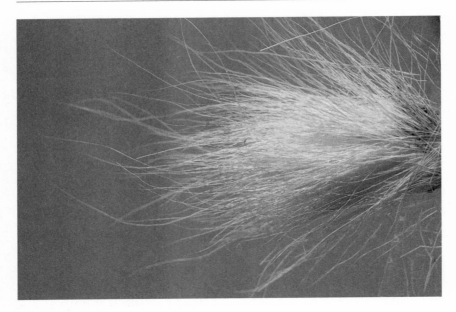

Hair between rear legs.

Tail hair.

Belly hair.

8. BRISKET HAIR

This is grayish-black, stiff, curly and coarse.

Brisket hair.

Heart-lung area hair.

9. HEART-LIVER-LUNG AREA HAIR

It is basically grayish in color but there are long dark guard hairs that will turn gray with age. Lung-area hair is similar but tends to be more brownish-gray.

10. LOW FRONT LEG (OUTSIDE)

Hair found on the front legs on the outside will be short, dark grayish-black with brownish colored tips.

11. LOW FRONT LEG (INSIDE)

This hair is short and a grayish-white color.

12. LOW REAR LEG (NEAR GAMBREL)

It is short and a whitish-gray color.

Knowing deer hair color, length and texture near a hit can give hunters a better opportunity to tag their deer if they use this

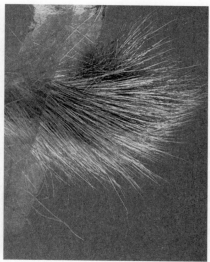

Low front leg hair (outside of leg).   *Low front leg hair (inside of leg).*

Low back leg hair near gambrel.

knowledge in combination with information about how animals act when wounded in various organs or major arteries.

Blood trailing deer requires knowledge. The more information a hunter has at hand, the better the chance of recovering the wounded animal. After all, trailing wounded deer is a combination of using common sense, possessing some indepth knowledge of deer habits and habitat, and the willingness to put in the time required to reduce a whitetail to possession.

A whitetail deer is a beautiful animal. It deserves a better fate than being lost by a hunter only to be ripped apart by predators. Part of the code of conduct for deer hunters is to make every possible effort, regardless of how long it may take, to find a wounded deer.

Anything less is a waste of a wounded deer. And in this day and age where hunting has come under criticism from antihunters and some nonhunters, it's up to sportsmen to prove they have made the ultimate effort to find the animal.